SOUTH AFRICA *Versus* ENGLAND

A Test Cricket History

Ray Knowles

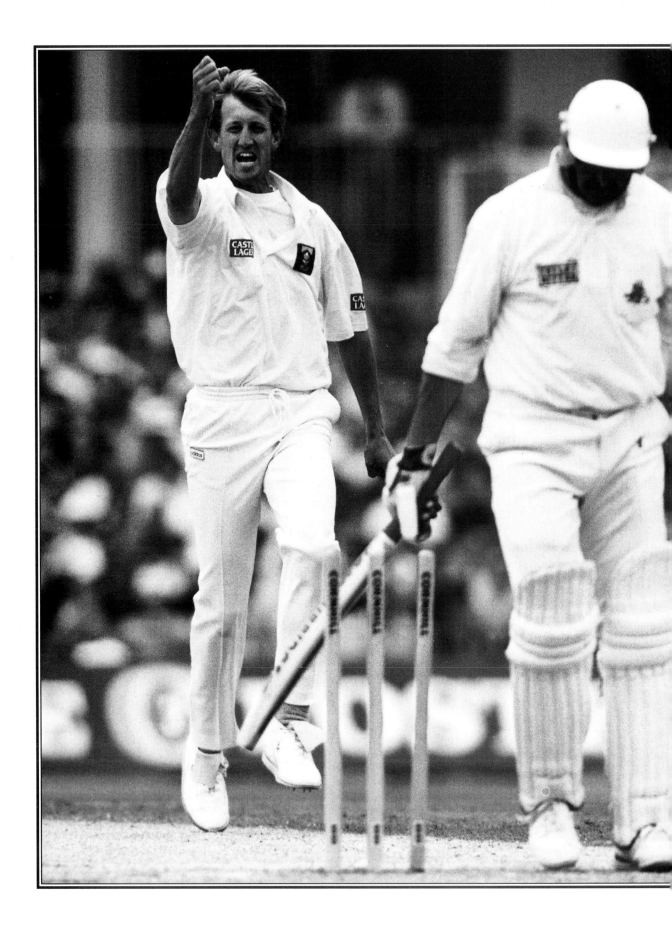

SOUTH AFRICA *Versus* ENGLAND

A Test Cricket History

Ray Knowles

For Penny
the ideal 'Twelfth Man'

First published by New Holland (Publishers) Ltd
London • Cape Town • Sydney • Singapore

24 Nutford Place
London W1H 6DQ
UK

ISBN: 1-85368-750-2

DTP and Cover Design: Rob House/Arden House Associates
Project Manager: Tracey Hawthorne
Project Assistant: Donald Reid
Production: Ingeborg Jones
Picture Research: Tracey Derrick
Illustrations: John Marques

Reproduction: Hirt and Carter (Pty) Ltd, Cape Town, South Africa
Printed and bound by CTP Book Printers (Pty) Ltd
PO Box 6060 Parow East 7501, South Africa

The publishers would like to thank the following people and organizations for their help in producing this book:
Dougie Ettlinger; Maureen Payne; South African Library, United Cricket Board of South Africa,
Western Province Cricket Association, Western Province Cricket Club.

ABOUT THE AUTHOR: A Yorkshire-born South African, cricket lover and historian, Ray Knowles has had a lifelong interest in the 'Noble Game'. He was a founder member of the Cricket Society of South Africa and has played club cricket in Yorkshire, Uganda and Malawi. He has a career batting average of 7.36.

CONTENTS

INTRODUCTION

The three founder members of the Imperial Cricket Conference – England, Australia and South Africa – have enjoyed a long association. Matches between two of those countries, South Africa and England, have often produced excellent cricket and tours by the two sides have been popular with players and spectators alike.

The climate and natural beauty of South Africa, together with the hospitality it offers, have made it an appealing and enjoyable destination for English touring sides. On the other hand, the opportunity to visit the home of cricket has always held a special attraction for South Africans.

Early tours were organized by cricket-loving individuals who regarded the social aspect of an overseas excursion as important as the results. The first of these took place in 1888, and only in 1903 did the MCC take control of the organization of tours.

South Africa announced its arrival in international cricket with a three-one series victory over the first official MCC tour in 1905/06. South Africa also recorded a victory against the 1909/10 tourists, but standards deteriorated either side of the First World War and it was not until the late 1920s that cricket in the Republic fully regained its strength. Herbie Wade's tour in 1935 was the first to really capture the imagination of the British public, but following this tour there was hardly an occasion when the South Africans failed to prove exciting and popular visitors.

The MCC tour in 1938/39 saw the playing of the famous 'Timeless Test' in Durban, which ended on its 13th day. Matches after the Second World War and through the 1950s were closely fought and included memorable performances by players such as Compton, Edrich, Eric Rowan, Hutton, Nourse and Tayfield.

For all these years and until relatively recently, the South Africans played as amateurs and many brilliant players came to the fore, playing their particular brand of sunshine cricket and holding their own against the more professional English sides. Many joined English county sides and performed well, while a number of English cricketers stayed behind following tours, with many engaged to coach and play in South Africa during the northern winters.

Political problems that affected contact between the two countries from the 1960s onwards prevented probably the finest ever South African side from performing in England in 1970. In the event, no Test matches were played between South Africa and England between the years 1965 and 1994. In that time some outstanding players were prevented from showing their skills in representative matches and individuals were forced to leave their homeland to be able to perform on the world stage. Many South Africans played county cricket in England and others forsook their home nationalities to further their ambitions in international cricket. While South African cricketers openly objected to their government's racial policy, the country's cricket authorities for many years pleaded for readmittance to the International Cricket Conference, but without success.

A series of privately organized tours were arranged through the 1970s, followed by various controversial rebel tours. The ostracism of South African cricket, together with a general dissatisfaction among cricketers of all nationalities and the opportunities offered by the Packer 'Revolution', paved the way for such tours, which made a significant impact on the cricketing world. For South Africa, 'Cheque-book cricket' had become a means to keeping cricket alive.

The massive changes announced by President de Klerk in 1990 encouraged the racially separate South African cricket authorities to join together and gain readmittance to the international body. The way was open for matches between South Africa and England to be resumed and, for the first time, South Africans of all race groups could support their team in this most compelling of fixtures.

Action from the Oval Test match of the 1955 tour. South African batsman Jackie McGlew survived this run out appeal and went onto make 30 on a difficult pitch. South Africa were unable to take advantage of it, however, and lost the match by 92 runs.

BACKGROUND TO CRICKET TOURING

Tours have been an important part of cricket from the very beginning. William Clarke's 'All England XI' toured all over England in the early 1800s. Professionals were paid between 50 shillings and £4 pounds per match, depending on their skills. Ironically, amateurs were paid £4.

In 1859 a twelve-man squad toured Canada and the United States of America, the twelfth man acting as umpire. The Montreal Club guaranteed £50 per man for the two-month tour. Two years later, Spiers and Pond, a catering firm, offered £150 per man to tour Australia as a substitute for a cancelled lecture tour by Charles Dickens. The tour made over £12 000 profit for the promoters.

Dr WG Grace took his own cricketing party with him on his honeymoon to Australia. His wife's expenses were paid by the Melbourne Club but the professionals travelled second class and were offered £50 plus £20 pocket money for the four-month tour. Later, Grace undertook a second tour to Australia, which netted him £3 000 plus expenses and a locum to look after his medical practice while he was away. In those days professionals were expected to travel separately from the amateurs, stay at separate hotels, use different change rooms and take to the field from separate entrances.

Between 1859 and 1888, when the first tour to South Africa took place, 18 tours abroad were made by English teams, chiefly to North America and Australia. Twelve cricket sides toured England, including a team of Australian Aborigines, who also demonstrated their skill at throwing boomerangs. Other tourists included an American baseball side which also played cricket, Canadians, Philadelphians and Australians. All the tours were organized by entrepreneurs.

In 1888, when the first tour to South Africa took place, two rival English sides were touring in Australia. They both lost money and the touring situation had become a free-for-all.

BACKGROUND TO SOUTH AFRICAN CRICKET

This most English of games was brought to South Africa by British troops during the first occupation of the Cape between 1795 and 1797, and in the second occupation of 1809. On 5 January 1808, a match was played between 'Officers of the Artillery Mess (having Colonel Austen of the 60th Regiment)' and 'Officers of the Colony (with General Clavering)' for a stake of 1 000 Rix Dollars.

Records exist of a match played in 1810 on the Green Point Common, Cape Town, between 'The Ordinance Department plus the 87th Regiment' and 'The Officers of the other Regiments', also for a stake of 1 000 Rix Dollars.

Stake money had been part of the game from very early days, while betting on games, and the resultant bribery, was common. During one match in England, both sides were so determined to lose that the spectators ended up rioting when neither side attempted to score any runs.

In 1842, B Taylor scored the first recorded century made in South Africa while playing for 'Civilians' against the 'Army' at Wynberg in the Cape. The military continued to spread the game

Colin Bland, one of many South Africans who were to make a big impression on the British public during a South Africa tour.

Captains Norman Yardley and Alan Melville toss in the final Test of the first post-war series in 1947 in the United Kingdom.

to Natal and matches were played in Maritzburg in 1843/44, coinciding with Natal's official declaration as a British colony.

In Bloemfontein, the 'Army and Navy' played against 'Indians and Civilians' in 1845, while the 45th Foot challenged the inhabitants of Bloemfontein to a match in 1850.

English settlers followed the military. One of the 1820 Settlers is pictured wading onto the beach holding a cricket bat over his head. Once the Settlers became established, cricket clubs were formed in all the main centres.

Western Province Cricket Club was formed in 1864 and, until the formation of the Western Province Union in 1890, became responsible for organizing teams to represent the Cape Colony. In 1871, three Men of War from the English Flying Squadron, based in the West Indies, paid a visit to Cape Town and played a match against Western Province Cricket Club. This could be regarded as the first unofficial tour by visiting English cricketers.

South Africans Hugh Tayfield and Trevor Goddard lead their team off the field at Headingley after bowling their side to a Test victory in 1955.

Many local matches took place between such sides as 'Mother Country' versus 'Colonial Born', 'Married' versus 'Single' and even 'Ugly' versus 'Handsome'. The latter teams were naturally selected by the ladies.

Travel between the centres was extremely difficult before the arrival of the railways. When the 'Stray Klips' of Kimberley challenged the 'Cape Town Wanderers' in 1887/88, the Inland Transport Company boasted a service taking only eight days for the journey between Cape Town and Kimberley. Even the journey from Durban to Maritzburg took up to three days by wagon.

In 1886, Australian-born cricket enthusiast Captain R Gardner Warton was the only Western Province Cricket Club (WPCC) committee member to vote against the acquisition of Lot 27, a portion of Meriandal farm, belonging to the Vicomtesse de Montmart. The farm had been granted to a brewer, Jacob Letterstedt, who gave it to his daughter when she married the Vicomte de Montmart. The rental was to be £100 per annum for 25 years with the option of a further ten years at £150 per annum.

Fortunately, Captain Warton was outvoted and the farm developed into Newlands Cricket ground, one of the most beautiful in the world, and one of the few with a brewery situated beside it.

Warton, by then a Major, retired from the general staff a year later and returned to England, determined to bring out the first cricket touring team to South Africa. The WPCC offered a guarantee of £450 and other centres followed suit. This provided the spark that South African cricket needed.

There was a frenzy to prepare grounds suitable to host the visitors. Newlands was developing in Cape Town, St George's Park was available in Port Elizabeth, and the Albert Park Oval in Durban was opened in 1887. Johannesburg was only four years old and still a mining camp, but was granted a piece of land, known as Kruger Park in Braamfontein, by President Kruger. This was to be developed as a sporting club called the Wanderers. A corrugated iron fence was built around the ground, which was roughly levelled. There was not a blade of grass, but a pavilion, which included a ballroom, was built. Other than the pavilion, there was no seating accommodation. The admission charge for the week's matches against the English tourists was three guineas, a formidable sum in those days.

Everything was ready for South Africa's entry into the international cricket scene.

CHAPTER I

1888/89

MAJOR WARTON'S TOUR
OF SOUTH AFRICA

Captain: CA Smith

The first international tour from England with matches played against local sides and against a South African side in two 'Tests'. The visitors were powerful, with Briggs and Abel outstanding but there were good individual performances from the South Africans. The tour helped consolidate South African cricket administration.

The first English team to travel to South Africa in 1888/89. Back: JH Roberts, M Read, F Hearne, J Briggs; middle: AJ Fothergill, H Wood, Major RG Warton, CA Smith (capt), Hon CJ Coventry, BAF Greive; front: E McMaster, MP Bowden, AC Skinner, R Abel.

As the strength of South African cricket was unknown and untested, the task of choosing an English touring team was a difficult one. Major Warton chose a mixed side, consisting of seven men who played regularly for their counties and five amateurs of good club standing.

Social acceptability was as important as cricketing ability in the selection of the touring team, which was led by CA Smith, a successful bowler who played for Sussex. He had toured Australia the previous season as the captain of one of the two rival teams to tour that country.

The team boarded the *Garth Castle* on 21 November 1888 and, after calling at Lisbon and Madeira, landed at Cape Town on 14 December 1888. Roberts returned home shortly after the team arrived in South Africa due to the death of his mother. Major Warton telegraphed back to obtain the services of George Ulyett, the

TOURING SIDE	
AMATEURS	PROFESSIONALS
CA Smith (captain) (Sussex)	R Abel (Surrey)
MP Bowden (Surrey)	JM Read (Surrey)
Hon CJ Coventry	H Wood (Surrey)
JEP McMaster	J Briggs (Lancashire)
JH Roberts	F Hearne (Kent)
BAF Greive	AJ Fothergill (Somerset)
AC Skinner	
Major Warton was to act as Manager and 'touring umpire'	

Yorkshire batsman, who joined the team in Pietermaritzburg.

Nineteen matches were to be played, including two against a full South African side. These were to become accepted as the first

Charles Aubrey Smith, the captain of the first touring party. He was only to play one test match for England, but he later took up a career in Hollywood as an actor and was knighted in 1944.

JOHN BRIGGS

John Briggs, the devastating Lancashire bowler who bamboozled every South African batsman. He took 15 for 28 in the second Test match.

forming on matting wickets, laid on rock hard surfaces where the ball came through quicker and rose higher than in England.

Johannesburg was booming; prospectors were flooding in from all over the world and were starved of entertainment. The Wanderers Club was virtually complete and everyone was ready for a party. The visitors were feted and the public banquet in their honour went on all night.

The next day, XXII of Johannesburg scored 138 and then dismissed the English side for 60, no doubt as a result of the entertainment. Then the match and the tour turned. The tourists pulled themselves together and Johannesburg were dismissed for 58 with the English captain, CA Smith, taking ten wickets. The English openers scored 138 without loss to win the game by ten wickets. They were not to lose another match throughout the tour.

The following games against XV of the Transvaal, XXII of Pietermaritzburg, and XV of Natal, provided decisive victories for the tourists. The humidity in Durban affected the English players, although the grassy outfields were a welcome change after the dust of the interior. The match against XVIII of Durban was the first draw of the series, when GA Kempis took five for 32 for Durban.

Briggs and Smith were too good for the XXII of the Cape Mounted Rifles when Briggs took 27 wickets for 23 runs. Similar results were obtained against XXII of Grahamstown and XXII of Midlands District in Graaff-Reinet.

The team travelled to Port Elizabeth full of confidence to prepare for the first 'eleven-a-side'

Test matches between the two countries. The remaining 17 matches were all to be played 'against odds' when the local side could have as many as 22 players.

The first games against Cape sides were a disaster for the tourists. Although Johnny Briggs, the Lancashire bowler, was taking plenty of wickets, the South Africans were showing that they were not to be overawed. Theunissen and CH Vintcent, in particular, were matching the Englishmen's skills and the Cape sides were successful. Having lost four of the first six matches, the tourists came in for criticism from the local press. The English batsmen were not per-match of the tour. This was to be against a full South African side in what is now regarded as the first Test match between the two countries. The South African side was the strongest available apart from the lack of Theunissen. It was captained by OR Dunell from Port Elizabeth, and the team included AR Innes, AB Tancred, P Hutchinson, CH Vintcent, AE Ochse, WH Milton, Lieutenant Stewart, F Smith, CE Finlason, and GA Kempis. For the first time, the South African team sported olive-green caps with 'SA' embroidered in gold on the front.

Between two and three thousand people watched the start of play at St George's Park and disaster for South Africa. By the second over, the South African score was no runs for two wickets, and it was soon 17 for five wickets. Dunell and Tancred were the only two players to reach double figures and South Africa were all out for 84. Briggs and Smith took the wickets.

England scored 148, but only due to a last wicket partnership of 35. In the second innings, South Africa fared only slightly better by scoring 129 and the Englishmen won the game easily by eight wickets.

Charles Aubrey Smith went down with a fever after this match and took no further part in the tour. He therefore holds the distinction of being the only player to have captained his country in his only Test match. Monty Bowden took over the captaincy for the last match of the tour, the second Test match at Newlands, played on 25 and 26 March 1889.

England made 292, with Bobby Abel scoring 120, the first century in South African first-class cricket. WH Ashley was the most successful bowler for South Africa, with a good seven wickets for 95. For England, Johnny Briggs was unplayable, with seven for 17, AB Tancred batted through the South African innings for 26 and South Africa could manage only 47. Briggs then took eight wickets for 11 runs in the second innings of 43 so that South Africa were thrashed by an innings and 202 runs. Briggs took 15 wickets for only 28 runs in the match.

After the match, Smith awarded the first Currie Cup, donated

The South African team which lost the first Test match in 1889. Back: A Rose-Innes, AB Tancred, CE Finlason, CH Vintcent, FW Smith; middle: P Hutchinson, OR Dunell (captain), WH Milton; front: AE Ochse, RB Stewart, GA Kempis.

AB Tancred, the batsman from Kimberley who carried his bat in the first innings of the second Test match, scoring 26 out of a team total of 47.

by Sir Donald Currie, the head of the Castle Mail Packet Company, to Kimberley for the best performance against the tourists.

On the whole tour Bobby Abel scored over a thousand runs, including three centuries. Johnny Briggs was unplayable with 290

wickets at under six runs per wicket. Smith and Fothergill took over 100 wickets each.

Major Warton's experiment of bringing out a team of English cricketers was a success after a very shaky start. In spite of reasonable attendances, he did not cover his expenses, although the WPCC showed a profit of £575 from matches against the tourists.

From a South African cricket point of view it was a most important tour and put South Africa on the international map. However, apart from one or two good individual performances, particularly from Theunissen, Vintcent and Ashley, it was clear that South African cricket still had a lot to learn.

The tourists embarked on the *Garth Castle* and arrived back in England on 16 April 1889. Frank Hearne stayed behind to join WPCC as coach at £250 per annum, with a free house and an annual benefit.

Basil Greive, the Honorable Charles Coventry, Emile McMaster and Major Warton also stayed in South Africa. C Aubrey Smith and Bowden formed a partnership as stockbrokers in Johannesburg. Smith was to lead Transvaal in the Currie Cup match the following season and then return to England to form a film company with Leslie Howard. He later went on to Hollywood and became famous as Sir C Aubrey Smith, the film star.

Wisden summed up the tour by stating that 'All the beatings were sustained in the early part of the trip, and it is no libel to state that, for a time, generous hospitality had an effect on the cricket.' This was to become a regular feature of future tours to South Africa.

The most luxurious building in South Africa. Wanderers Pavilion, complete with ballroom, was built in 1888/89 specifically for the English tour.

CHAPTER 2

1891/92

WW READ'S TOUR OF SOUTH AFRICA

Captain: WW Read

*Another tour against 'odds' with little interest
from the public. The professionalism of the
Englishmen was too strong for the locals.
The Hearne family represented both England
and South Africa, but the tour belonged to
the bowling of JJ Ferris.*

Western Province XVIII versus WW Read's Team 1891. Back: G Cripps, VA van der Byl, V van der Byl, Lieutenant Boyle, ES Steytler, GP Pemberton, CN Thomas (umpire); middle: H Calder, C Mills, Captain Wright, WH Milton (capt), HH Castens, F Hearne, CS Hickley, T Routledge; front: E Allen, M Bisset, Drummer Ellis, J Middleton.

Efforts were made to bring the full-strength Australian side to South Africa during the 1889/90 season, but these were unsuccessful. This was perhaps fortunate given the lack of experience of the South Africans. There were also misgivings about the advisability of this second cricket tour, following the financial failure of Warton's tour and the fact that a rugby tour had just been completed.

WG Grace was leading another side to Australia at the time and it was thought there would be little interest from the South African public. This proved to be the case. However, a strong side arrived in Cape Town on 8 December 1891 aboard the *Dunnottar Castle*.

The Hearne family was well represented. JT (Young Jack) was a cousin to brothers George and Alec. A third brother, Frank, having stayed behind following the previous tour, was playing for Western Province and was eligible to play for South Africa.

Twenty matches were scheduled, all except the last to be 'against odds'. The last game, against South Africa, was to be regarded as a Test match. In fact, an additional game was played in Cape Town against a Malay side for the benefit of the Professionals.

The Cape Colony sides, with up to 22 players, proved no problem for the tourists, although both Hearne and Grimmer put up good performances. Teams in the Transvaal also suffered and only PH de Villiers proved worthy of the occasion so that the matches were poorly attended. The

TOURING SIDE	
AMATEURS	PROFESSIONALS
WW Read (captain) (Surrey)	W Brockwell (Surrey)
JJ Ferris (Gloucester)	H Wood (Surrey)
WL Murdock (Sussex)	GW Ayres (Surrey)
G Brann (Sussex)	AD Pougher (Leicestershire)
	W Chatterton (Derby)
	VA Barton (Hants)
	F Martin (Kent)
	E Leaney (Kent)
	A Hearne (Kent)
	G Hearne (Kent)
	JT Hearne (Middlesex)

powerful English side carried on triumphantly through Natal, Border, Eastern Province, Free State and Kimberley before returning to Cape Town. XV of Western Province and XXII of Country Clubs were hammered, so an undefeated English team prepared to meet South Africa on even terms in the only Test match of the tour.

The South African team was led by William Milton, and included Frank Hearne, who had previously played for England, while on the English side both Murdock and Ferris had previously played for Australia against England.

South Africa was thrashed by an innings and 189 runs. England's wicket-keeper Harry Wood scored 134*, his only century in 316 first-class matches. England went on to a total of 392, and South Africa were dismissed for 97 and 83. Frank Hearne was top scorer for South Africa in both innings with 24 and 23, while skipper Milton managed 21 and 16.

As the match was over so quickly, an extra match was arranged for the tourists against a Malay XIII at Newlands, with the proceeds of the game going towards the English professionals. This was the first time a Malay team had played against a touring side. L Samoodien became only the second South African to score a half century against the tourists.

With 14 wins, seven draws and no defeats, the touring side was obviously too strong for the South Africans. Once more the bowlers had dominated. JJ Ferris took 234 wickets, JT Hearne 163 and F Martin 106. Chatterton scored 955 runs, Murdock 633, and Alec Hearne 516.

But it was JJ Ferris's tour. He was a great left-arm bowler who had played regularly for Australia. Following two tours of England with the Australians, he agreed to qualify for Gloucestershire, for whom he was an utter failure. However, on this tour he was a brilliant success. He returned to Australia and joined the Imperial Light Horse to serve in South Africa, where he died at the age of 34.

The tour had been a social success, but as with the previous visit proved financially unsuccessful.

WW Read, who captained the tourists. He had previously led England abroad in Australia, winning the one test match played on that tour. He was a fast round arm bowler and good bat for Surrey.

JJ Ferris, who played for both Australia and England, the top wicket taker on the tour with 234. He died of enteric fever during the South African War in 1900 and is buried in Durban.

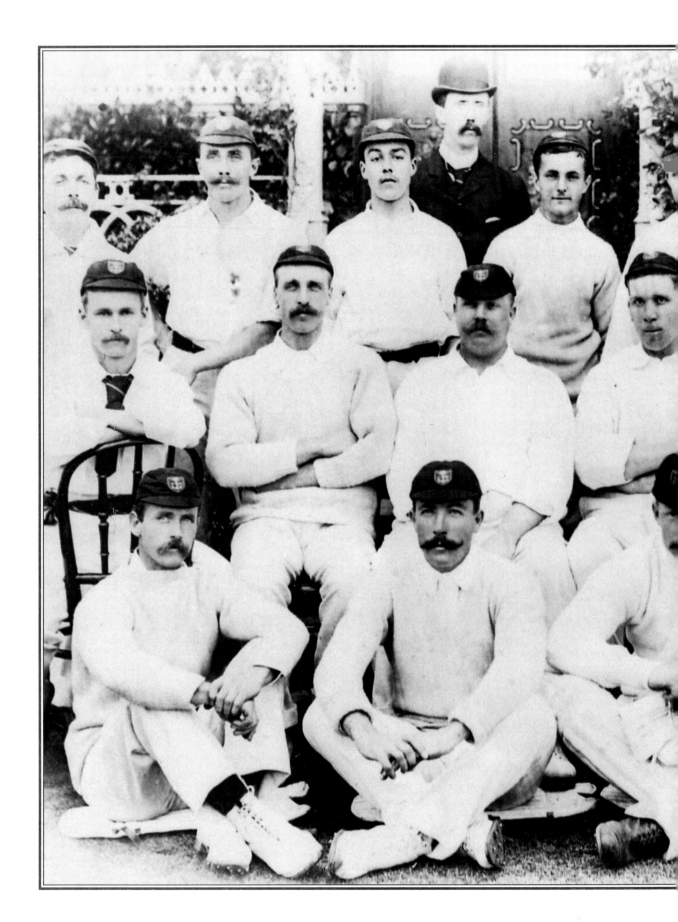

CHAPTER 3

1894

FIRST SOUTH AFRICA TOUR OF THE UNITED KINGDOM

Captain: HH Castens

The first tour abroad played against second class sides. WG Grace almost beat them single-handedly but Middleton, Rowe and Sewell showed that they were world class. Money problems almost caused the cancellation of the tour until it was bailed out by Randlords.

The greatest cricketer of all time, WG Grace, who aged 46 beat South Africa virtually single-handedly playing for Gloucestershire.

HH Castens (Captain)(W Province)	
J Middleton (W Province)	COH Sewell (Natal)
G Rowe (W Province)	D Davey (Natal)
F Hearne (W Province)	T Routledge (Transvaal)
AW Seccull (W Province)	CL Johnson (Transvaal)
G Mills (W Province)	GS Kempis (Transvaal)
G Cripps (W Province)	EA Halliwell (Transvaal)
DC Parkin (E Province)	G Glover (GW)

The Manager was WV Simkins from Cape Town

Cricket had become very popular in South Africa following the visits by the two English sides and the introduction of the Currie Cup competition. More clubs were being formed, fortunes were being made (and lost) on the diamond and gold fields, so there was no shortage of sponsors for a tour to England.

Individuals had put up good performances against the English tourists, and it was thought to be a good time to arrange the first tour by a South African side to the home of cricket. The tour was originally intended to be organized by the Western Province Cricket Club but the newly formed South African Cricket Association took over and it was agreed that the team should represent all South Africa. The captain chosen to lead the 15-man squad was HH Castens, who had previously captained South Africa in its first rugby Test in 1891.

Cecil John Rhodes gave £500 towards the guarantee fund of £3 000 and the Honourable JD Logan of Matjiesfontein promised another £500. But he withdrew his offer when his choice of manager, HG Cadwallader, was not selected.

Twenty-four fixtures were arranged, but none of them was regarded as first-class, much to the disappointment of the South Africans. In 1894, only the original nine counties forming the County Championship were granted first-class status.

Tancred was unable to go for business reasons and brilliant Jimmy Sinclair, barely 18, was thought to be too young. It was considered 'impolitic' to include T Hendricks, a Malay fast bowler, who was omitted as a result of 'the greatest pressure by those in high authority in Cape Colony'. The South African publication *The Cricket Field* predicted: 'The team would regret before the season was out that they were so particular about the colour of their men.'

Most of the side arrived at Southampton aboard the SS *Tartar* on 29 April 1894. On arrival they practised at the Private Banks ground at Catford for three weeks to become accustomed to turf wickets before the first game against Lord Sheffield's XI at his home, Sheffield Park, in Sussex.

No charge was made for admission to the match, although cabs were excluded from the park. This caused a demonstration by the 'cabbies' who barricaded the gates when the South Africans wanted to leave. This was the first, but regrettably not the last demonstration concerning a South African team.

The South Africans lost this match and the one against a weak Surrey side but beat Oxford University and were fortunate to draw against Hampshire.

Two defeats in the first four matches was a poor start and the next match was to be against the MCC at Lord's, led by the great WG Grace himself. There was no play on the first day because of rain and Grace, against all his principles, sent South Africa in to bat. Frank

Hearne was the only one able to cope with his bowling, and South Africa were dismissed for 126. Middleton and Rowe bowled beautifully, however, and gave South Africa a lead of 23.

Disaster struck in South Africa's second innings when they were all out for 57. Grace took another six wickets, leaving MCC needing only 81 to win. At 63 for three it was decided to extend the normal hours of play in the hope of obtaining a result. Middleton and Rowe again bowled superbly to take the next seven wickets for seven runs and to win the exciting match by 11 runs. Middleton and Rowe took 19 of the 20 MCC wickets.

Having beaten Leicester, Chatham and District, and Glamorgan, at Gloucestershire the side again met 'The Old Master' who virtually took on South Africa single-handedly. In the South Africans' first innings he took nine wickets and then caught the last man off his brother's bowling. He then scored 129 not out in a total of 301. Centuries by EA Halliwell and Frank Hearne helped the tourists, but Gloucestershire won by five wickets.

Charles William Wright, who was due to tour South Africa with Lord Hawke the following year, organized a match at Portsmouth.

His eleven included the 'prince of cricketers', KS Ranjitsinhji, who was still at University prior to joining Sussex. Ranji scored 53 in the first innings and 146* in the second. Thanks to 152 from Routledge, the game ended in a draw.

Matches against Warwickshire and Derbyshire were drawn, but there were convincing wins against teams from Scotland, Glasgow and District, and Liverpool and District.

The team then travelled to Ireland for matches against the gentlemen of Ireland and Dublin University. Both matches ended in easy victories for the South Africans, but at this point it was found that the money had run out.

The Manager, WV Simkins, was forced to canvass the wealthy South African mining magnates living in England, who fortunately subscribed sufficient funds to complete the tour and a series of holiday matches.

The South Africans gained valuable experience during the tour, and proved that they were a team of reasonable county standard, with some players of higher standard. Sewell reached third place in the national batting averages by scoring over a thousand runs. Routledge and wicket-keeper Halliwell scored over 700 runs. Slow bowler Rowe took 136 wickets and Middleton 83.

The public was not interested in watching second-class matches and the gate receipts during the tour were only £500 compared to expenses of £3 600.

The team split after the last game to see more of Europe. Sewell, however, stayed behind to qualify for Grace's team, Gloucestershire.

Frank Hearne, who had toured as part of Major Warton's team and returned to England in 1894 to represent South Africa.

Twenty-year-old George Rowe, a slow bowler from Cape Town who was the principal wicket taker on the tour with 136.

CHAPTER 4

1895/96

LORD HAWKE'S FIRST TOUR OF SOUTH AFRICA

Captain: Lord Hawke

A strong English side led by the intrepid organiser Lord Hawke came to South Africa in a period of political uncertainty at the time of the Jameson Raid. Lohmann was outstanding, but there were few good performances by the South Africans who were dismissed on one occasion for 30 runs.

George Lohmann was the star of the tour, with his performances including a hat trick in Port Elizabeth. He stayed behind after the tour and became a stalwart of South African cricket.

Lord Hawke's first love was Yorkshire cricket. He had transformed the team from being 'ten drunks and a parson' (Lockwood was a lay preacher) into the most powerful and successful county cricket team. His second love was organizing cricket tours to all parts of the world. Having been to Australia in 1887, USA and Canada in 1891, Ceylon and India in 1892 and North America in 1894, he arranged the third tour to South Africa in 1895.

It was a time of political uncertainty in South Africa. The *uitlanders* in the Transvaal had for some time been expressing their grievances, with little sympathy from the Transvaal Republic. Cecil John Rhodes, the prime minister of the Cape Colony, was giving the movement his support and it was common knowledge that insurrection was planned.

In the meantime, Lord Hawke had organized a very strong squad. With most of the players playing regular county cricket and two or three worth their places in the England team, it was the strongest squad to arrive in South Africa to date.

Lord Hawke, Sir TC O'Brien and HT Hewett travelled separately from the rest of the team and an accident to their steamer caused them to miss the first match at Newlands against XV of Western Province. George Lohmann bowled out Western Province for 115, but Middleton, also with seven for 50, dismissed the tourists for only 79. Although Lohmann took another seven wickets in the second innings, J Willoughby took six for 15 to win the game for XV of Western Province.

As the game was over in two days, a challenge was issued to a one-day, eleven-a-side match, which Western Province also won by one wicket. When Lord Hawke arrived, he was not amused.

The team was invited to Groote Schuur, the home of the prime minister of the Cape Colony and, during lunch with Cecil Rhodes, word was received that Dr Leander Starr Jameson had marched on Johannesburg. On the second day of the match, news arrived that Jameson had been arrested and that the invasion of the Transvaal had failed. This was a problem, not only for Cecil Rhodes, but also for Lord Hawke, as the next match was scheduled for Johannesburg.

After a delay, the team set off and were surrounded by an armed party of Boers. However, they demonstrated the game of cricket, presented the Boers with two bats, and carried on safely having made good friends.

On their arrival in Johannesburg they watched Cronje march his prisoners through the streets and were allowed to dine with them in prison after the match. Jimmy Sinclair scored 75 and took seven wickets in the match.

Johannesburg had changed considerably since the first tour by CA Smith six years earlier. The slump in 1889, which had forced Smith to leave, was followed by an enormous boom. This, in turn, had been followed by a slump in 1895 when the stock market

TOURING SIDE	
AMATEURS	PROFESSIONALS
Lord Hawke (captain) (Yorkshire)	TW Hayward (Surrey)
AJL Hill (Hants)	GA Lohmann (Surrey)
C Hesseltine (Hants)	HR Butt (Sussex)
CB Fry (Sussex)	EJ Tyler (Somerset)
Sir TC O'Brien (Middlesex)	
HR Bromley-Davenport (Middlesex)	
SMJ Woods (Somerset)	
HT Hewett (Somerset)	
AM Miller (Wiltshire)	
CW Wright (Nottinghamshire)	

George Lohmann was to act as Manager

collapsed. Johannesburg comprised 25 000 white men, 14 000 women, including 1 000 prostitutes, 97 brothels and 50 000 black mine workers.

Nine years after the gold reef had been discovered, the corrugated iron shacks of 1889 had given way to a more solid city. There were horse-drawn trams, large solid stone buildings, a stock exchange, several banks, mining company offices and the rand club.

The newly built railway line between Johannesburg and Natal made it easier for the touring team to reach Pietermaritzburg for their next match against XV of Maritzburg. CB Fry and TC O'Brien scored centuries for the tourists and RM Poore scored 112 for Pietermaritzburg before the match was called off as a draw. Two days later, Poore was again in good form with 107 not out to win the game for XV of Natal by five wickets. Poore was in fact a major; he had been ADC to Lord Harris in India, where he is supposed to have learned his cricket from books. He was a great all-round sportsman and represented the army in several sports. He later joined Hampshire, where he became a prolific scorer and was instrumental in encouraging Natal-born Llewellyn to join the side.

In the warm-up for the first Test match, XVIII of Port Elizabeth were easily beaten when Lohmann took 26 wickets in the match.

Innes, Rowe, Tancred and Richards were not available for South Africa in the first Test, which was to be played on a turf wicket for the first time in South Africa. England's batting in the first innings of this Test was mediocre. They scored a modest 185 runs. J Middleton took five for 64.

South Africa's performance with the bat was worse – they collapsed for 93, George Lohmann taking seven for 38. Worse was to come when South Africa batted again in response to England's second innings of 226. This time Lohmann took eight wickets for seven runs to dismiss South Africa for 30 runs, leaving England winners by 288 runs.

The total of 30 runs was to remain a blot on South Africa's Test record as the lowest-ever Test score until 1924, when it was equalled, unfortunately again by South Africa. Lord Hawke invited President Kruger of the Transvaal to the match against XV of Pretoria but President Kruger declined.

South Africa was again humiliated in the second Test match in Johannesburg when England amassed 482 runs in the first innings. All the English batsmen made runs and the only South African bowler to be reasonably successful was GA Rowe. George Lohmann took nine wickets for only 28 to dismiss South Africa for 151 in the first innings and for 134 in the follow-on.

Kimberley hosted the tourists and there was great excitement when the Englishmen were bowled out for only 95. 'Diamondopolis' led on the first innings and lost a very close game by only 13 runs.

The team called at Matjiesfontein to play a match against the Honourable JD Logan's XX, strengthened by the addition of one of the tourists, George Lohmann. Logan had built Matjiesfontein as a health resort in the middle of the Karoo and included a cricket field in the village. He was to form a close association with George Lohmann when the latter, suffering ill health, went to live in Matjiesfontein.

There was very little interest in the match against Western Province or the third Test match. A reasonably representative South African side was available but they had no answer to George Lohmann and could make only 115 and 117. England's first innings of 265 was sufficient to win the match by an innings.

Lohmann, who played for Surrey, had a wonderful tour, taking 157 wickets at an average of under seven, including his career best of nine for 28 in Johannesburg. The next best bowler took only 46 wickets. Hayward and CB Fry topped the batting averages while Sammy Woods played in every match on the tour.

It was a tour full of incidents, made in uncertain times, and showed once again that, in spite of good individual performances by the South Africans, they could not match the professionalism of English cricketers such as George Lohmann, CB Fry, AJL Hill and Tom Hayward.

The tour made a small profit and the main group arrived back in England in April 1896.

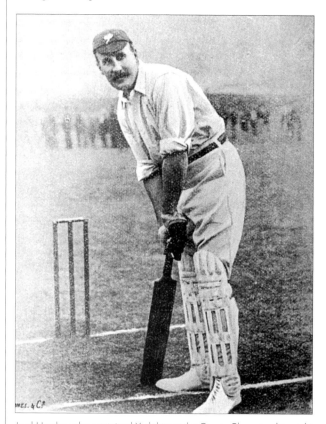

Lord Hawke, who captained Yorkshire to the County Championship eight times and was a compulsive tourist.

CHAPTER 5

1898/99

LORD HAWKE'S SECOND TOUR OF SOUTH AFRICA

Captain: Lord Hawke

Another strong side led by Lord Hawke, with young 'Plum' Warner, Schofield Haigh and Albert Trott outstanding, toured in South Africa amid more political uncertainty. The South Africans performed better, with Middleton and Rowe matching the Englishmen. South Africa's giant all-rounder, Jimmy Sinclair, came to the fore.

The South African team which lost an exciting first Test match against the English tourists in 1898/99. Back: GH Shepstone, JH Sinclair, WRT Solomon; middle: J Middleton, VM Tancred, M Bisset (capt), HH Francis, RR Dower; front: CB Llewellyn, GA Rowe, R Graham.

Since his last visit to South Africa, Lord Hawke had taken a team of amateurs to the West Indies. After just one winter at home, he was persuaded to bring out a second tour to South Africa by the Honourable JD Logan, the Laird of Matjiesfontein.

The railway had been extended from Kimberley to Bulawayo in 1897 and two matches were to be played for the first time in Rhodesia. Cecil Rhodes had resigned as prime minister of the Cape Colony as a result of the Jameson Raid but was again involved in Cape politics. Lord Milner, Governor and High Commissioner of the Cape Colony, was in London to discuss the Transvaal problem with the foreign minister, Chamberlain. War was imminent.

Meanwhile, in Pretoria, President Kruger was host at a banquet

TOURING SIDE	
AMATEURS	PROFESSIONALS
Lord Hawke (captain) (Yorkshire)	S Haigh (Yorkshire)
HR Bromley-Davenport (Middlesex)	JT Tyldesley (Lancashire)
PF Warner (Middlesex)	WR Cuttell (Lancashire)
F Mitchell (Yorkshire)	JH Board (Gloucestershire)
CEM Wilson (Yorkshire)	AE Trott (Middlesex)
FW Milligan (Yorkshire)	
AG Archer (Shropshire)	

Lord Hawke, captaining his second tour. With the political situation in southern Africa tense, the tour was to prove eventful both on and off the field.

to celebrate the end of half a dozen wars against African chiefs.

Johannesburg had grown to a city of 50 000 Europeans and 88 000 Africans, but all the grievances that had led to the Jameson Raid remained and it only needed a spark to cause a blaze.

AA White was brought out as touring umpire and H Kirk, the Trent Bridge dressing room attendant, was to act as dogsbody. George Lohmann, now living in Matjiesfontein, was to act as manager for the team.

Once more the side was a good mix of socially acceptable amateur 'gentlemen' and professional 'players', the equivalent of a good county side. They sailed from Southampton on 3 December 1898 on board the *Scot* and arrived in Cape Town on 20 December.

The Englishmen found difficulty with the matting wicket but won a close game against XIII of Western Province. A second game was scheduled against Western Province, strengthened by Brown, Tate, Gutteridge and Sidney Barnes, four English professionals who were coaching in South Africa. However, the professionals declined the offer made by the Western Province Cricket Union.

The result was similar but with a margin of 106 runs. Middleton and Rowe took all but one of the English wickets. Trott and Haigh took all but two of the Province wickets.

Trott took 20 wickets against XXII of Midlands, then hit 84 and took another 15 wickets in the match against Port Elizabeth XV.

The next match was supposed to have been a Test match. However, there was unpleasantness between the Transvaal cricket administration and Port Elizabeth so that the match was changed to one against Cape Colony. Lord Hawke expressed his disappointment at a smoking concert held at the local Drill Hall, while Bromley-Davenport entertained the guests to songs at the piano.

A plague of locusts at St George's Park, which stopped play on the last afternoon, could not prevent a victory for the Englishmen. Young Plum Warner got a duck in each innings.

On to Johannesburg where, remarkably, Trott did not take a wicket against XV of Johannesburg.

Albert Trott, England's great all-rounder. A demon bowler and the only batsman to have hit a ball over the pavillion at Lord's.

Jimmy Sinclair took five wickets and scored a fifty to force a draw. Another match was played on even terms against Transvaal. The English XI had their best innings of the tour scoring 537 for six declared. Plum Warner managed another duck.

Lord Hawke, rather naïvely perhaps, again invited President Kruger to the match against XV of Transvaal at Pretoria; Kruger

James Middleton, South Africa's left arm spinner from Cape Town.

again declined. The Transvaal team included LC Braund, the English professional who was approaching top form when he appeared for Transvaal. Trott was again on form with ten for 29 and Plum Warner's bad spell was broken with an innings of 92.

Large crowds attended the Test match at the Wanderers where Murray Bisset led the South Africans out to dismiss England for 145. Then Jimmy Sinclair hit a brilliant 86 to give South Africa a useful lead of 106 on the first innings. With the tourists on 173 for seven, South Africa seemed certain to win. However, Plum Warner carried his bat for 132* in his first Test match. For this feat he was given a gold signet ring by Lord Hawke. Cuttell was the next highest scorer, with 21. Middleton took five for 51, leaving South Africa with a target of only 132 to win the Test. However, Trott took over with five wickets and dismissed South Africa for 99 to win the match by 32 runs. This was the closest Test match result between the two countries to date.

Using the newly completed railway from Kimberley through Bechuanaland to the terminus at Bulawayo, a journey that started early Friday morning and ended only late Sunday, the team played its first major match in Rhodesia. The tourists were far too strong for the Rhodesians, but sat down to a ten-course meal at the Bulawayo Club on the last evening of the match.

A match had been arranged in Mafeking on the way back from Rhodesia, but the locals had been unable to raise a side and yet another match was quickly arranged in Kimberley against Griqualand

West. This time the locals gave the visitors the biggest fright of the tour when the Englishmen were on 54 for nine; but a last wicket partnership of 72 brought the score to 126. Brilliant hitting by A W Powell enabled Griquas to reach 200, in spite of Schofield Haigh's hat-trick in his nine for 44. Unfortunately, a thunderstorm stopped the fascinating match.

More drama was to befall Lord Hawke's side when, travelling by rail from Kimberley to Cape Town, the brakes failed and the train ran backwards to collide with another train. Windows were smashed and the party was badly shaken. Trott's thumb was put out of joint and Milligan suffered a black eye and cut nose. The team were all thankful to arrive in Matjiesfontein to rest for a few days with Logan.

Back at Newlands, the Cape Colony team was again outclassed by Haigh and Trott before the second Test. There was some criticism of the choice of the South African team, with two wicket-keepers, Halliwell and Price, chosen. Twenty-three-year-old Murray Bisset led the team and there was sensation when, having been 60 for one, England were dismissed for only 92. Jimmy Sinclair took six for 26 and Middleton four for 18 as nine wickets fell for 32 runs. Sinclair then followed up his performance with a century, the first by a South African. He thus became the first South African to take five wickets and to score a century in a Test match.

South Africa's total of 177 gave them a lead of 85 and the crowd grew to 7 000 anticipating a great victory. England pulled themselves together in the second innings, Tyldesley scoring 112 and Trott wading in with two sixes out of the ground for England to reach 330. South Africa needed 246 to win. Shalders and Powell were 11 without loss at lunch and then the unbelievable happened. In a total innings time of 45 minutes, South Africa were all out for 35 runs. Haigh and Trott bowled an incredible spell during which Haigh took six wickets for 11 runs and Trott took four wickets for 19 runs. South Africa had lost decisively.

It was a very successful tour. Apart from the two light-hearted games at Newlands and Matjiesfontein, the English XI played 17 matches, won 15 and drew two.

Plum Warner headed the averages followed by Mitchell and Tyldesley. Cuttell and Schofield Haigh played well. But the tour belonged to Trott with 168 wickets and 472 runs.

Albert Edwin Trott was one of three Australian brothers to make their marks on cricket. Playing for Middlesex, he was regarded as one of the best all-rounders of his day. Every ball was different and he was the only man to have hit a ball over the pavilion at Lord's. During 1899 and 1900 he was at the peak of his career but later became heavy and muscle-bound. He became ill and shot himself at the age of 42.

South African cricket had shown a remarkable improvement since the previous tour. Jimmy Sinclair in particular had shown that he was a world-class all-rounder, heading the Test averages in both the batting and bowling. The previous season, while playing for

Villagers against Roodeport, he had scored a record 301 not out. Left-arm spinner James Middleton, who had been bought out of the army by Cape Town Cricket Club and was now their professional, had also shown his class.

The touring side left Cape Town on the *Norman* and arrived back in England on 21 April 1899. The Yorkshire amateur, Milligan, stayed behind and died in action during the relief of Mafeking at the age of 30.

South Africa was to have no more serious cricket for four years.

Jimmy Sinclair, the great all-rounder on the South African side, a giant fast bowler and enormous hitter.

CHAPTER 6

1901

SECOND SOUTH AFRICA TOUR OF THE UNITED KINGDOM

Organizer: The Hon. JD Logan
Captain: M Bisset

A controversial second class tour, with little public interest, organised by Logan. Kotze's fast bowling impressed and Halliwell's wicket-keeping was world class. Jimmy Sinclair had a variable tour. Brilliant South African all-rounder Llewellyn, now playing for Hampshire, joined the side occasionally.

JJ Kotze, claimed to be the fastest bowler in the world in his time. He was to tour the United Kingdom three times, in 1901, 1904 and 1907.

TOURING SIDE

M Bisset (captain) (W Province)	GA Rowe (W Province)
ACV Bisset (W Province)	CMH Hathorn (Transvaal)
A Reid (W Province)	LJ Tancred (Transvaal)
CFH Prince (W Province)	EA Halliwell (Transvaal)
R Graham (W Province)	JH Sinclair (Transvaal)
JD Logan jun. (W Province)	WA Shalders (Griqualand West)
JJ Kotze (W Province)	BC Cooley (Natal)

GA Lohmann was to act as Manager

The Anglo-Boer War was not over and the country was split in two when the Honourable JD Logan announced that he had decided to send a cricket team on tour to the United Kingdom.

Jimmy Sinclair had joined the British forces, was captured by the Boers, then escaped to play cricket. PH de Villiers, who had played against the previous touring teams, was in a British prisoner-of-war camp in Ceylon, where he spent his time organizing cricket matches, both inside and outside the camp. De Villiers had been captured, dressed in his cricket gear, by a Lancashire regiment. His captors were duly impressed when they discovered that he had played against their beloved Johnny Briggs.

Napier van Ryneveldt had also been in a prisoner-of-war camp in Cape Town. As a result of being absent from the camp while playing cricket for the British forces, he missed the boat to join De Villiers in the camp in Ceylon and instead found himself sent to St Helena.

Logan's announcement caused controversy. The English press, led by Arthur Conan Doyle, believed they should be fighting the Boers and not playing cricket. On the other hand, the South African press stated that the tour was a private venture by Logan, and should not be designated a South African side as it was not chosen by the South African Cricket Union. In any case only half-a-dozen of those selected stood a chance of being selected for South Africa.

COH Sewell, now playing for Gloucestershire, was billed to play for the tourists but in fact never did. CB Llewellyn, now playing for Hampshire, turned out twice for the team.

Unlike the previous tour, 15 of the 25 matches to be played were granted first-class status.

The squad left Cape Town aboard SS *Briton* on 17 April 1901, and arrived in Southampton on 3 May.

Two weeks later, Llewellyn, playing for Hampshire, scored 216 and took four wickets for six runs to help beat his countrymen by an innings. CB Llewellyn was born in Pietermaritzburg, the son of an English father and a St Helenan mother. He was a brilliant all-rounder; the 216 scored in this match was the highest of his 15 centuries and took only three hours, including 30 boundaries. Llewellyn was in top form during 1901 and, although he did not play, was among the squad from which the England team was chosen in 1902. He severed his connections with Hampshire and returned to play for South Africa on many occasions. Later he returned to England to play league cricket for Accrington.

The second match was at Crystal Palace against London Counties, a team organized by WG Grace, after he had broken his connections with Gloucestershire. Llewellyn, now playing for the South Africans, took 13 wickets and scored most of the runs to enable the tourists to win.

The next matches against Kent, Leicestershire, Warwickshire and MCC at Lord's exposed the shortcomings of the South African batsmen in the strange conditions. However a fine 184 by skipper Bisset gave the tourists a much-needed victory against Derbyshire.

The batsmen came into form on the good batting

Ernest Halliwell, one of South Afirca's true world class performers. He kept wicket for Middlesex, as his father had done before him, and was noted for his skill in standing up to Kotze.

Unfortunately, five of the first six matches had been defeats so there was little public interest in the team's progress. In fact, five of the 15 first-class matches were won by the South Africans.

Sinclair's batting only came good towards the end of the tour, although his bowling, together with that of Rowe, was very successful throughout. Hathorn, Shalders, Tancred, M Bisset and Halliwell had good games while Kotze was compared to Kortright, generally regarded as the fastest bowler in the world. Halliwell's wicket-keeping was world class.

Several players stayed on for a holiday and the rest sailed home on the SS *Briton* on 14 September.

The visit was not a financial success and the Honourable JD Logan lost money on the tour. His friend, George Lohmann, died and was buried at Matjiesfontein shortly after the team returned from the tour.

wicket against Cambridge University when they scored 692. Rowe then took 13 wickets in the match to win the game by an innings. The form was not to last, however, and Somerset thrashed the South Africans. Matches against the Gentlemen of Ireland, Dublin University, Liverpool and District, and Durham were won comfortably. Lancashire and Surrey beat the South Africans but Kotze bowled well to defeat Nottinghamshire.

The match against Worcestershire ended in a remarkable tie. R Graham took eight wickets for 90 and the last man was out with the scores level.

Northamptonshire, Staffordshire and Wiltshire provided no opposition but Yorkshire provided a sterner challenge at Harrogate. Sinclair had another good match when he took 14 wickets and scored 80 runs, but the visitors lost by 155 runs.

A short tour of Scotland provided two victories against East of Scotland at Edinburgh and West of Scotland at Glasgow.

The tour ended on a good note when Sinclair, with seven for 20, dismissed Gloucestershire for 40, the lowest score of the tour. He then took another six wickets in the second innings to achieve a victory by an innings. Glamorgan were also easily beaten.

Most of the first-class matches were arranged at the beginning of the tour, before the side became accustomed to the turf wickets.

Jimmy Sinclair of South Africa – devastating bowler, exciting batsman, and a representative of his country at both rugby and cricket.

CHAPTER 7

1904

THIRD SOUTH AFRICA TOUR OF THE UNITED KINGDOM

Captain: Frank Mitchell

An improved South African side played attractive cricket and became influenced by Bosanquet's bowling. There were good performances by Kotze, Halliwell, Hathorn and Mitchell. The South Africans beat a strong All England XI but there was still a lack of public interest. South African cricket was becoming a force.

Frank Mitchell, the Yorkshire and England amateur who stayed behind after Lord Hawke's tour in 1888/89 and went on to lead two South African touring teams to the United Kingdom.

TOURING SIDE

F Mitchell (captain) (Transvaal) GC White (Transvaal)
JH Sinclair (Transvaal) B Wallach (Transvaal)
EA Halliwell (Transvaal) GH Shepstone (Transvaal)
CMH Hathorn (Transvaal) J Middleton (W Province)
RO Schwarz (Transvaal) SJ Snooke (W Province)
WA Shalders (Transvaal) SE Horwood (W Province)
LJ Tancred (Transvaal) JJ Kotze (W Province)

Horwood was a late replacement for A Reid
G Allsop was the Manager

The Anglo-Boer war was over, South African cricket had improved, and reasonable success against the visiting Australians two years previously had made them more hopeful for the third tour of Britain.

Frank Mitchell, the Yorkshire amateur who had stayed behind after the Lord Hawke tour, was chosen as captain. Abe Bailey, the mining magnate and one of the founders of the Wanderers Club, guaranteed the finances of the tour.

Twenty-six matches had been arranged. All but four were to be first-class. No Tests were to be played, but a match against an England XI was included in the itinerary. It was hoped that Llewellyn would be available but in fact he played in only a few games.

The team arrived in England on 7 May and spent three weeks practising at Lord's before the first match against MCC. Bosanquet, who was to have such an influence on the South African game, took nine wickets for MCC with his googlies.

Batsmen came into form against the Universities and in games against Gloucestershire and Warwickshire. Rain prevented the tourists from winning the first, but the second was won in two days when 150 runs were scored in 90 minutes by Snooke and White.

There was a fascinating match against Middlesex at Lord's. Kotze took the first two wickets without a run on the board, then Bosanquet hit a century for Middlesex. After an even first innings, Middlesex left the South Africans to score 211 to win. Tancred managed 75 and Llewellyn 60, but with the scores level on 210 for eight, Trott had Snooke LBW and clean bowled Kotze for the match to end in an exciting tie. This was the second time a match involving the South Africans on tour had ended in a tie.

London Counties were not the side they had been when WG Grace was at his best and provided an easy victory for the South Africans. The traditional trip to Ireland ended in a surprising manner when the Gentlemen of Ireland beat the tourists by 93 runs on a rain-affected pitch. Llewellyn, playing for Hampshire, could not prevent an innings victory for the tourists and Somerset were also beaten by an innings.

A very strong 'All England' side, including Ranji, Gilbert Jessop, JT Hearne and John Gunn, was chosen to play in the most important game of the tour at Lord's. Schwarz made a century while Frank Mitchell and Hathorn helped to put on a useful 352. The South Africans broke through early and Sinclair, with Schwarz, bowled the All England XI out for 167. Mitchell did not enforce the follow-on and must have been worried when the first five South African wickets fell for only 44. Hathorn and Halliwell then each scored 50s and left the All England XI needing 397 to win. Sinclair and Schwarz bowled them out for 203 to win a very important victory by 193 runs.

Second-class matches against Scotland, and Liverpool and District were no problem, but the South Africans were lucky to hold out for a draw against Yorkshire at Hull. Leicestershire and Lancashire put up weak sides and Nottinghamshire lost by an innings in a very high-scoring match. The South Africans managed their highest score of the tour, 611, with the help of centuries by White and Tancred.

It was intended that an Indian touring side would play against the South Africans at Lord's, but the Indian visit to England was called off and a second match against MCC was substituted. Another weak MCC side was chosen and the South Africans won easily by ten wickets.

Gilbert Jessop of England, known as 'the Croucher'. Playing for the South of England team against the tourists at Hastings he scored a memorable 159 not out in only two hours.

Rain badly affected the following matches against Derbyshire and Sussex, which ended in draws. Ranji made 178 of the runs for Sussex and passed the 2 000 runs for the season before CB Fry declared on 357 for 3. The South Africans surprised everyone by passing this total with seven wickets down, thanks to Hathorn and Sinclair. The match ended early to allow the South Africans time to travel to Kent for their next match. They suffered their third and final defeat. The South Africans were also lucky not to lose the following match against Surrey at the Oval and were saved by the rain. Rain also interrupted the festival games at Scarborough against Yorkshire and at Hastings against the South of England.

The latter match was memorable for the hitting of Gilbert Jessop who scored 159 not out in two hours. The first 50 took him one hour; he then added another 100 to his score in the next hour.

The lack of public interest in the tour was partly because of poor publicity and partly because the stronger counties preferred to rest their better players for the more important County Championship.

Having lost only three, and winning thirteen matches, including the match against the All England XI, South Africa had every reason to be proud of her team. Kotze was the fastest bowler of the season and Halliwell stood up to the wicket to him. On one occasion he had two leg side stumpings off consecutive balls. As a result of his performance, Kotze was asked by WG Grace to join his team, London Counties. Hathorn and Mitchell batted well but Sinclair was very variable, although he did well with the bat. Schwarz learned how to bowl the googly early on in the season and was very effective. Surprisingly the fielding was mediocre.

While South Africa would never capture the interest of an Australian tour in the eyes of the British public, they had shown such an improvement that they were to become a close second.

In a charming reflection on modern training regimes, the South African tourists are shown skipping to keep in trim during the passage from Cape Town to England.

CHAPTER 8

1905/06

FIRST MCC TOUR OF SOUTH AFRICA

Captain: PF Warner

The first official MCC tour by a mediocre English side. South Africa recorded victory in both the 'Greatest game ever' and the Test rubber. Vogler, Schwarz, Faulkner and White had taken Bosanquet's lessons to heart and South African cricket had become world class.

The South African team for all the 1905/06 Tests. Back: J Phillips (umpire), AW Nourse, WM Reid (manager), AEE Vogler, F Hearne (umpire); middle: SJ Snooke, RO Schwarz, CMH Hathorn, PW Sherwell (capt), JH Sinclair, LJ Tancred; front: WA Shalders, GC White, GA Faulkner.

Previous tours had all been arranged by individuals, but in 1903 the MCC took over the organization of all cricket tours, on the condition that guarantees against financial loss were given by the local cricket authorities. South Africa had performed better than the English public had given them credit for on the previous year's tour and had justified an official tour by MCC.

Twenty-six games were to be played, which included five Test matches. A well-balanced side was chosen that was considered strong enough to uphold the honour of England but not so strong as to make the series a farce. Plum Warner, who had toured South Africa as a youngster in a previous series, was to lead the side.

TOURING SIDE	
AMATEURS	PROFESSIONALS
PF Warner (captain) (Middlesex)	D Denton (Yorkshire)
LJ Moon (Middlesex)	S Haigh (Yorkshire)
FL Fane (Essex)	EG Hayes (Surrey)
JN Crawford (Surrey)	WS Lees (Surrey)
HDG Leveson-Gower (Surrey)	C Blythe (Kent)
EG Wynyard (Hants)	EA Relf (Sussex)
JC Hartley (Sussex)	JH Board (Gloucester)

AW (Dave) Nourse, who for forty seasons was 'the Grand Old Man' of South African cricket.

The voyage out on the *Kinfauns Castle* was a particularly rough one. Windows in the smoking room and cabins were smashed by waves that broke over the ship, and the team was relieved to arrive in Cape Town on 28 November 1905.

The first two games at Newlands were played against Western Province and provided a good start for the tourists. Western Province were going through a bad patch in the Currie Cup and were easily beaten.

XVIII of Worcester and XV of Griqualand West provided no competition and an unbeaten side went to the Transvaal for Christmas. The Wanderers field still had no grass but had been surfaced with red gravel instead of the dusty soil of the past. The wicket was coir matting laid on fine, anthill soil.

Transvaal had a good side this season, but could score only 135. MCC found the Transvaal bowling of Schwarz and Faulkner equally difficult and only a good innings by Denton of 132 not out allowed them to gain a first innings lead of 130. Transvaal batted consistently in the second innings to set the tourists a reasonably easy target of 176 to win. But Schwarz and Faulkner bowled MCC out for 115 to win the memorable match for Transvaal.

XVIII of Western Transvaal at Potchefstroom provided batting practice for the tourists before the first Test match at the Wanderers. This was the first meeting of the

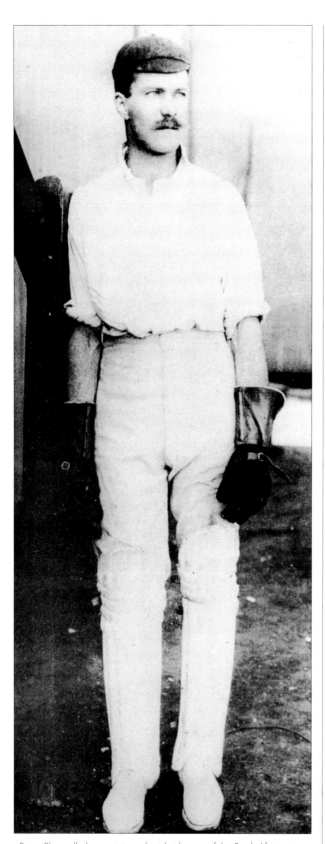

Percy Sherwell, the captain and wicket keeper of the South African team
He was to hit the winning runs in the first Test match at the Wanderers.

two countries since Lord Hawke's tour seven years previously and both sides were the strongest available. The South African team comprised PW Sherwell (captain), LJ Tancred, WA Shalders, M Hathorn, G White, SJ Snooke, JH Sinclair, A Faulkner, AW Nourse, AE Vogler and R Schwarz.

Virtually all the South Africans could be regarded as genuine all-rounders. There was sensation when Sherwell opened the bowling with two leg-break bowlers, Schwarz and Faulkner, who had the wickets of Warner, Fane and Denton with only 15 runs on the board. The others managed to bring the total to a not very flattering 184. However, South Africa also struggled against the bowling of Blythe and Lees and were all out for 91, a deficit of 93. England were in a very strong position at 253 runs on, with five wickets in hand. However, Faulkner and Nourse polished off the tail-enders and England finished with a lead of 283.

Wickets fell so that South Africa were six down for 105 and a defeat was staring them in the face. Dave Nourse joined White and they put on 121 runs before White was out for 81. With the last man, skipper Sherwell, at the wicket, South Africa still needed 45 to win. Sherwell cracked the first ball he received for four and gradually the score mounted. Scores were tied. Sherwell survived three balls from Relf then hit a full toss down the leg side for four to win the match. Nourse had batted beautifully for 93* but it was last man Sherwell with 22* who saved the match and forced the historic victory, the first for South Africa. Plum Warner called it the greatest game that he had ever played in and the crowd went wild, carrying Nourse and Sherwell off the field shoulder-high.

A series of minor matches against Pretoria, Middleburg and District, and the Army at Robert's Heights were an anti-climax before the next major match at Durban. Natal lost the match but Dave Nourse received a collection of £46 for his efforts in this and the previous Test match.

Minor matches were played along the coast and it was back to Johannesburg for another Test. The itinerary was arranged rather unusually with four Tests being played in the last month of the tour, two in succession in Johannesburg to be followed by two in Cape Town. The South African team for all the Tests remained unchanged. Once more the English batsmen collapsed and it was only the tail-enders who helped the team to reach 148. South African batsmen all got runs, Sinclair hit a six and seven fours in his 66, and South Africa had a lead of 129 on the first innings. England lost their first four wickets for 25 and the game was as good as won. Schwarz took the last four wickets cheaply and South Africa scored 33 to win the second Test.

England made two changes for the third Test two days later, but it made very little difference. South Africa put on 385 with Hathorn making 102 and

Nourse 61, and everyone getting into double figures. England again got off to a disastrous start when Schwarz bowled Warner, Crawford and Denton for under 30. Fane came to the rescue with a fine 143 but there was a slump at the end and England were all out for 295, 90 behind. South African batsmen continued their dominance over the English bowlers in the second innings when they declared at 349 for the loss of only five wickets and a formidable lead of 439. Gordon White hit two sixes and 19 fours in an innings of 147. Yet again the English openers Warner and Fane were out early and only Denton and Crawford showed any ability to cope with the bowling of Snooke who took eight for 70. South Africa had won the third Test and the rubber, with two more matches to play.

A minor match was played in Bloemfontein before returning to Cape Town for the last two Tests and the final matches of the series. South Africa made a shaky start and Colin Blythe took the first five wickets cheaply, but some lusty hitting by the tail-enders brought the first innings score to 218. It was only some aggressive hitting by Denton, Moon and Crawford that brought the English total to 198, a deficit of 20. Blythe and Lees bowled well to dismiss South Africa for 138, with White hitting a beautiful 73 in 105 minutes. England needed 159 to win. Warner, Crawford and Denton were out for 34 before Fane managed to stay for a solid 66 not out and win the game for England.

The score in the series was now three Tests to one for South Africa with one more to play.

Four Test matches inside a month at the end of a long and exhausting tour was bad planning and it was not surprising that the tourists were jaded. The last Test was to be an anti-climax after the excitement of the others.

England batted first and, apart from Crawford, could do little against the bowling of Sinclair, Vogler, Snooke and Schwarz to post a first innings total of 187. At 107 for six, South Africa looked to be in trouble but good hitting in a last wicket stand of 94 by Snooke 60 and last man Vogler 66*, enabled South Africa to gain a first innings lead of 146. Nourse and Schwarz bowled England out for 130 to win the Test by an innings and 16 runs. A collection was taken for Vogler's efforts.

South Africa had won the series by four games to one. Apart from the unsatisfactory itinerary, which was long and arduous even before the all-important Tests were played at the end, MCC underestimated the strength of the South African national side. The South African bowlers, particularly the leg-spinners, were proved to be too good for the Englishmen, yet the failure by established and renowned batsmen was surprising, even given that they were playing on matting wickets.

The squad arrived back in England on 21 April 1906, Wynyard having travelled home earlier due to illness. Leveson-Gower and Moon stayed behind.

South Africa had arrived in international cricket at last.

Pelham (Plum) Warner, the unsuccessful captain of the first MCC touring team to South Africa. He was later to become President of the MCC.

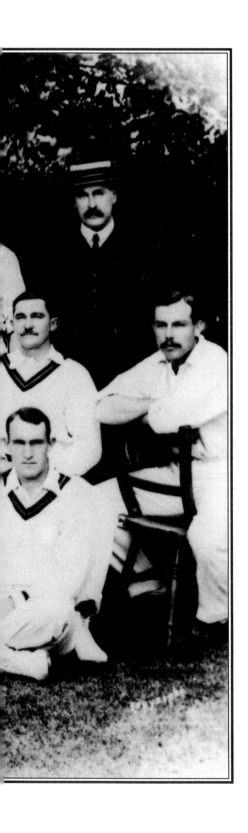

CHAPTER 9

1907

FOURTH SOUTH AFRICA TOUR OF THE UNITED KINGDOM

Captain: PW Sherwell

A strong South African side with good batting, brilliant fielding and devastating googly bowlers in Vogler, Schwarz, Faulkner and White. They played exciting cricket and the tour made a profit for the first time. They lost the Test series narrowly but proved to be formidable opponents.

The English team which drew the rain-interrupted first Test match against the touring South Africans at Lord's. CB Fry (wearing the striped blazer in the middle row) captained the side in all three Tests and was the most impressive English batsman.

Cricket authorities in South Africa worked together for the first time to organize and guarantee the finances, estimated at £2 900, for a tour of Britain. South African cricket had improved and the success of the team against Plum Warner's side in South Africa the previous season meant that there were high expectations for a successful tour.

AE Halliwell and CE Floquet had been originally chosen but were unable to travel. Rev CD Robinson and SD Snooke took their places. There were eight bowlers in the squad, four of whom had taken the lessons of Bosanquet to heart, and could bowl the googly. The batting strength was good. It was by far the strongest team to represent South Africa to date.

TOURING SIDE	
PW Sherwell (captain) (Transvaal)	
AEE Vogler (Transvaal)	JH Sinclair (Transvaal)
HE Smith (Transvaal)	LJ Tancred (Transvaal)
CD Robinson (Natal)	WA Shalders (Transvaal)
AW Nourse (Natal)	CMH Hathorn (Transvaal)
JJ Kotze (W Province)	RO Schwarz (Transvaal)
SJ Snooke (W Province)	GC White (Transvaal)
SD Snooke (W Province)	GA Faulkner (Transvaal)
Manager: G Allsop	

African batsmen managed to get runs in what was a very important victory for the tourists.

The South Africans lost the first five wickets for 46 against Warwickshire but went on to win by 276 runs. Hathorn scored his only century of the tour in the first innings and Nourse a century in the second. Nourse and SJ Snooke both scored centuries against Derbyshire, then Vogler took six for 17 to dismiss them for 46.

The South African bowlers were proving too good for the English batsmen. Kent provided more opposition when, on the last morning, the South Africans needed 124 to avoid an innings defeat with five men out. No one gave them a chance of surviving, let alone winning. However, Snooke and Faulkner added 93 then Sinclair and Snooke put on another 110, leaving Kent to score only 104 to win. Three wickets were down for seven, and six down for 79, and the South Africans won by two runs in a memorable victory.

The South Africans were proving to be an exciting team to watch and, with eight wins and no defeats out of the first eleven matches, public interest was high. Fifty thousand people flocked to the three days of the first Test at Lord's. Rain again interfered with the match and, with England's first innings of 428, compared with South

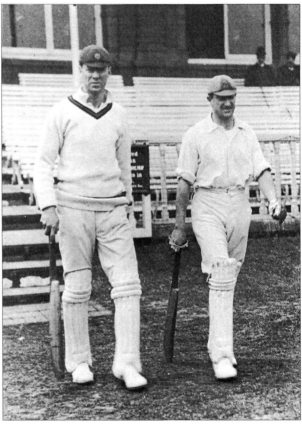

Jimmy Sinclair (left) and Aubrey Faulkner, South Africa's two great all-rounders, walk out to bat.

Following the success of previous tours, 31 matches were to be played including three Test matches. Sailing on the *Durham Castle* on 9 April, the team played a one-day match at Las Palmas and arrived on 30 April. The team took three weeks to acclimatize to the turf wickets and then beat Leicestershire and Essex comfortably.

A match against the MCC could easily have been won in two days when, shortly before lunch on the second day, MCC were seven wickets down and still needed 46 runs to avoid an innings defeat. The next three wickets produced 138 runs. Needing only 93 to win, six South African wickets fell for 58. Fortunately Sinclair knocked off the required runs and what should have been a resounding victory became a narrow one. Rain completely disrupted matches against the Universities and Northamptonshire, but Middlesex failed against the bowling of Schwarz and Kotze. All the South

One of South Africa's quartet of googly bowlers, Aubrey Faulkner took 73 wickets and scored over 1000 runs on the tour.

The South African tourists in 1907, who lost the rubber by one Test to nil. The captain, Percy Sherwell, is fourth from the left in the middle row.

Africa's reply of only 140, probably saved South Africa. Jessop hit 93 in just over an hour out of 145, and only Vogler stood out among the bowlers. In the follow-on, Sherwell and Hathorn scored 140 for the second wicket but, at 185 for three, rain stopped play and the match was drawn.

A drying pitch at Brighton caused the South Africans to be dismissed for 49, their lowest score of the tour. Sussex scored 186 and Sinclair was sent in with Tancred to open the second innings. He scored 92 out of 135 in an hour and forty minutes and the South Africans finished with 327. Nourse was given out 'handled the ball' during the innings. Vogler, Schwarz and Sinclair bowled Sussex out for 151 to win another exciting match.

The South Africans suffered their first defeat at the Oval against Surrey on a fast pitch that should have suited them. Vogler's seven wickets could not prevent a defeat by 85 runs.

After an even first innings against Yorkshire at Bradford, Schwarz was hit for 12 runs off his first over. An hour later he had taken five for only 19. Needing 116 to win, the last 40 runs came in 20 minutes for another good win.

High-scoring matches were played in Scotland and Durham before the second Test match at Leeds. On a soft wicket, England were 34 for the loss of CB Fry at lunch on the first day. In the next 75 minutes they were all out for 74, thanks to Faulkner. He took seven wickets for 17 runs in 11 overs. Colin Blythe of Kent was equally successful with eight for 59 and South Africa held a lead of only 34 runs. Rain interfered with the play throughout the next day but Fry played a very good innings of 54 out of 162. The South African bowlers kept up the pressure in spite of the wet ball. Needing 129 to win, South Africa were in trouble from the start and five wickets were down for 18. Sinclair hit Blythe for a dozen runs off an over but the conditions were right for Blythe and he took another seven wickets for 40 to bring his total to 15. Thus he equalled a Test record and won the match by 53 runs.

It was agreed that South Africa had the worst of the conditions throughout the match, but they were now one down and one to play.

Lancashire played badly at Old Trafford and were well beaten by an innings. Two light-hearted matches were played in Ireland before returning to play the champion county, Nottinghamshire. The South Africans lost this match by seven wickets, but they took their revenge against Essex at Leyton. For once the conditions favoured the South Africans.

Rain again affected the third Test match at the Oval and prevented a result. England lost two early wickets but recovered, thanks to 129 from CB Fry, the highest score made against the tourists.

The South African team aboard the *Durham Castle* on the way to England. In the middle of their three-week passage they stopped in the Canary Islands to play a one-day match at Las Palmas.

Facing a total of 295, South Africa reached 149 for five before the wicket deteriorated and five wickets fell for 29 runs, Blythe taking four of them. Leading by 117 runs, England lost three for 20 and, in trying to force the pace, then lost the last six wickets for 49 runs giving England a lead of 255 with two hours and forty minutes remaining. South Africa went for the runs but Hirst took three quick wickets and they had to settle for a draw.

Gloucestershire were 162 for three at lunch on the first day and all out for 183, Schwarz taking five of the wickets. The South Africans could have been in trouble when their seventh wicket fell, but Schwarz joined White and an incredible 221 runs were added in an hour and a quarter. 156 runs were scored in 63 minutes. White hit 162*, the highest score of the tour. In the second innings, Gloucestershire were bowled out for 151 and the South Africans had another brilliant victory.

The South Africans beat South Wales in a light-hearted match and then Somerset at Bath, scoring at an average of 100 runs an hour, before a match at Lord's against MCC. For once, the South Africans did not play well and were badly beaten on a soft wicket.

Two light-hearted festival games rounded off a very successful tour. The first was won convincingly and the second, played at Scarborough, was noted for the batting of fast bowler Kotze. As a traditional number 11, Kotze had more wickets than runs but opened the innings and top-scored with 60.

It had been the most successful tour so far. English crowds had never seen bowlers like the four South African spinners before. Schwarz took 143 wickets and Vogler 133, while White and Faulkner took over 70 each. Sinclair and Kotze, the successes of the previous tour, had little to do. Schwarz and Vogler were included in Wisden's five Cricketers of the Year.

The batting was consistent, with someone usually getting the runs at a fast pace. The side played exciting cricket; the fielding was good, often brilliant, and the team was extremely popular wherever they went. A profit of £1 400 was made on the tour, in contrast to the losses sustained on the previous tours, and South African cricket had truly become world class.

As usual, the team disbanded to have a holiday, but Schwarz and Snooke went on tour with the England side to Philadelphia.

CHAPTER 10

1909/10

SECOND MCC TOUR OF SOUTH AFRICA

Captain: HDG Leveson-Gower

A good MCC side met the four South African spinners on matting and lost an exciting Test series three-one. Hobbs was magnificent throughout while Rhodes and Denton played well and Simpson-Hayward's 'lobs' were very effective. South Africa was on a high.

HDG Leveson-Gower, captain of the MCC side in 1909/10 and a life-long patron of the game.

TOURING SIDE

AMATEURS	PROFESSIONALS
HDG Leveson-Gower (captain) (Surrey)	JB Hobbs (Surrey)
MC Bird (Surrey)	H Strudwick (Surrey)
FL Fane (Essex)	D Denton (Yorkshire)
GHT Simpson-Hayward (Worcester)	W Rhodes (Yorkshire)
EG Wynyard (Hants)	CJ Thompson (Northamptonshire)
NC Tufnel (Cambridge University)	FE Woolley (Kent)
C Blythe (Kent)	CP Buckenham (Essex)

Following the lack of success of the MCC's previous tour to South Africa in 1905/06, the side chosen was much stronger, but still not a fully representative one. Nevertheless, on paper it was a good side containing Jack Hobbs, Frank Woolley, Colin Blythe and the two Yorkshiremen, David Denton and Wilfred Rhodes.

Eighteen matches were to be played including five Test matches. Once more the three final Test matches were organized to be played in succession at the end of the tour. The team left Southampton on board RMS *Saxon* on 6 November 1909 and arrived in Cape Town on 23 November.

In the warm-up match against XVI Colts at Newlands, Hobbs scored his first century of the tour in a drawn match. He scored his second two days later against Western Province. In the home team's innings, Thompson took seven for 26 to dismiss them for 67.

The team moved on to Kimberley, where it was so hot that the umpires used umbrellas to protect themselves. MCC beat XV of Griqualand West easily. Jack Hobbs showed that he could also bowl when he took four wickets against XV of Free State. MCC won comfortably again.

Rain washed out two of the four days' play in the match at Vogelfontein against The Reef , a team that included Tancred, Snooke, White, Vogler and Ward.

Christmas was celebrated in Johannesburg before the match against a strong Transvaal side. Snooke scored fifties in both innings, while Faulkner, with 46 and 148*, also took nine wickets in the match. Only Denton and Bird scored more than 30 and it appears that the traditional South African hospitality once more was at work because Transvaal won overwhelmingly by 308 runs: not a very good omen for the visitors with the first Test match imminent.

The South African side was made up of SJ Snooke (captain), JW Zulch, L Stricker, A Faulkner, AW Nourse, GC White, JG Sinclair, M Commaille, RG Schwarz, AE Vogler and T Campbell. Colin Blythe had taken only one wicket in the game against Transvaal and was left out of the side. Simpson-Hayward, the last of the underarm 'lob' spin bowlers, was included in the England side.

Ten thousand spectators watched Faulkner and Nourse batting well but none of the South Africans could really cope with the 'lobs'

Sibley Snooke, South African captain. His eight for 70 in the previous MCC tour remained the best figures by a South African for 50 years.

of Simpson-Hayward who took six for 43 on the matting wicket and South Africa collapsed from 133 for three to 208 all out. When England batted, Rhodes and Hobbs attacked the bowling and put on 159 runs before falling to Vogler. The last eight wickets fell to Vogler and Faulkner for 120 and England had lost the commanding position to be only 102 runs on. In the second innings, South Africa lost three wickets before they knocked off the first innings deficit but Faulkner and Snooke then put on 99 runs for the sixth wicket. Then Faulkner and Commaille put on 74 for the eighth wicket and South Africa were all out for 345, a lead of 243, built on a great knock of 123 by Faulkner. The wicket was still good and there seemed no reason why England should not get the 244 runs needed, but Vogler bowled beautifully and at the close of play seven wickets were down for 144. Next morning the Englishmen hit out and with the last man, Strudwick, at the crease, still needed 34 to win. He and Thompson scored 14 of them and then Faulkner bowled Thompson for 63 and won an exciting game for South Africa by 19 runs. Aubrey Faulkner was carried off the ground shoulder-high. He and Ernie Vogler had taken all 20 English wickets between them in front of the 29 600 spectators who watched the game.

Following the exciting Test the next match against Natal in Durban had to be an anti-climax. For the first time the tourists played at Lord's, a ground which Natal were to use until 1920, when it was bought by the railways and cricket transferred to Kingsmead.

In addition to being 'The Master' with the bat, Jack Hobbs was a superb fielder in the covers. He was to score a brilliant 187 in the final Test and topped the tourists' batting averages by a clear margin.

Wilfred Rhodes, possibly the best all-rounder ever. His opening partnerships with Hobbs were the cornerstone of the English batting.

Wilfred Rhodes and Jack Hobbs had an opening partnership of 207 with Hobbs scoring 163 out of MCC's 331. Rhodes also took seven wickets in the match which was drawn. Dave Nourse scored 129 and 54 not out and received £46 from a collection made at the ground on his behalf.

Several players were rested for the return match at Pietermaritzburg and the tourists gave a game to R Ponsonby, the private secretary to the Governor of Natal. Blythe took seven for 20 to dismiss Natal for 50 in the first innings and the tourists won easily.

There were no changes in the sides to play the second Test at Durban. Oddly enough both sides scored 199 in the first innings. In the second innings, South Africa lost three quick wickets but White and Nourse added 143 together and White went on to 118. All the other batsmen made runs and South Africa ended up with 347. Hobbs and Rhodes gave England another good start, but five wickets were down for 111 and the game was as good as lost. Hobbs however started to hit out and his 70 came out of 106 in 75 minutes. Thompson and Bird did the same and the final score of 252 flattered the Englishmen, but the South Africans had won the second Test with three still to play.

Matches against Border in East London, North-Eastern Districts at Queenstown and Eastern Province at Port Elizabeth proved no obstacles to the tourists. In the match against Transvaal, which was won comfortably, David Denton scored 139 in the first innings and 138 in the second.

South Africa substituted Sinclair and Schwarz with SJ Pegler and CE Floquet for the third Test match at the Wanderers but England kept the same team.

Rain prevented a full day's play but South Africa, having won the toss for the third time, scored well. Faulkner, White and Vogler helped bring the South African score to 305. Hobbs was indisposed and Fane opened the batting with Rhodes, Denton hit 104 out of 161 in an hour and forty minutes and England finished the day only 104 runs behind with five wickets standing. Spectators collected £88 to show their appreciation of Denton's innings. Wickets fell quickly and only the last wicket partnership between Woolley and Strudwick of 69 brought the score to 322. South Africa were 123 for seven, and the game seemed as good as over when Snooke was joined by Vogler and Pegler, who helped carry the score to 237, a lead of 220. Faulkner and Vogler took four wickets for 42, and South Africa's chances looked good. Hobbs, having recovered, came in and played a brilliant innings. He and Fane put on 50, Woolley was out for a duck and with six wickets down South Africa looked forward to victory. However Bird came in and, with Hobbs, put on 95 runs before being run out in sight of an England victory. Leveson-Gower joined Hobbs and they knocked off the required runs to win an exciting match which could have gone either way. Hobbs was undefeated on 93 not out, but the crowd gave a collection of £60 to Vogler for his magnificent bowling.

The two teams travelled to Cape Town for the final two Tests and the last matches of the tour.

Sinclair and Schwarz were brought into the South African side in place of Pegler and Floquet whereas Colin Blythe was brought into the England side for the first time on this tour. Fane took over the England captaincy from Leveson-Gower.

There was drama at Newlands when Hobbs, Rhodes and Denton were back in the pavilion with only two runs on the board. It was left to Frank Woolley and Bird to save the side. South Africa, facing a total of 203, did a little better but only achieved the four run lead thanks to big hitting by Schwarz and Vogler. Unbelievably the first three England batsmen were once more back in the pavilion, this time for only 17. Three celebrated batsmen like Hobbs, Rhodes and Denton only scored 16 runs between them in two innings. Once more it was up to Frank Woolley, this time with his skipper Fane, to put on 100 runs and to save the team. South Africa, facing an apparently easy task of scoring 175 runs for victory, lost five wickets for 91 and the game had swung again. However, Faulkner and Sinclair saved the day with a stand of 71 to win the game for South Africa.

The fifth and last Test started two days later and it was a complete reversal. Hobbs and Rhodes could not fail a third time and they put on an opening partnership of 221 runs before Rhodes was out for 77. Hobbs continued playing brilliantly and was fifth out with 187 out of 327. The rest of the batting was disappointing and the innings ended on 417. South Africa were bundled out for 103 by Colin Blythe on a good wicket. Zulch batted through the innings for 43. South Africa followed on 314 runs behind and this was a hopeless task. Faulkner scored 99 out of the 327 runs made by South Africa and England knocked off the required 16 runs for the loss of Bird to win by nine wickets. South Africa had won the Test series by three games to two.

Hobbs was brilliant and headed the batting averages with over 66, the next highest being Denton with 36. Colin Blythe headed the bowling averages but was erratic and only played in the final two Tests. The South Africa spin bowlers were once more formidable on the matting wickets and were chiefly responsible for South Africa's success.

The Englishmen sailed on the *Armadale Castle* and arrived home on 2 April, having had a financially rewarding tour. Leveson-Gower, Fane, Bird and Simpson-Hayward joined a party of seven South Africans on a social cricket trip to Rhodesia. The only disquieting feature of the tour was the fact that several of the English players had been contracted by newspapers to write articles during the tour and these caused some embarrassment to their South African hosts. However this could perhaps be overlooked in view of the fact that South Africa had won the Test series.

The powerful Transvaal side which beat MCC by 308 runs. Back: BdeR Malraison (scorer), JW Zulch, TH Tandy (12th man), L Stricker, T Campbell, CE Floquet, GC White, JH Moulder; front: AE Vogler, GA Faulkner, JH Sinclair, SJ Snooke (capt), RO Schwarz.

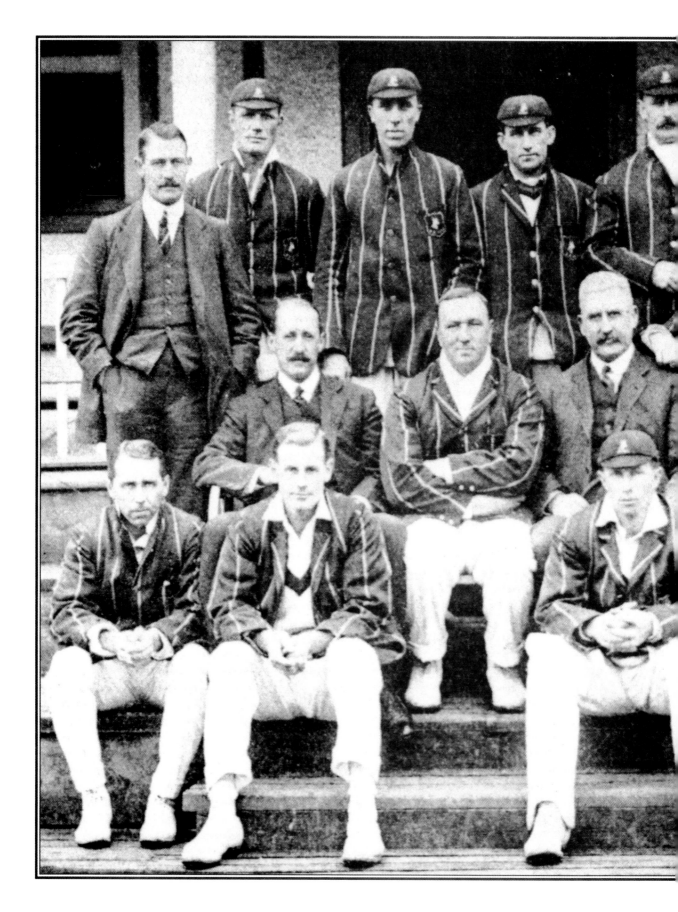

CHAPTER II

1912

FIFTH SOUTH AFRICA TOUR OF THE UNITED KINGDOM

Captain: F Mitchell

*A disastrous Triangular tournament in
England with poor weather and treacherous
wickets. The side did well against county sides
but were dismissed for 30 runs in a Test and
offered no threat to England or Australia.
An enormous set back for South Africa.*

The Australian team which joined South Africa in England to play a triangular tournament in 1912. The event, sponsored by Sir Abe Bailey, did not prove a success as both touring teams were under-strength.

South Africa had suggested a triangular competition but the Australians only agreed to take part on condition that South Africa paid them a visit beforehand. South Africa performed reasonably well in Australia with very good performances from Aubrey Faulkner. However, the experiment of holding a triangular competition in England was to prove a disaster. Thirty-seven matches were arranged to be played, including three Test matches against both England and Australia.

Two important omissions from the party were Vogler, who was rumoured to be at loggerheads with Sir Abe Bailey, one of the sponsors, and Zulch. The squad sailed on the *Balmoral Castle* and arrived in mid-April. White followed on the *Walmer Castle* on 24 April 1912 and missed the first few matches.

TOURING SIDE

F Mitchell (captain) (Transvaal)	
LJ Tancred (Transvaal)	TA Ward (Transvaal)
GA Faulkner (Transvaal)	SJ Pegler (Transvaal)
SJ Snooke (Transvaal)	HW Taylor (Natal)
GC White (Transvaal)	AW Nourse (Natal)
L Stricker (Transvaal)	CB Llewellyn (Natal)
R Beaumont (Transvaal)	CP Carter (Natal)
RO Schwarz (Transvaal)	JL Cox (Natal)
T Campbell (Transvaal)	GPD Hartigan (Border)

G Allsop acted as manager

two days. Australia batted on a soft wicket and, in just over five hours, scored 448. The next day's play was sensational. White was batting well with a split hand and Faulkner, who was dropped off an easy catch on 31, then went on to 122 not out, his best innings of the tour. At four o'clock only 30 runs were needed to avoid the follow-on with three wickets standing when Matthews performed his first hat-trick of the day. Going in again at quarter-to-five South Africa collapsed, and were 70 for five when Matthews performed his second hat-trick of the day – a feat never before accomplished in a Test match, and unlikely to be matched in the future. South Africa were all out for 95 before the close of play to lose by an innings and 88 runs.

The tour started well with wins over Derbyshire and Surrey. Schwarz scored a hundred and took seven wickets in the latter match. Hobbs was bowled cheaply by Dave Nourse in both innings.

CB Fry captained a strong MCC side, containing eight good batsmen and six first-class bowlers, at Lord's. The South Africans were well beaten by 108 runs.

Pegler took a hat-trick and Frank Mitchell, playing against his former county, Yorkshire, saved the South Africans from defeat. Two good innings by Nourse, together with rain on the last day, then saved the tourists from an embarrassing defeat at the hands of Oxford University.

The tourists made amends in the following game against Worcestershire when, after the first day was washed out, they played well to achieve a victory by an innings. The first Test match of the tournament was at Old Trafford against Australia and lasted only

An early photograph of Frank Mitchell, the Yorkshire-born captain of the South African side in 1912.

CB Fry, a brilliant scholar who captained England at cricket, played soccer in a Cup Final and for England, was the world long jump champion and was even asked to become King of Albania!

The public decided that South Africa were not up to Test match standard and this affected both the tournament and interest in the rest of the tour.

Following their crushing defeat, the South Africans batted well against Northamptonshire but rainy conditions continued in matches against Cambridge University and Surrey.

The second Test match, against England at Lord's, put South Africa out of the running for the tournament. No play was possible until three o'clock on the first day and the pitch had to be changed at the last minute. Mitchell elected to bat and by half-past-four all the South Africans were back in the pavilion for 58. Barnes and Forster were unplayable on the drying pitch. Hobbs was out in the first over but Spooner and Rhodes put on 124 and the score was 303 for four at lunch the next day. Pegler then became unplayable and he took the next six wickets for 34 runs so that England were all out for 337. Facing a deficit of 279, South Africa lost the first three wickets for 36. Then Faulkner and Llewellyn came together. Faulkner scored five runs in fifty minutes and Llewellyn hit out for 75, but the task was hopeless and South Africa were all out for 217 to lose by an innings and 62 runs. Barnes and Forster took 19 wickets in the match.

In the next fixture, Nottinghamshire left the South Africans to score 255 to win in two hours and ten minutes. Taylor and Tancred, with a brilliant century, were not out at the closing score of 203 for one for the match to end in a draw.

After a tame draw against Somerset, all the South Africans got runs to win the match against South Wales at Swansea. Faulkner was outstanding against Scotland and both matches proved to be easy wins for the tourists.

Warwickshire were beaten comfortably before the third Test against England at Leeds but the crowds stayed away, having decided that the South Africans were no competition.

Fry won the toss and batted, although the pitch was damp. Rhodes, Hobbs, Spooner and Fry lost their wickets in the first hour and Hearne was missed at the wicket on five. He and Woolley put on 110 and England were all out for a moderate 242. South Africa were in trouble with four wickets down for 43 and it was soon 80 for seven. Snooke and Pegler put up a stand and South Africa's innings ended on 147, a deficit of 95. Although the wicket had improved since the first day the English batting was once again laboured. Faulkner bowled as well as at any time in the tour and England were all out for 238, a lead of 333. Seven wickets were down for 85 and a ninth wicket partnership by Carter and Tancred only postponed the inevitable.

The Test against England at Leeds was followed a few days later by a Test against Australia at Lord's. Now regarded as no opposition in the Test arena, the crowd was better than might have been expected, but this was due chiefly to the fact that King George V arrived to be introduced to the two teams. South Africa batted first

Sidney Pegler of Transvaal and South Africa. He was by far the most successful South African bowler on the 1912 tour, and achieved a haul of seven for 65 in the Lord's Test against England.

on a good wicket and, after losing five wickets for 74, they totalled 263. Australia missed no fewer than nine chances in the innings. Nourse bowled Jennings and McCartney with only 14 on the board, but Kelleway and Bardsley took the score from 86 to 256 in under two hours. The Australian innings closed at 390, a lead of 127. Llewellyn was playing well when the deficit was knocked off with four wickets down but South Africa were all out for 173, a lead of only 46. Very few people bothered to watch the end of the match the following day, and South Africa had lost by ten wickets.

Contrasting sharply with the dismal showing in the Test matches, the South Africans provided a sparkling display of batting against Kent, scoring at 83 runs an hour on the first day. Rain again interrupted play and the match was drawn.

Matches in Ireland, and the match against Minor Counties at Stoke, were badly affected by rain. Rain again held up play until after lunch in the match against Lancashire. Needing 270 to win, on a treacherous pitch, the tourists were skittled out for 44 in an hour and a quarter. Lancashire had already beaten the Australian tourists twice and were the only county to beat the South Africans.

Unfortunately the only Test match in which the South Africans did themselves justice was ruined by rain at Trent Bridge against the Australians. An indication of the lack of interest was that only 2 400 attended on a bank holiday.

Taylor was out for two but all the others got runs and, after a cautious start, hit out freely to score 329. The Australians struggled on the heavy ground but reached 165 for 4 before Bardsley threw his wicket away and the last five wickets fell for 48 runs for the Australians to be all out for 219. Faulkner and Pegler bowled extremely well. Rain ruined the match and a draw was called with South Africa in a commanding position.

On a very treacherous wicket at Leicester, the South African spinners made short work of the opposition to win by 60 runs. Rain affected the Oval wicket and the Test match against England was another disaster for South Africa. Winning the toss, Tancred had no option but to bat in bad light and Sid Barnes and Woolley each took five wickets to have South Africa back in the pavilion for 95. Rhodes was out early but Hobbs and Spooner put on 61 for the second wicket. Hobbs went on to a very good 68 but England could only achieve 176. Faulkner was turning the ball on the sticky wicket and ended with seven wickets. In the second innings only Nourse and Faulkner managed anything approaching a stand and the tourists were all out for 93 to lose by ten wickets. Sid Barnes took eight wickets in the second innings to add to his five in the first.

Rain washed out most of the return match against Yorkshire and the match against Lancashire was called off. The tourists had the better of the drawn game against Hampshire when Nourse scored 213 not out, carrying his bat in a total of 432.

Three festival matches concluded the exhausting itinerary for the tourists. The team had failed to live up to expectations in the Test matches and that was all the public demanded. The googly bowlers of the previous tours were unsuccessful in the international matches and the batting was not up to standard. Only Pegler and Faulkner played to their potential.

While the team was successful in the matches against the counties and in fact only lost once, winning 13 matches compared with nine Australian wins, they were not good enough in the international matches.

The atrocious weather undoubtedly had an effect on the team but the triangular tournament was written off as a failure and not repeated until the limited overs matches in the 1970s. South African cricket was at a low ebb.

CHAPTER 12

1913/14

THIRD MCC TOUR OF SOUTH AFRICA

Captain: JWHT Douglas

A strong MCC side met a weak South African side. Jack Hobbs was brilliant and no-one could cope with the outstanding bowling of Sidney Barnes except Herbie Taylor, the pick of the home side. South Africa's poor performance continued.

Jack Hobbs of Surrey and England. One of the greatest ever batsmen and one of the stars of JWHT Douglas's team.

The MCC squad chosen to tour was a strong one at a time when South Africa was going through a lean period. Schwarz, Vogler and Faulkner who made the great team of 1907, and Pegler of the 1912 side, had all settled in England and there was no-one to take their place. Victory for the tourists was a foregone conclusion and in the event they lost only one match of the 22 played. In the Test series England won four and the fifth was drawn. This was to be the only time that no Test was allocated to Newlands. Guarantees of over £5 000 were given to the MCC by the South African authorities but the Rhodesian clubs could not raise the guarantee and were excluded from the tour.

On arrival at Cape Town, DC Robinson, the reserve

TOURING SIDE	
AMATEURS	PROFESSIONALS
JWHT Douglas (captain) (Essex)	JB Hobbs (Surrey)
MC Bird (Surrey)	H Strudwick (Surrey)
Hon LH Tennyson (Hants)	CP Mead (Hants)
DC Robinson (Gloucester)	JW Hearne (Middlesex)
FE Woolley (Kent)	AE Relf (Sussex)
SF Barnes (Staffordshire)	MW Booth (Yorkshire)
W Rhodes (Yorkshire)	

wicket-keeper, fell ill and returned home. EJ Smith (Warwickshire) was sent for as a replacement. Barnes was rested for the first game and the other bowlers were still recovering from the voyage. PT Lewis hit 151 in 185 minutes and Western Province scored 375. Hobbs soon struck form with 72 but MCC followed on 176 runs behind. Hobbs and Hearne avoided defeat in a second innings of 330.

Hobbs continued his brilliant form with a century against Fifteen of SW Districts and 170 out of 385 at Port Elizabeth. This was sufficient to force an innings victory when Barnes took seven wickets in the second innings to dismiss Cape Province for 60. Wicket-keeper Strudwick opened the bowling in the second innings against Border, but did not take a wicket.

The first Test was played at Durban.

FIRST TEST TEAMS—DURBAN	
SOUTH AFRICA	ENGLAND
HW Taylor (captain)	JB Hobbs
GPD Hartigan	W Rhodes
PAM Hands	AE Relf
AD Nourse	Hon LH Tennyson
PT Lewis	CP Mead
AHC Cooper	JWHT Douglas (captain)
LG Tapscott	FE Woolley
TA Ward	MC Bird
HV Baumgartner	MW Booth
JM Blanckenberg	SF Barnes
JL Cox	H Strudwick

Herbie Taylor won the toss and elected to bat, but got no support from his team and was last man out on a magnificent 109, scored out of a total of 182. MCC's innings of 450 was interrupted by rain and several catches were dropped. Jack Hobbs was once more brilliant in his innings of 82 but Douglas took over four hours for his century. In South Africa's second innings, only Nourse could cope with Barnes, Woolley and Relf and they were dismissed for 111. Barnes took five wickets in both innings, and England won the match by an innings and 157 runs.

Transvaal were not the side they had been a few years previously and, although Barnes was more expensive than usual, Hobbs and Woolley both scored centuries and MCC won by an innings.

Four changes were made to the home team for the second Test at Johannesburg. Zulch, Beaumont, Tancred and Newberry took the place of Tapscott, Lewis, Cooper and Baumgartner.

South Africa batted when Taylor won the toss and were soon in trouble. Barnes took eight wickets for 56 and South Africa were all out for 160. Relf and Rhodes put on 141 for the first wicket and then Rhodes and Mead added 152 for the third for Rhodes to finish on 152 and England 403 all out. South Africa's second innings started reasonably with Taylor, Zulch, Hands and Nourse getting runs. But Barnes was outstanding and took another nine wickets to end the match with South Africa on 231 all out and a defeat by an innings and 12 runs. Sid Barnes had taken 17 wickets in the match and was quite unplayable on the last day.

The third Test took place a day later, again in Johannesburg, to decide the rubber. Dixon and Tucker replaced Tancred and Cox in the South African team. Hobbs and Rhodes opened the England innings with Hearne returning to the team after a bout of influenza had kept him out for over a month. Hobbs scored 92 and England were all out for 238. Hearne and Barnes bowled well to dismiss the home team for 151, a deficit of 87. Rhodes and Hearne were out

without scoring but Hobbs with 41, and Mead with 86, recovered the situation and with Douglas scoring 77, the tourists' innings ended on 308 leaving South Africa to score 396 to win. Taylor and Zulch put on an opening partnership of 153. After this, there was a collapse, and with only four wickets standing, 223 runs were still needed. Newberry and Ward added 44 and Ward and last man Blanckenberg added 78, but when Ward was dismissed South Africa were all out for 304, 91 runs behind, following a fine fight-back.

Labour troubles were at their height when A Transvaal XI played the MCC at Vogelfontein and there was very little interest. Hobbs scored 137 and Hearne 96 for MCC to declare at 350 for four. Rain prevented any more play.

Both Griqualand West and Orange Free State had no pretensions when facing the MCC on equal terms and Hobbs hit out merrily. The MCC batsmen and Barnes had field days in fun games.

Back in Johannesburg, Transvaal had a stronger side and for once collared Barnes in a high-scoring match. 1 089 runs were scored and the match ended in a draw. Hearne scored 136 out of 386 and Transvaal responded with 347. When MCC batted a second time, Hobbs scored 131 and Rhodes 76 to allow a declaration at 211 without loss. Transvaal were 145 for six when play was ended.

Northern Natal XV only offered hitting practice for the Englishmen. Natal offered more of a challenge and, in fact, became the only team to beat the tourists. MCC were dismissed for 132.

Spectators line the boundary at Newlands Cricket Ground in Cape Town for the game between Western Province and the touring English team. This was the only time that there was no Test scheduled against the tourists at Newlands.

A large Test Match crowd spills over the ground at Wanderers in Johannesburg during a lunchtime interval in the second Test between South Africa and England. England won the match by an innings.

Barnes then took five wickets to dismiss Natal for 153 of which Herbie Taylor scored 91. All the MCC batsmen got runs in the second innings but were all out for 235, a lead of 214. Taylor had a third wicket partnership with Nourse of 145 and hit Barnes for 32 runs off three overs. This caused Barnes to leave the field in disgust, allegedly to drown his sorrows. Hobbs was not playing and the MCC batting looked ordinary.

The fourth Test match took place in Durban a few days later. Barnes took seven wickets and Rhodes the other three in South Africa's innings of 170. Hobbs scored 64 but there was a collapse and Carter took six wickets in England's 163. Taylor batted with caution but scored an admirable 93 in South Africa's second

innings and all the others waded in to declare at 305 for nine, a lead of 312. Barnes took another seven wickets. Hobbs and Rhodes scored 133 to make any thought of defeat out of the question and rain ended the proceedings early for the match to end in an honourable draw.

The fifth and last Test match was played in Port Elizabeth and the English side were without Barnes, who was reported to be ill. South Africa started well but then collapsed before Douglas and Woolley. Hands hit a chanceless 83 and Taylor 42 to end with 193. Hobbs and Rhodes started well and England totalled 411 with Mead scoring a century. The faster wicket than normal suited the English batsmen more than the South Africans, although the South African openers again got the side off to a good start, with Zulch and Taylor putting on 121. Apart from Hands with 49, the others did not get into double figures and South Africa were all out for 228 to lose by ten wickets. MCC played a final drawn game against Western Province before leaving for home.

The pleasures of the tour were marred by the labour troubles in the Transvaal but apart from that, JWHT Douglas' team had a very successful tour. The wonderful batting of Taylor, particularly against Barnes, and the bowling of Blanckenberg had impressed the visitors, but the tour belonged to Hobbs and Barnes. Hobbs had an outstanding tour, scoring 1 596 runs at an average of 76, while his consistency in the Test matches gave him an average of 63. Barnes was often unplayable on the matting wickets. In the four Tests he took 49 wickets for less than 11 runs each and in all the matches 125 wickets for under ten runs per wicket. No one else came close although Rhodes played a role as an all-rounder.

Sidney Francis Barnes ranked amongst the finest bowlers ever. However he could be a difficult man to deal with and it is rumoured that he refused to play in the last Test at Port Elizabeth because the South African authorities reneged on their promise of a special reward if he took part in the tour.

The team sailed home in March 1914 and, soon after their arrival in England, WG Grace wrote an article for *The Sportsman* in which he stated that it was the duty of every cricketer to volunteer his

Herbie Taylor, the captain of South Africa and the only man able to tame the bowling of Sidney Barnes.

services in the approaching Great War. There was to be no more serious cricket played for four years.

Natal, the only side to beat MCC on the tour. Herbie Taylor, captaining the Natal side, scored 91 out of a team total of 153 in the first innings and then exactly 100 in the second to nurse his team to a four-wicket victory.

CHAPTER 13

1922/23

FOURTH MCC TOUR OF SOUTH AFRICA

Captain: FT Mann

An average MCC side met an ageing South African side in a close series with Russell's innings in the final Test deciding the issue in favour of the English. No thought had been given to the future, although Alf Hall impressed and Taylor was outstanding.

The South African side for the first Test at the Wanderers in 1922/23. Back: JM Blankenberg, TA Ward, ID Buys, CM Francois, CA Munroe (12th man), WH Brann, EP Nupen; front: VVS Ling, GAL Hearne, HW Taylor (capt), AW Nourse, RH Catterall.

The horrors of World War I were over. South African cricket had taken a long time to recover from losses suffered in the war, although two Australian sides had visited South Africa following successful tours of England. MCC had suffered crushing defeats in a disastrous tour of Australia the previous season, but South Africa had not performed well since 1907, 15 years previously.

The squad leaving England under Frank Mann was considered more than strong enough even without Hobbs, Sutcliffe, Parkin and Hearne, who all declined the invitation to tour. Twenty-two matches were to be played including five Tests and eight non-first-class matches. Livsey, the wicket-keeper, broke his finger in the sixth match and was replaced by G Street of Sussex.

The team landed at Cape Town on 9 November 1922 and played the next day against Western Province. Despite the lack of practice, and magnificent fielding from the Province players, MCC won comfortably.

Matches against South Western Districts, Eastern Province, XV of Grahamstown, Border, Griqualand West, and North Eastern Districts provided no problems, but a dust-storm caused play to be abandoned in the match against East Rand at Benoni.

The tourists had met with little opposition on the tour so far,

TOURING SIDE	
AMATEURS	PROFESSIONALS
FT Mann (captain) (Middlesex)	AC Russell (Essex)
PGH Fender (Surrey)	A Sandham (Surrey)
AW Carr (Nottinghamshire)	CP Mead (Hants)
GTS Stevens (Oxford University)	FE Woolley (Kent)
VWC Jupp (Sussex)	CG Macaulay (Yorks)
AER Gilligan (Sussex)	G Brown (Hants)
	WH Livsey (Hants)
	A Kennedy (Hants)

but this was to change against Transvaal prior to the first Test, in front of a crowd of 14 000. Sandham and Woolley put on 109 runs, but Nupen then took five wickets and MCC were all out for their lowest score of the tour so far – 240. Catterall scored the first century against the tourists and almost everyone got runs in Transvaal's innings of 291. Sandham and Russell put on 119, then a thunderstorm prevented any more play and the match ended in a draw.

Ten thousand people watched the first Test at the Wanderers over the Christmas holidays.

FIRST TEST TEAMS—JOHANNESBURG

SOUTH AFRICA	ENGLAND
RH Catterall (Transvaal)	A Sandham
G Hearne (W Province)	FT Mann (captain)
HW Taylor (captain) (Natal)	FE Woolley
AD Nourse (Natal)	AW Carr
WV Ling (Griqualand West)	CP Mead
W Brann (Eastern Province)	PGH Fender
CM Francois (Griqualand West)	VWC Jupp
JM Blanckenberg (W Province)	GTS Stevens
EP Nupen (Transvaal)	G Brown
TA Ward (Transvaal)	A Kennedy
ID Buys (Western Province)	AER Gilligan

South Africa batted well until after lunch when they suffered a collapse and they were all out for 148. Blanckenberg bowled particularly well with support from Nupen and England could only achieve a 34-run lead through hitting by the tail enders. South Africa batted out the day with Taylor on 121*. He carried on the next day to 176 before being caught, having made the highest score to date by a South African against England. South Africa ended the innings at 420, a lead of 386, and four England wickets fell for 123 before close of play. It was all over after lunch when England were dismissed for 218 and South Africa had achieved their first victory in 11 years. During the match, Blanckenberg had taken nine wickets, and Nupen six, and the fielding had been brilliant, but the match-winner was Taylor with his 176.

The second Test started three days later in Cape Town. South Africa were all out for a disappointing 113 and England replied with 183. South Africa's second innings got off to a bad start when Hearne was out without scoring. Taylor and Catterall took the score to 157, but then Macaulay and Kennedy bowled South Africa out for 242. Needing 173 to win, only Sandham and Mead could cope with the bowling of Hall and at the end of the day's play England were 86 for six. Mann and Jupp put on 68 runs and, with three wickets remaining, England needed just 19 to win. Mann was caught in the slips, Brown was run out with a direct throw at the stumps from the deep and, with the last man in, five runs were still needed. Kennedy swung the bat and scored a boundary to bring the scores level. Macaulay was beaten twice but scored a single to settle the exciting match, which could have gone either way, to England.

With England nine wickets down at Newlands Yorkshireman George Macaulay puts the ball away to clinch a thrilling win for the tourists and level the series one-all after South Africa had won the first Test.

South African captain Herbie Taylor (front left) leads his team out onto field at the Wanderers. In this first match of the series, the South Africans were to record their first victory over the English in 11 years.

After his performance of seven wickets in the first innings and four in the second, Hall was carried from the field shoulder-high.

With both teams having won one Test each, there was a lot of interest in the third Test in Durban. Rain affected the outfield and England lost two early wickets, but Mead and Fender then put on 154 runs together. Mann then joined Mead and hit two sixes and 11 fours in his 84. Mead went on to 181 and the innings closed on 428. Catterall and Taylor stayed together in bad light to score 70 without loss and the next day was washed out. Taylor went on to 91 and Catterall 52, which, together with contributions from Nourse and Francois brought the South African total to 368.

England had only a few minutes batting before the game was called off as a draw.

Another two fun matches were played, against Zululand at Eshowe and Northern Districts at Newcastle. A return match against Transvaal preceded the fourth Test. Sandham completed his 1 000 runs for the tour with a century, and MCC declared at 288 for four, leaving Transvaal a target of 380 on a crumbling pitch. Transvaal were bowled out for 180 with 15 minutes to spare.

Wanderers was the scene of the fourth Test with the score still one-all. England's batsmen struggled on the first day and good bowling combined with brilliant fielding kept the England score down to 244. Nourse and Ward scored patient fifties while Tapscott and Francois hit out to give South Africa a lead of 51 runs. Russell and

Sandham put on 150 for the first wicket then Woolley found his form and, with Mann, put on 124. This allowed Mann to declare on 376 for six, a lead of 326. Two South African wickets were down for 32, but Taylor and Nourse stayed until a draw was certain and then hit out freely. Nourse scored 63 and Taylor 101. Stumps were drawn with the South African score on 247 for four.

As the rubber depended on the last Test to be played in Durban, the MCC in London agreed by cable to play the match out to a finish. Russell scored 140 out of a modest 281, then took a beautiful catch at slip to dismiss Taylor with the score on seven. Nourse and Francois were the only ones to offer any resistance and South Africa struggled to 173. There was heavy rain overnight and next morning four English wickets were down for 26. Russell was ill but came out to join Sandham and they took the score to 102. After Sandham went, Russell could get no support until joined by last man Gilligan. They put on 92 in 80 minutes and the innings closed at 241, a lead of 343.

Russell had batted for four and a half hours for his second century in the Test match, a feat accomplished only once before, by Bardsley. A collection was taken for him which raised £90.

Set to score 344, South Africa reached 111 for three before bad light stopped play. The next day was interrupted several times by rain. Taylor was ninth out on 102 and South Africa were all out for 234 to lose by 109 runs. South Africa lost the rubber on the sixth day of the final Test.

Orange Free State proved no match for the MCC and the MCC wound up their tour with an easy victory against Western Province at Newlands.

The tour must be remembered for the outstanding batting of the South African captain, Herbie Taylor, with three Test centuries and an average of over 50. Russell's centuries in each innings of the fifth Test to win the series were also memorable. When the MCC left England, it was thought that they would have no difficulty in beating South Africa. The narrow win in the series did not convince the people back home that the England side had recovered from the beatings handed out by the Australians, in spite of the success of the team in the non-Test matches. Only Test matches count in the public's view.

South Africa were still reliant on the old stalwarts and even Snooke was brought back, after an absence of ten years, into the Test side. Alf Hall of Transvaal was the exception with a match analysis of 11 for 112 on his Test debut.

Alf Hall, the Transvaal bowler, being carried by the crowd from the field at Newlands after an outstanding debut performance of 11 for 112. It was not enough, however, to prevent England from winning the match.

CHAPTER 14

1924

SIXTH SOUTH AFRICA TOUR OF THE UNITED KINGDOM

Captain: HW Taylor

*The Old Guard was again chosen to tour.
Parker, from the Bradford League, and
43-year-old Faulkner were both called upon.
South Africa were dismissed for 30 once again
and failed to win a Test match. A very
disappointing tour from a second-rate side.*

Herbie Taylor leads the South African tourists onto the field during the first Test in 1924. From left to right: RH Catterall, TA Ward, AW Nourse, JM Blankenberg, Taylor, JMM Commaille and SJ Pegler.

The selectors relied on the Old Guard once more and gave little thought to the future. In fact, of the 18 chosen, only six played for South Africa following the tour. The average age of those selected was 33. Pegler was on holiday in Europe at the time but was co-opted when it became obvious that the bowling strength was not up to standard. GM Parker, a South African now living in England and playing in the Bradford League, together with veteran Aubrey Faulkner, were also needed – a sad indictment on the choice of the selectors.

The team arrived in Southampton on Easter Monday. Rain interrupted the first three matches so that draws were inevitable. Nourse played his best innings of the tour to score 147* against Nottinghamshire, but the tourists suffered their first defeat. Then disaster struck again at Old Trafford when the South Africans were bowled out in an hour and a half for 60. Richard Tyldesley took seven wickets for 28. Rain could not save the South Africans and the English public became convinced that the South Africans posed no threat in the Test matches. Rain spoiled the match against Gloucestershire and yet again, no play was possible on the first day of the game against MCC at Lord's. Both games against Scotland were interrupted by rain and the Yorkshire public objected to paying 2s 6d to watch the second-rate tourists, so stayed away from another rain-interrupted

TOURING SIDE	
HW Taylor (captain) (Natal)	G Hearne (SWD)
C Carter (Natal)	HG Deane (Transvaal)
AW Nourse (Natal)	MJ Susskind (Transvaal)
JM Blanckenberg (Natal)	EP Nupen (Transvaal)
JMM Commaille (W Province)	DJ Meintjes (Transvaal)
PAM Hands (W Province)	CD Dixon (Transvaal)
RH Catterall (Rhodesia)	TA Ward (Transvaal)
GF Bissett (Griqualand West)	SJ Pegler (Transvaal)
G Allsop was to be manager	

drawn match. Cambridge University provided the South Africans their much-needed second win out of ten matches when Dave Nourse scored 144.

Only half a day's play was possible against Oxford University, and the opportunity was taken to give Parker a trial. He took four wickets and had four catches dropped off his bowling and so played himself into the side for the first Test at Birmingham, having played only half a day's first-class cricket.

After being put in to bat, Hobbs and Sutcliffe put on 136 for the first wicket. Then Parker took six wickets but had to leave the field suffering from exhaustion. The England innings closed on 438 and, incredibly, three-quarters of an hour later, South Africa were

FIRST TEST TEAMS—BIRMINGHAM

SOUTH AFRICA	ENGLAND
HW Taylor (captain)	JB Hobbs
RH Catterall	H Sutcliffe
MJ Susskind	FE Woolley
AD Nourse	E Hendren
JMM Commaille	APF Chapman
JM Blanckenberg	PGH Fender
HG Deane	R Kilner
EP Nupen	MW Tate
SJ Pegler	AER Gilligan (captain)
TA Ward	GEC Wood
GM Parker	C Parkin

all out for 30. No-one got into double figures but there were 11 extras. Gilligan took six wickets for seven runs and Tate took the rest. Taylor and Commaille started well in the follow-on, and Catterall was last man out, hitting out for 120 in a vain attempt to avoid an innings defeat. South Africa were all out for 390. Gilligan took 11 wickets in his first match as England's captain, and Tate took eight, but the other bowlers did not look at all difficult. The 30 run total equalled the lowest score achieved by South Africa and resulted in the crowds staying away from the rest of the matches in the tour. Only 10 000 watched the whole of this Test.

There was some consolation in the next match against Essex at Colchester when the last man, Bissett, scored 28 of the 31 runs required and the exciting match was won with a few minutes to spare. Matches against Hampshire and a Leveson-Gower's side helped to restore the South Africans' spirits when they won both games in exciting finishes. Parker was again asked to play for South Africa in the Test at Lord's. Taylor also asked Aubrey Faulkner, who was busy running his cricket school in London and was now way past his prime.

Despite the high entrance fee of three shillings, there was a crowd of 20 000 to greet the King when he visited the match and saw South Africa score 273 on a good batting wicket. Taylor, Commaille and Nourse were out with 17 on the board but Catterall went on to 120, the same score as the previous Test, and saved the side from disaster. Hobbs and Sutcliffe opened for England and scored 200 runs in two and a half hours. Their partnership went on to 268 before Sutcliffe was out for 122. Woolley was sent in to keep up the momentum and at 410 for one, Hobbs was out for 211, having put on 142 runs in 80 minutes. Hendren joined Woolley and in 55 minutes took the score from 410 to a massive 531 for two. To everyone's surprise Gilligan declared, leaving South Africa to score 259 in order to make England bat again. South Africa were bowled out for 240 to lose by an innings. Parker, the League player, took

The England team which dismissed South Africa for 30 in the first Test. Back: Umpire, R Kilner, MW Tate, APF Chapman, GEC Wood, E Tyldesley, C Parkin, E Hendren, H Sutcliffe; front: PGH Fender, AER Gilligan (capt), JB Hobbs, FE Woolley.

Patsy Hendren batting for England in the fifth and final Test match at the Oval. The South African wicket-keeper is TA Ward of Transvaal and the fielder RH Catterall, the batsman from Rhodesia.

all the English wickets to fall in the match (mind you, that was only two). Faulkner was not asked to play again.

Following a drawn match against Yorkshire, Northants were thrashed when Blanckenberg and Pegler bowled superbly. Taylor scored a century and there was a good innings from Nourse. Some 1 141 runs were scored in the game against Warwickshire and the match ended in a draw. Taylor scored a century in the second innings to add to his 94 in the first and the game became light-hearted on the last afternoon. Nupen and Carter came into the side and Parker did not play in the Test at Leeds. Sutcliffe was in great form and scored 83, while Hendren's brilliant 132 took England's first innings to 396. Three South African wickets fell in the first half-hour and the score became 34 for five. Taylor and Catterall were the only ones able to cope with the bowling of Tate and they were all out for 132.

In the follow-on, four wickets had fallen for 135, but again Taylor and Catterall added 97 and the tail-enders hit out to force England to bat again in order to get 60.

Matches against Lancashire, Middlesex and Durham were called off because of rain. The fourth Test at Manchester was abandoned because the ground was waterlogged after only a few hours' play. The crowd demonstrated, but fortunately they were given tickets for the far more important upcoming Roses match against Yorkshire and they dispersed. Matches against Sussex, Glamorgan and Surrey were ruined by rain.

A Combined Services side shocked the tourists by bowling them out for 182 and then scoring 418. Lieutenant GJ Bryan scored the highest total against the South Africans on tour with 229. Taylor and Catterall recovered the situation with centuries and saved the embarrassment of another defeat.

A match against Harlequins provided an easy victory before the fifth and final Test at the Oval. South Africa lost two early wickets but recovered to score 342. Susskind scored 65 and Catterall narrowly missed his century. Rain interfered with England's innings but Hendren scored 142 and they were on 421 for eight when the match was abandoned.

Minor Counties beat the tourists by 25 runs with 2 minutes left to play. Then Kent were far too strong for the South Africans and scored 418 for six declared. Woolley was in magnificent form and scored 176 while Hardinge also scored a century. Wright and Tich Freeman bowled the tourists out to win by an innings.

The second-rate tourists managed to win against Somerset and Worcestershire in the final matches against the counties. Then three holiday games closed a long and arduous tour. Veteran Sidney Barnes played for North Wales and took five wickets but the game was ruined by rain. At the Scarborough Festival the tourists were perhaps appropriately beaten by an innings. Percy Holmes scored 202 not out and Patsy Hendren scored a century. South African cricket suffered a major setback on this tour. Although the weather was atrocious the bowlers were ineffectual on turf wickets. The English public and players regarded the tour as secondary to the approaching tour of Australia and stayed away. Out of 38 matches played the South Africans won only eight, against weak sides, and lost nine. The other 21 were drawn.

Taylor and Catterall, along with Nourse, had their days but were inconsistent and the fielding of the team was ordinary, with the exception of wicket-keeper Ward, who proved that he was a worthy successor to Halliwell and Sherwell. Pegler, the man not originally chosen, became invaluable, and the fact that substitutes in the form of Parker and Faulkner were required was a sad indictment of South African cricket.

Having played in only half a day's first-class match and two Tests, in all of which he performed creditably, Parker returned to Eccleshill in the Bradford League. Brilliant Aubrey Faulkner was 43 years old when he was co-opted into the side. Six years later he was to gas himself in his world famous cricket school in London.

South African cricket was not to be considered world class while most matches were still played on matting wickets. It was becoming vital that the players became accustomed to playing on turf wickets at home.

The team sailed for home on the *Armadale Castle* on 26 September 1924, following a very disappointing tour which showed a small profit.

Herbie Taylor, South African captain and outstanding opening batsman. On this tour, however, he was unable to repeat his earlier success.

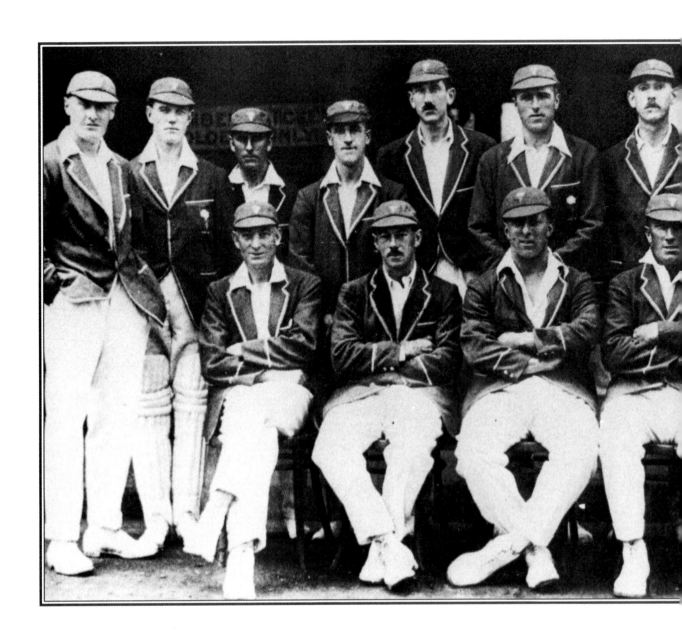

SB JOEL'S ENGLISH TEAM IN SOUTH AFRICA

*Captain: The Honourable
LH Tennyson*

*A second-rate, sponsored, unofficial English side
halved the 'Test' series two matches all.
Only Nupen and Hall enhanced their
reputations in a lacklustre tour. South African
cricket continued to be at a low ebb.*

The South African team for the fourth 'Test' at the Wanderers. Back: HW Taylor, IJ Siedle, VSW Ling, MJ Susskind, HG Deane, DJ Meintjes; front: AE Hall, EP Nupen, VH Neser (capt), AW Nourse, RH Catterall.

SB Joel, the mining magnate and nephew of Barnie Barnato, sponsored the tour of South Africa by a team of English cricketers chosen from those who were not selected to go to Australia as part of the official MCC tour.

The Honourable LH Tennyson, grandson of the poet, was invited to lead the side. It was a strong side, but could not be regarded as the representative English side and thus the matches against South Africa could not be classed as 'Test matches'.

Following the disastrous tour of United Kingdom by the 1924 South African side, the strength of South African cricket was suspect. No Currie Cup matches were played and the season was used to rebuild the South African Test side. In fact 22 players were selected to play for South Africa in the five Test matches.

Twenty-two games were to be played including five against South Africa.

WE Astill (Leicestershire), who was in South Africa coaching, was asked to join the side for several matches. The side travelled out on the *Edinburgh Castle* and arrived in Cape Town on 13 November 1924. Parker took a hat-trick in a one-day match which was played against a Schools and Colleges XV as soon as they arrived.

TOURING SIDE	
AMATEURS	PROFESSIONALS
Hon LH Tennyson (captain) (Hants)	E Tyldesley (Lancashire)
Captain TO Jameson (Hants)	EH Bowley (Sussex)
JCW MacBryan (Somerset)	P Holmes (Yorkshire)
AHH Gilligan (Sussex)	AC Russell (Essex)
Lt. ELD Bartley (RN)	A Kennedy (Hants)
CS Marriott (Kent)	C Parker (Gloucestershire)
G Geary (Leicestershire)	

Matches against Western Province and Natal were drawn, and both Pretoria and Griqualand West surprised the tourists by gaining first-innings leads. However these matches were also drawn. Tyldesley hit the highest score of the tour with a magnificent 174 but Tapscott and McKay scored centuries, while Ling made 91 and 75 for Griquas. Tapscott, McKay and Ling had all been considered for the previous tour of the United Kingdom.

Matches against Rhodesia and Transvaal gave the tourists much-needed victories before the first match against South Africa at the Wanderers. After a reasonable start, the visitors were all out for 198. Nupen took five wickets for 54. South Africa scored 295 with good contributions from the captain, 'Boet' Neser, who made 80, and Dave Nourse with 71. Seven English batsmen failed to get into double figures and the Englishmen were all out for 149, a lead of only 52. Nupen again took five wickets. South Africa knocked off the required runs for the loss of only one wicket.

The teams went down to Durban for the second 'Test' on New Year's Day where they played a well-fought game. Bowley scored the only century of the series against South Africa in the first innings total of 285. Taylor replied with a century but he had little support and the South African innings was a disappointing 211. Percy Holmes had recovered and scored 81 in the second innings, but he also had little support and Tennyson's side scored 174, a lead of 248. Nupen, with five wickets in the first innings and seven in the second, had an outstanding match. Catterall, Susskind and Taylor all failed and it was left to Nourse, together with skipper Neser, Nupen and Francois to try to retrieve the situation. This they were unable to do and they were all out for 200 to lose by 48 runs.

It was one-all in the series with three to play.

Matches against Northern Natal at Ladysmith and XV of the OFS Northern Districts at Bethlehem ended in draws.

Susskind, Nupen, Deane and Ling were replaced for the third match against South Africa at Newlands. Geary took six wickets for 37 to dismiss South Africa for 113 and then Joel's XI scored 224 with fifties from Tyldesley and Russell. Catterall and Siedle gave South Africa a good start in the second innings but the tail was too long and they were dismissed for 150, a lead of only 39.

The Englishmen won by ten wickets. Hall with six for 62 was the only South African to come out of the game with credit.

In the match against Country District teams at Mossel Bay, the only matter of note was the fact that Vintcent, the Country Districts' captain and wicket-keeper, wore an artificial leg as a result of a motoring accident.

Kennedy and Geary were in deadly form to dismiss Eastern Province for 62 at Grahamstown. Needing only 16 to win, the two bowlers, Bartley and Marriott, opened the batting in the second innings and both lost their wickets for a duck. Back at the Wanderers for the fourth 'Test' there was some inconsistent batting from the visitors with only Tyldesley, Russell and Jameson being at all confident to reach 239. Equally the South African batsmen all got a few runs but not one of them had a big innings and they were all out for 193. In the second innings Nupen and Hall bowled well to dismiss the Englishmen for 164, giving them a lead of 210 with a day to play. Unfortunately rain prevented any further play and the interesting situation was unresolved.

On their way down to Port Elizabeth the tourists played at Bloemfontein against Orange Free State in what proved to be a high-scoring match. In reply to a score of 442, the Free Staters scored 384 with a century from S Coen. There was no time for a second innings and the match ended in an honourable draw.

A final, well-contested 'Test' was played at St George's Park, Port Elizabeth. South Africa scored 183, then Nupen and Hall bowled beautifully to dismiss the Englishmen for 94 in the first innings for a lead of 89. When South Africa batted a second time, Catterall scored 86 and they were all out for 200. Needing 290 to win, Holmes and Tyldesley had 234 on the board with only four wickets down, but then Hall bowled so well that the remaining six wickets fell for only 34 more runs and South Africa had won the match by 21 runs. The series was halved with two victories each and one draw.

Nupen, who had not been a success in the United Kingdom, had taken 37 wickets in four games and was the most successful bowler, although Hall was also dangerous. Neither had been chosen to go to England on the previous tour. VH Neser captained the South Africans and proved a good replacement for Ward as wicket-keeper, but business commitments kept him out of the future South African sides. Dave Nourse, having played in 52 consecutive matches for South Africa, came to the end of a highly successful international career. No outstanding youngsters came to the fore.

Ernest Tyldesley was the most successful English batsman, but they had a long tail. Out of the 21 matches played, eight were won, two lost and 11 drawn. The tour was a social success: the team was very popular but financially a failure, losing about £4 000.

Vivian Neser, captain of the South Africans in the five unofficial 'Tests' played against SB Joel's tourists.

CHAPTER 16

1927/28

FIFTH MCC TOUR OF SOUTH AFRICA

Captain: RT Stanyforth

A reasonable MCC side under an inexperienced captain drew the series two-all. Sutcliffe, Holmes, Tyldesley and Hammond all scored runs but their bowlers could not penetrate. Jock Cameron and Cyril Vincent provided hope for the future for the home side and George Bissett impressed.

'Nummy' Deane, the South African captain, walks from the field having made the winning hit in the fourth Test at the Wanderers. Following him from the field are (from left) Stevens, Stanyforth, Hammond, Peebles, Astill, Freeman, Wyatt, Staples and Sutcliffe.

The English press criticized the choice of the party as a whole and particularly the choice of Stanyforth as captain. He had never played in county cricket as captain, but was only selected by MCC when the original choice, GR Jackson of Derbyshire, was forced to decline through ill health.

The team could in no way represent the full strength of English cricket as it was without Hobbs, Hendren, Tate, Larwood, Jardine and Chapman, and it was thought that the strength of South African cricket had been underestimated. Eighteen matches were to be played including five Tests.

The team sailed from Southampton on the *Kenilworth Castle* on 21 October 1927, and arrived at Cape Town on 7 November.

As usual, Western Province provided the opening game. On the only day that play was possible, Tich Freeman took five of the six wickets to fall for 15 runs.

Sutcliffe and Tyldesley put on 216 for the second wicket against Griqualand West at Kimberley. Only Tapscott with 75 showed any resistance and MCC won by an innings.

Holmes and Sutcliffe shared the opening berth for Yorkshire and

TOURING SIDE	
AMATEURS	PROFESSIONALS
RT Stanyforth (captain) (Army)	WE Astill (Leicestershire)
GTS Stevens (Middlesex)	E Tyldesley (Lancashire)
EW Dawson (Leicestershire)	H Sutcliffe (Yorks)
GB Legge (Kent)	P Holmes (Yorkshire)
RES Wyatt (Warwickshire)	WR Hammond (Gloucestershire)
IAR Peebles (Middlesex)	G Geary (Leicestershire)
	SJ Staples (Nottinghamshire)
	AP Freeman (Kent)
	H Elliott (Derby)

also the same birthday. It was on their birthday that they put on 203 in 100 minutes for the first wicket against the Orange Free State. Holmes also had a 224 run partnership with Legge in just over two hours. He went on to 279 not out, the highest score made in matches between teams of the two countries.

Tyldesley scored 161 out of 333 against Natal, but rain then prevented more play and the match was drawn. A second match was

Hammond took six for 32. Holmes scored 128 giving the tourists a lead of 237. In the second innings the South African XI had no difficulty and scored 305 to avoid an innings defeat. Stanyforth and Elliott were injured and MCC had to borrow Hubble, an Englishman playing in South Africa, and 'Shunter' Coen from the Orange Free State to complete the side.

The first Test was played in Johannesburg over the Christmas holiday.

FIRST TEST TEAMS—JOHANNESBURG	
SOUTH AFRICA	ENGLAND
HW Taylor	H Sutcliffe
JP Duminy	P Holmes
JM Commaille	E Tyldesley
RH Catterall	WR Hammond
HG Deane (captain)	RES Wyatt
D Morkel	GTS Stevens
S Coen	GB Legge
HB Cameron	WE Astill
EP Nupen	Captain RT Stanyforth (captain)
CL Vincent	G Geary
H Promnitz	IAR Peebles

Geary's spin baffled all the South Africans, except Catterall who scored 86, and he took seven wickets for 70 in South Africa's first innings of 196. Sutcliffe and Tyldesley both made centuries and added 230 runs in a record second wicket partnership. Hammond hit briskly for 51, but the next seven English batsmen could only score 13 between them and England were 117 ahead. Hammond took three wickets in three overs without a run being scored off his bowling and ended with figures of five for 36. Geary supported him with the other five wickets, bringing his match total to 12, and South Africa were dismissed for 170, a lead of only 53. Sutcliffe and Holmes knocked off the deficit without loss for England to win by ten wickets.

George Bissett was brought into the South African side to strengthen the bowling in the second Test at Cape Town over the New Year. At the time, Bissett was playing second league cricket in Cape Town and had not played for Province. He justified his selection with five for 37 in England's first innings of 133. Herbie Taylor scored 68, Deane batted well and Nupen hit out in South Africa's 250 and gained a lead of 117. Holmes and Sutcliffe knocked off the deficit and went on to a first wicket partnership of 140. Tyldesley scored 87 while Wyatt hit a brisk 91 and England's second innings ended on 428, a lead of 312 with four hours and thirty-five minutes in which to get them. Taylor and Catterall started off in fine style by scoring 115 in 100 minutes but then Astill

played against Natal at Durban, this time on a turf wicket. Holmes and Sutcliffe put on a century opening partnership and when Tyldesley joined Sutcliffe, they put on another century. Stanyforth was able to declare at 354 for four. Siedle scored 80 for Natal but they were only five runs on with six wickets down when the game ended in a draw.

MCC struggled against Transvaal at Pretoria. Duminy, playing in his début, hammered the MCC bowling for 95 not out and Transvaal declared with seven wickets down for 382, a lead of 177. Holmes made 71 out of the first 100 and, after putting on 108 with Tyldesley, then put on another 100 with Hammond. Thanks to Holmes's 184 not out, MCC were 151 runs on with the loss of three wickets when the match was left drawn.

A second game was played against a stronger Transvaal side. The last five English batsmen added only ten runs when Nupen took five wickets and Vincent four. Transvaal passed the MCC score with only two wickets down but could only manage a lead of 70 on the first innings. MCC brought the score to 360 for nine with 132 from Hammond. Duminy played himself into the Test side with a third good innings against the tourists and the match ended in a draw.

A South African XI could only score 86 at Benoni when

The South African team that played the fourth Test of the 1927/28 series. Back: RH Catterall, GF Bissett, CL Vincent, DPB Morkel, AL Ochse, IJ Siedle, LTH Trotter (12th man); front: EP Nupen, HL Crockett (manager), HG Deane (capt), HW Taylor, HB Cameron (JFW Nicolson absent).

and Freeman dismissed the last eight South African batsmen for 98 runs to win by 87 runs with half-an-hour remaining to play.

Geary injured himself in this match and was unable to play in the following Tests.

MCC collapsed in dramatic fashion against Eastern Province. The pace of Ochse was devastating and the tourists were dismissed for the lowest total of any side to date, 49. Eastern Province had a lead of 185, but Sutcliffe opened with Wyatt and they were not separated in knocking off the runs.

Freeman took eight Border wickets for 48, then Hammond hit two sixes and 13 fours in his innings of 166 out of 289. The fifth wicket stand with Dawson, who scored 59, was 198. Astill bowled Border out for 107, and so to the third Test at Durban.

Arthur Ochse, from Eastern Province, Jack Siedle and John Nicolson from Natal were brought into the South African side. Once more South Africa started badly and things could have been worse if Stanyforth had not taken off Wyatt, who had bowled 11 overs for one run and taken the wicket of Taylor. He only came back on to break an eighth-wicket partnership when the score had reached 241 by bowling both Deane and Nupen in the first three balls he sent down, end-ing with three wickets for four runs. Holmes was missed three times in his 70, Stevens twice in his 69 and Tyldesley once in his 78. Hammond scored 90 and the England innings closed on 430. Nicolson had stands with Taylor, Catterall and Morkel and wore down the English bowling, thus paving the way for another partnership between Deane and Nupen so that Deane was able to declare at 464 for 8, a lead of 280. Holmes and Tyldesley gave a delightful display of batting in their partnership of 102 but the match was drawn.

The total number of runs in the match, 1 272 for the loss of 30 wickets, was a record between the two countries.

Johannesburg hosted the fourth Test which South Africa had to win to keep the series alive. Aware of this, Deane gambled and put England in to bat. Hall's slow left arm bowling, combined with Bissett's fast, troubled the English batsmen and between them they took 17 of the 20 wickets to fall. Wyatt played a good innings while Astill and Peebles waded in to give England a first innings score of 265. Hammond bowled Duminy and Morkel with only seven runs on the board. However, Taylor managed to rescue the situation and hit 101 out of 170. He and Catterall mastered the bowling and allowed Deane and Cameron to score 89 together in 47 minutes, and the South Africans took a lead of 63. Holmes, with a damaged

94

finger, scored 63 of the first 83 runs, but the rest of the side could do nothing and England were dismissed for 215. Needing 153 to win, South Africa scored freely after Taylor and Duminy were out and Morkel and Nicolson saw them to a victory which saved the series for the home team.

The fifth and final Test was played at Durban and rain prevented any play on the first day of the four-day match. Stanyforth was injured and Stevens took over the captaincy with Elliott keeping wicket. Deane won the toss for the fifth time and again put England in to bat. Holmes went almost immediately but Sutcliffe and Tyldesley had a partnership of 130 runs and the score rose to 240 for three. At this point, Nupen took five for seven runs and the innings closed for the addition of only 42 runs to end on 282. Catterall and Cameron had a stand of 136 runs in 90 minutes. With a lead of only 50 runs, Deane declared and this adventurous move won the match. Holmes was again out in the first over and Bissett bowled with such fire that England were bowled out for 118. Bissett took seven for 29 and was unplayable. Taylor, Coen and Nupen knocked off the required runs and South Africa had saved the rubber in great style with two victories each and one draw.

A match was played at Grahamstown against a Combined Schools XI, who surprised the tourists. Holmes and Sutcliffe scored

John Nicolson (Natal) and Jacobus Duminy (Transvaal), both left-handed batsmen, made their Test debuts in the 1927/28 series.

quickly, and MCC were able to declare at 222 for five. The schoolboys then scored 291, thanks to a century from Byron and fifties from Rees and Owen-Smith.

The last match of the tour was against Western Province and Stanyforth had his highest score of the tour, 71. Until this match he had scored only 83 in 17 innings. MCC declared at 415 for nine and only L Serrurier managed to cope with the bowling of Freeman and Astill. He batted through the innings of 162 for 74 not out. In the follow-on, Western Province did better and all got runs to score 339, leaving MCC to score 87 runs in an hour and a quarter. They won by eight wickets in an exciting finish.

Tyldesley, Holmes and Sutcliffe all scored over 1 000 runs on the tour with Hammond scoring 908. When these recognized batsmen failed, however, there was a long tail. The injury to Geary undoubtedly affected the penetration of the English bowlers, particularly in the Tests.

Cameron and Vincent, who were to play a large part in the future South African cricket, had been blooded, but the bowling of George Bissett was the factor which impressed everyone. Unfortunately he lost his form in the next season and never played for South Africa again. Stanyforth's team was popular and he proved a reasonable captain in spite of his poor performances on the field.

Dawson became engaged to a South African and stayed behind. The rest of the team sailed home on the *Saxon* with Tyldesley and Sutcliffe getting off in Madeira for a well-deserved holiday before the rigours of another county season.

George Finlay Bissett, whose seven for 29 in England's second innings of the fifth Test match enabled South Africa to square the series.

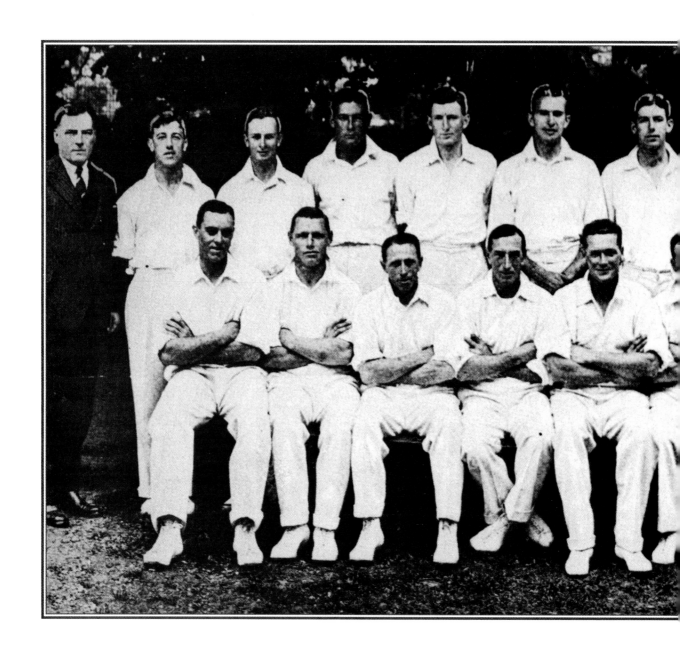

CHAPTER 17

1929

SEVENTH SOUTH AFRICA TOUR OF THE UNITED KINGDOM

Captain: HG Deane

A new side in which the youngsters batted well and the fielding was brilliant. Jock Cameron played well behind the stumps. Although they lost the series, things looked a little brighter for South African cricket.

Herbert Sutcliffe of England strokes the ball past Denys Morkel to reach his century in the fifth Test at the Oval. Wicket-keeper Jock Cameron and Bruce Mitchell at slip look on. In the match Sutcliffe scored a century in both innings.

No Currie Cup competition was held in the 1928/29 season and emphasis was given to a series of trial matches to select a team for the forthcoming tour of the United Kingdom. Following the failure of the 1924 tour, the selectors decided on a clean sweep with an eye to the future. Only three of the 1924 party were included in the side and nine of the 16 chosen were under 24.

Thirty-seven matches were to be played of which thirty-four were first-class, including five Test matches.

The team arrived early in April and played two one-day matches before the start of the tour proper. Although the first two first-class games were drawn, the South Africans had totals of 444 for 8 against Worcestershire and 354 for 8 against Leicestershire, and the dry summer obviously suited their game.

They lost to Surrey at the Oval on a soft pitch but had good wins against Middlesex, Oxford University and Glamorgan. Having lost to Gloucestershire the team did well against Yorkshire at Bramall Lane by scoring 441 for 5 before the game was drawn. Cambridge University proved no problem and there was an honourable draw

TOURING SIDE	
HG Deane (captain) (Transvaal)	AJ Bell (W Province)
HB Cameron (Transvaal)	DPB Morkel (W Province)
JAJ Christy (Transvaal)	HG Owen-Smith (W Province)
B Mitchell (Transvaal)	RH Catterall (Natal)
Q McMillan (Transvaal)	EL Dalton (Natal)
HW Taylor (Transvaal)	IJ Siedle (Natal)
EA van der Merwe (Transvaal)	AL Ochse (E Province)
CL Vincent (Transvaal)	NA Quinn (Griqualand West)

Honorary General Manager: HO Frielinghaus
Secretary: AS Frames

against a strong MCC side at Lord's. The match against Derbyshire was drawn due to rain but Lancashire were too strong for the tourists, although they were without Tyldesley, Hallows and Duckworth.

Against Minor Counties they then came up against their old foe in the form of Sid Barnes, who showed that he was still a force

Ochse had five slips when England batted again and England were 117 for five when Leyland and Tate hit out and both scored centuries. Tate's century was his first. White was able to declare at 312 for eight leaving South Africa needing 293 to win. South Africa had lost five wickets for 85 when a fast rising ball from Larwood hit Cameron and knocked him unconscious. The light was bad and everyone trooped off the field feeling bad about the incident. Cameron was out of the game for a month.

At this point of the tour Siedle, Taylor, Quinn, Vincent and Cameron were all injured and so the team selection was no problem – the others were automatically chosen.

Games against Northamptonshire and Nottinghamshire were interrupted by rain and drawn, while a very exciting match against Wales was won. Sidney Barnes took ten wickets in the latter match, including a spell of four for ten and another of six for eight. Set to make 273 to win, Wales needed only 49 with 7 wickets still in hand. Vincent and McMillan then took the seven wickets for 38 runs to win the match by ten runs.

Siedle, Quinn and Vincent were fit, but JP Duminy, who was on business in Europe, was invited to play in the third Test at Leeds. Freeman had 34 knocked off his bowling before taking a wicket and then took seven wickets in the afternoon. Catterall batted well and Vincent waded in with four sixes and six fours for South Africa to score 236. Hammond, Woolley and Leyland batted well and

to be reckoned with at the age of 54 by taking eight wickets. Injuries to several South Africans made the team selection difficult and put pressure on the fit to play without the opportunity of a rest.

The first Test at Birmingham ended in a draw, when, after an even first innings, England scored 308 for 4 declared, leaving South Africa to get 304 to win in three hours. Catterall and Mitchell put on 171 for the first wicket before the stumps were drawn.

Morkel and Taylor played attractive cricket in a drawn match against Yorkshire and the South Africans scored 628 runs in the match against Surrey, but again rain prevented a result. Norfolk provided a relaxed match and were hammered by Taylor, who scored a brisk 170, to win by an innings.

Vincent, Quinn and Taylor were not fit for the second Test at Lord's and Bell came into the side. Morkel bowled so well that the first three England wickets were down for 18. Sutcliffe was missed at slip by Mitchell with his score on 14, and went on to his century. Together with Leyland, they made a recovery and England were all out for 302. Bell took the last six wickets to fall. Catterall was out first ball but Mitchell and Christy put on 82 and, on a nasty wicket, South Africa brought the score to 322.

Bob Catterall and debutant Bruce Mitchell open the batting in the first Test. Catterall scored 67 and 98, Mitchell 88 and 61 not out.

South African captain 'Nummy' Deane en route to England. Deane's young tourists showed a great deal of promise in England, but they were unable to record a Test match victory and lost the series two-nil.

England were 270 for 5 at lunch and then Quinn and Vincent took the last five wickets for 58, leaving England with a lead of 92. Larwood injured a tendon and was unable to bowl, but Tate and Woolley bowled well and seven wickets were down for 116 at close of play. Next morning Owen-Smith and Quinn put on 51 and then the last wicket partnership between Owen-Smith and Bell put on 103 runs in 65 minutes. This last-wicket record for South Africa was cheered as though they had won the match and added life to the game. Needing 184 to win, England lost five for 110 but Woolley and Tate hit the required runs to win the match.

Lancashire handed out another beating when Richard Tyldesley took seven wickets in the second innings. Richard was the youngest of four Tyldesley brothers at Lancashire and no relation to the other two Tyldesleys, JT and Ernest, who also played for the Lancashire team.

Owen-Smith took four wickets in five balls including a hat-trick against Scotland. Both Scotland and Durham were beaten by an innings before the fourth Test at Manchester.

Hammond, Tate and Larwood were injured and their places taken by Wyatt, Geary and Barratt. Carr took over the captaincy from White. Taylor and Cameron were fit for the match but it was a very moderate performance by the South Africans and Tich Freeman proved too much for them, taking 12 wickets. Wyatt and Woolley came together at 36 for 2 and scored 245 before being separated. Woolley went on to 154 before being caught and bowled by Vincent while Wyatt scored the first century to be made by an amateur in a representative match since the War. Carr declared on 427 for seven. Five South African wickets were down for 39 and poor batting had them all out for 130. Freeman took seven for 71. In the follow-on, South Africa lost three wickets for 15 and, although Taylor and Morkel tried to stop the rot and Cameron hit bravely, they were all out for 265 to lose by an innings. England, having won two Tests with one more to play, had made sure of the rubber.

Following the disappointment of the Test, the South Africans played well against Somerset and Essex to win. Rain ruined the game against Glamorgan and the game against Warwickshire was a draw although Owen-Smith scored a century. Skipper Deane scored his first century of the tour against Hampshire but a game which was developing nicely ran out of time.

McMillan came into the side for the fifth and last Test at the Oval on a beautiful pitch. Sutcliffe had the distinction of scoring a century in each innings, the first time this had happened in a Test. After a good start, England collapsed and were all out for 258 with Vincent taking 5 wickets. South Africa had a terrible start with Catterall, Siedle and Mitchell out for 25. Taylor and Deane led the recovery with a partnership of 214 in the best batting of the series. Taylor scored 121 and Deane narrowly missed his century. Cameron, Morkel and McMillan consolidated the position and South Africa declared at 492 for eight. Hobbs and Sutcliffe put on a century opening partnership and then Sutcliffe and Hammond both scored centuries before the three-day game was called off as a draw. Some 47 298 people paid for admission during the three days.

The South Africans declared at 491 for seven against Kent and almost lost the match. Kent replied with 436 with wicket-keeper Les Ames scoring 145. In the second innings six South Africans were out with a lead of only 114, when Dalton chanced his arm and despite being dropped five times, scored his second century of the match and saved the game. Dalton scored another century in the match against Sussex in the first innings and Mitchell a century in the second. McMillan was backed up by brilliant fielding once more and took nine wickets for the South Africans to win by 217 runs.

The traditional Scarborough Festival match against a powerful CI Thornton's XI provided an exciting finish. Jack Hobbs scored 151, his tenth century of the season, and Patsy Hendren 114. The tourists were left to score 308 to win in three hours. Only 35 runs were needed with two wickets in hand when stumps were drawn.

Following a long journey through the night, another festival game was played at Folkestone against An England XI. Freeman and Fender dismissed the tourists for 153 and then Hearne and Woolley put on a marvellous display, each scoring a century to put on 450. Catterall, Morkel and last man Bell tried to prevent a complete disaster to no avail and the game was over in two days to end the tour. As an experiment, the wickets were enlarged in this match and the experiment was judged to be very successful.

Having lost two of the five Tests, won nine and lost seven of the 34 first-class matches played, the side did not improve on the previous tour. However the team impressed everyone in England with some brilliant fielding, in particular that of the 20-year-old Tuppy Owen-Smith.

The side was hard hit by injuries at the beginning of the tour and it was a long, hard season. Taylor led the batting but was not the dominating person of the past. Siedle was successful in the non-Test matches while Mitchell was determined, without being attractive to watch. Christy and Morkel looked good and Dalton came to form in the last few matches. Seven of the team scored over a thousand runs and ten scored centuries. There was no fast bowler of the standard of Kotze although Ochse worked hard. The two left arm spinners, Vincent and Quinn, found the conditions not to their liking and Morkel was the best all-rounder in the side. Cameron impressed everyone with his wicket-keeping and the fielding was outstanding throughout the tour.

The experiment of choosing a young side was successful and the outlook for the future looked promising.

Brilliant all-round sportsman 'Tuppy' Owen-Smith takes a tumble at the crease on the way to a Test match century at Leeds. The 20-year old went up to Oxford University after the tour, and was later to captain England at rugby.

CHAPTER 18

1930/31

SIXTH MCC TOUR OF SOUTH AFRICA

Captain: APF Chapman

An average MCC side, badly hit by injuries, lost the series on wickets that were changing from matting to turf. Nupen, Deane and Cameron all captained South Africa and there was strife among the administrators.

Jock Cameron, South Africa's third captain in the series, and Percy Chapman, the captain of the English tourists, walk out to toss in the fourth Test at the Wanderers.

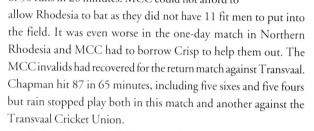

Once more the MCC chose a team which did not include the full strength of English cricket. Sutcliffe, Larwood and Woolley were missing and only Wyatt, Peebles and Hammond were included of those who had been on the previous tour. Les Ames was originally chosen but was unable to travel and stood down in favour of Farrimond.

The team sailed from Southampton on 17 October 1930 aboard the *Edinburgh Castle* and played the first warm-up match against a Western Province Schools XV on 6 November. Maurice Leyland took seven schoolboy wickets for seven runs.

A lot of work had gone into preparing the turf wicket at Newlands for the first match. Sandham and Wyatt passed Province's score before being separated. Then Wyatt and Hammond put on 158. Leyland took three wickets for four runs in four overs to win by an innings. Griqualand West played on matting but Natal prepared a turf pitch for their drawn matches. Transvaal were the holders of the Currie Cup and a strong side when an interesting game developed, on matting. Sandham had been injured in a motoring

accident and was unable to play, which left MCC without an opening batsman, so Leyland took over the role. Requiring 258 in under three hours, Curnow and Taylor scored quickly and Transvaal needed only 52 to win with six wickets in hand at the close.

Hendren, Duckworth and Goddard were down with influenza, and Sandham was not available for the match against Rhodesia. Hammond and Chapman both retired ill in the second innings but Leyland scored 169 in three hours and Voce helped in a stand of 50 runs in 20 minutes. MCC could not afford to allow Rhodesia to bat as they did not have 11 fit men to put into the field. It was even worse in the one-day match in Northern Rhodesia and MCC had to borrow Crisp to help them out. The MCC invalids had recovered for the return match against Transvaal. Chapman hit 87 in 65 minutes, including five sixes and five fours but rain stopped play both in this match and another against the Transvaal Cricket Union.

Christy, Morkel and Owen-Smith were in England and not available for selection for the first Test. Herbie Taylor was unfit and surprisingly, Buster Nupen, who had not played in Transvaal's match against the tourists, was chosen to lead the South Africans. Chapman won the toss and asked South Africa to bat on a matting wicket. Tate, Voce and Peebles received help from the pitch and nine South African wickets were down for 81. Last man Newson, together with McMillan, added 45 to bring the total to a disappointing 126. Wyatt took 45 minutes to score eight runs and four more England wickets fell before the end of the first day's play. Nupen and Vincent bowled the rest out for 17 before a crowd of 20 000 and England's lead was only 67. Two South African wickets were down for 50 and then Mitchell and Catterall put on 122. Viljoen and Cameron continued and South Africa were 236 runs ahead with three wickets in hand. The next day Voce took those wickets for three runs and England needed 240 to win. Nupen raised eyebrows by opening the bowling with Catterall, who was regarded as a club bowler. The dismissal of Wyatt and Leyland justified

Herbie Taylor scored an attractive century at Newlands and was again one of the most successful South African batsmen.

TOURING SIDE	
APF Chapman (captain)(Kent)	JC White (Somerset)
WR Hammond (Glous)	W Voce (Notts)
RES Wyatt (Warwicks)	TW Goddard (Glous)
M Leyland (Yorks)	MJC Allom (Surrey)
E Hendren (Middlesex)	MW Tate (Sussex)
MJ Turnball (Glam)	IAR Peebles (Middlesex)
W Farrimond (Lancs)	G Duckworth (Lancs)
Manager: W Sewell	

this decision and then Nupen took the ball himself and had Hendren caught in the slips. Turnbull and Hammond hit 61 before the latter was brilliantly stumped. Tate lived dangerously before he was Mitchell's third victim in the slips and stayed as runner for Peebles. Nupen took his eleventh wicket and England had lost by 28 runs, less than South Africa's last wicket partnership in the first innings.

Jack Siedle, 141, and Bruce Mitchell, 123, who put on a record 260 runs for the first wicket in the second Test in Cape Town.

Having been the hero of the first Test, Nupen was dropped as captain and Deane brought out of retirement to lead the side in Cape Town. Taylor and Bell replaced Curnow and Newson. South Africa scored their highest total thus far with 513 for eight declared when Mitchell with 123, and Siedle 141, put on a record first wicket stand of 260. The turf wicket should have favoured the English bowlers but the South Africans had no problems and a century from Taylor together with 56 from Catterall put on an attractive 148 runs. Duckworth injured his hand during the innings and was unable to keep wicket so Hammond took his place. Hammond opened with Wyatt and they put on 75. Hammond and Leyland scored 50s and Hendren 93, so that England were all out for 350, 163 behind. In the follow-on, Hendren was dropped twice before settling down. He and Hammond were chiefly responsible for saving England and the backlog was cleared with six wickets in hand. Catterall came on and took three late wickets but the match was drawn.

The return match against Natal was played on a matting wicket which Voce found to his liking. MCC won by an innings.

As the injury to Sandham ruled out his participation in the rest of the tour, Chapman received permission to use HW Lee of Middlesex, who was coaching in South Africa.

The third Test was played on a matting wicket at Durban and was badly affected by rain. Four South African wickets were down for 51 before lunch on the first day, then rain prevented more play for the next day-and-a-half. They were all out for 177 with Voce taking five wickets. Hammond and Wyatt batted freely and Hammond scored his first century in South Africa with 136 not out. Chapman declared at 223 for one in the hopes of trying to force a win. Siedle was out first ball to Maurice Tate and Mitchell was third out at 47. However, Catterall and Taylor were able to bat out time and the match was drawn.

Hendren went to his highest score of the tour with 170 against Free State. In the space of 70 minutes, he added 132 with Tate.

The fourth Test was played in Johannesburg. Cameron was made

FIRST TEST TEAMS—JOHANNESBURG	
SOUTH AFRICA	ENGLAND
IJ Siedle	RES Wyatt
S Curnow	M Leyland
B Mitchell	WR Hammond
RH Catterall	E Hendren
KF Viljoen	MJ Turnbull
X Balaskas	APF Chapman (captain)
HB Cameron	JC White
Q McMillan	MW Tate
EP Nupen (captain)	IAR Peebles
CL Vincent	W Voce
ES Newson	G Duckworth

Capacity crowds enjoy play in the fourth Test of the series at the old Wanderers ground in Johannesburg. The site is now covered by a railway station and the Wanderers club has moved to its present ground in Illovo.

captain and Viljoen, Nupen and Hall came in for Deane, Quinn and Bell. Lee came into the England side.

England started well with 338 for six on the first day and the innings closed on 442. Hammond made 75 and Leyland a quick 91. Curnow went early but Mitchell and Siedle put on 96. Taylor received little support but managed to avoid the follow-on with a total of 295. Peebles took the wickets of Taylor, Vincent and Hall in the space of five balls and in his last spell took five for 18. Bad light and rain caused stoppages in England's second innings. Lee, Wyatt and Hammond were out for 23, but Leyland and Hendren pulled the side together and England were able to declare at 169 for eight, leaving South Africa to get 317 in four hours. Mitchell played more fluently than normal and scored 74 out of 121 but five wickets were down for 154. Cameron played well and 108 runs were needed in an hour but this proved impossible and South Africa failed to win by 37 runs with three wickets still standing.

The match was drawn. England needed to win the last Test at Durban in order to save the series.

Stumps for Test matches were larger and wider than for normal first-class matches. Having won the toss, Chapman led the English players onto the field where they had to wait until new bails were made. Chapman claimed that this delay was to his team's disadvantage and made an official protest. In the event this was debatable because rain limited play to just over an hour on the first day.

Siedle and Mitchell put on 127 but South Africa's

252 was slow and England's only hope was to score quickly with the hope of forcing a win. Vincent bowled well in the conditions and England were 101 for five. Only a partnership of 62 between Tate and Farrimond enabled them to reach 230, 22 behind. South Africa batted slowly to reach 219 before a token declaration by Cameron left England an impossible task and the game was drawn. South Africa had won the series by one game to nil.

The last match of the tour was against Western Province on a turf pitch. Having lost four for 54, Tate and Hendren put on 102 in 90 minutes to post a first innings score of 254. Western Province made 316. Wyatt was out first ball to Morkel, but Turnbull and Leyland put on 125 for the second wicket and enabled White to declare at 335 for six, but Western Province saved the game easily.

MCC won five of the 18 matches played and lost only the one Test Match, which could be regarded as a satisfactory tour in spite of the misfortunes with injuries. Hammond, Hendren and Leyland led the batting averages in both the Tests and other matches. Peebles and Voce were the most successful bowlers.

Mitchell, Taylor and Siedle were the most impressive South African batsmen in the Tests while Catterall and Nupen led the bowling averages. The tourists left Cape Town on board the *Balmoral Castle* and reached England again on 30 March 1930. South African cricket had shown much more promise on the field but internal strife among the administrators left a nasty taste. This resulted in Nupen and Catterall not being considered for the forthcoming tour of Australia and New Zealand 'for reasons other than cricketing ability.'

CHAPTER 19

1935

EIGHTH SOUTH AFRICA TOUR OF THE UNITED KINGDOM
Captain: HF Wade

A rejuvenated South African side won the Test rubber and lost only two matches on the whole tour, playing attractive cricket before huge crowds. Rowan, Siedle, Mitchell and Viljoen made runs while Jock Cameron, who sadly died soon after the tour, scored quickly.

Ken Viljoen of the Orange Free State batting at the Oval in the final Test. A valuable batsman who topped the averages on the tour, he was one of a succession of South Africans who, down the years, have thrilled English crowds with their brilliant fielding.

Four years had passed since a disappointing tour of Australia and the South Africans had changed to turf wickets at home so that the acclimatizing period used by previous teams was not required. It was to be a long tour. Thirty-nine matches, including 31 first-class games and five Test matches of three days, were to be played. Herbie Wade of Natal was selected as captain, which relieved Jock Cameron of the additional responsibility.

When the side was announced, there was some criticism in the choice of Langton, following an operation, and Rowan ahead of Briscoe, while the lack of a real off-spinner was regarded as folly. However, these criticisms proved to be unjustified.

The first-class programme started with impressive victories against Worcestershire, Leicestershire, and Cambridge University, a side which included two future England captains in Yardley and Griffiths. At the Oval, Nourse had the distinction of scoring a century in each innings against Surrey. Tomlinson finished the game on the last afternoon to win by 190 runs.

Nourse continued his good form with 148 against Oxford University in a total of 372. The match was abandoned with the South Africans on 369 for one.

Seidle carried his bat throughout the innings for his third successive century in the drawn match against MCC at Lord's. Hampshire, Middlesex and

TOURING SIDE
HF Wade (captain) (Natal)

HB Cameron (vice-captain) (Tvl)	B Mitchell (Transvaal)
EL Dalton (Natal)	CL Vincent (Transvaal)
AD Nourse (Natal)	ABC Langton (Transvaal)
RJ Williams (Natal)	EA Rowan (Transvaal)
IJ Siedle (Natal)	AJ Bell (Rhodesia)
RJ Crisp (W Province)	DS Tomlinson (Rhodesia)
X Balaskas (W Province)	KG Viljoen (Orange Free State)

Manager: SJ Snooke
Scorer and baggage-master: W Ferguson

Derbyshire provided exciting wins for the tourists who were proving too good for the counties. The South Africans were caught out on a drying wicket against Lancashire, but rain prevented a result in an interesting game. Following this Northamptonshire were beaten with 10 minutes to spare in a high wind which prevented the bails from being used.

At Cardiff there was a remarkable conclusion to the game. Glamorgan were asked to follow on 259 runs behind. Five wickets were down for 10 runs and the last pair were at the wicket with an hour to play. Smart hit three sixes and 11 fours in his 114 and last man Hughes, playing in his first match, hit four sixes and six fours

110

in an innings of 70 not out. The record last wicket partnership of 131 saved the match.

The first Test was played at Nottingham over three days. Sutcliffe and Wyatt had an opening partnership of 118. Then Wyatt and Leyland put on 139 for the innings to close at 384 for seven. Rain fell over the weekend and Siedle was the only batsman to be successful with 59, while Cameron hit out for 52. Rain fell continuously and the match was abandoned as a draw. Rain ruined the return match against Lancashire.

Yorkshire were unbeaten when they met the South Africans at Bramall Lane, Sheffield. Cameron hit 45 out of 53 in the first innings, then hit Verity for 4-4-4-6-6-6, in his second century of the tour. Balaskas found a worn patch and ended with match figures of 12 wickets. The South Africans won by 128 runs.

King George V visited Lord's while South Africa batted in the second Test. Four South African wickets had fallen for 98 on a difficult wicket when Cameron played a marvellous innings, scoring 90 out of 126 in an hour and three-quarters. The innings closed on 228 and then Balaskas bowled superbly so that England were all out for 198, a 30 run deficit. Mitchell played the game of his life in an innings of 164, his first century of the tour, and was at the crease when Wade declared at 278 for seven. Needing 309 to win in just under five hours, Sutcliffe and Ames both required the services of a runner. But apart from a stand of 44 by Sutcliffe and Hammond, the other batsmen did not shape against the bowling of Langton and

Balaskas to be dismissed for 151 and a notable victory for South Africa. Spectators numbered 79 000 for the three days' cricket.

Cameron joined the long list of wounded when he deflected a ball onto his head and was taken to hospital in the match against Somerset. For the first time on this tour, a county side gained a first-innings lead. Then Mitchell took five wickets to win the game.

In the match at Nottingham, facing Larwood and Voce, Bruce Mitchell scored a magnificent 142, including a century partnership with Nourse. Wade scored a century and put on 142 with Mitchell, then Wade and Dalton put on 114 in an hour. The innings closed on 512 and only the fact that Balaskas had also joined the long list of wounded saved Nottinghamshire. Bill Edrich was a nineteen-year-old professional at Lord's when he scored a century in an otherwise all amateur side for his home county, Norfolk. South Africans were to hear more of this young Edrich in future.

Following the announcement of the England team for the Test at Leeds there was an extraordinary number of injuries and Leyland had to drop out an hour before the match was due to start. A car was sent to find Yorkshire's Arthur Mitchell, who was in his garden tending his roses. In story-book style he was rushed to the ground and scored 58 and 72 on his début for England. Wyatt was out to the third ball of the innings but Hammond and Mitchell played well so that England managed 216. Only Rowan played with confidence for 62 and the tourists were all out for 171. The gardener, Arthur Mitchell, opened the second innings for England and his

England captain Bob Wyatt hits out at Trent Bridge as South African wicketkeeper Jock Cameron and slip Bruce Mitchell look on. A tower of strength for the touring team, Cameron died of typhoid fever shortly after his return to South Africa at the age of 30.

partnership with Smith of 128 in under two hours allowed the following batsmen, particularly Hammond, to hit out so that Wyatt was able to declare at 294 for seven, a lead of 339. The South Africans were content to play out time for a draw in spite of the bowlers sending down full tosses to tempt indiscretions. 55 000 people watched the three day match.

The South Africans were far too strong for Durham, Scotland and Northumberland.

England made five changes for the third Test at Manchester. Arthur Mitchell was selected but had to withdraw. Siedle was injured and replaced by Nourse in the South African side. For once South Africa's fielding was poor and a lot of catches went down off the bowling of Crisp and Bell. Robins scored a good century and England made 357 in the first innings. South African wickets fell early and then Viljoen rose to the occasion and, in spite of being injured, scored 124. Cameron wielded the bat with two sixes and five fours, and Dalton gave support for the innings to close on 318. Bill Bowes was by far the best bowler for England. Vincent and Langley bowled well in England's second innings at a time when they were looking for quick runs, and the fielding was brilliant. Hammond in particular and all the other England batsmen scored at an average of 75 runs an hour in a scintillating display. England declared at 231 for six, leaving South Africa to score 271 at 72 runs an hour to win. Despite a brisk start by Rowan, the challenge was not taken up and the match ended in a draw and the rubber was saved by South Africa.

Surrey were overwhelmed in the match at the Oval. Mitchell scored 195 and Rowan 171 in a partnership of 330 with only one chance between them. Dalton continued the onslaught and the South Africans ended their innings on 572. Surrey were beaten by an innings and 205 runs in two days. Crisp was added to the list of injuries on the first day.

Excitement ran high for the return match against Glamorgan and 17 000 spectators packed the ground to watch the match. Wade joined the long list of wounded and Louis Duffus, the South African journalist, acted as substitute to take an important catch. Mitchell and Vincent bowled out Glamorgan when it was thought that the match could be lost.

Rowan, Nourse and Crisp were in form against Warwickshire to win by an innings. Undefeated after 32 matches, the South Africans travelled to Gloucestershire and Essex to lose very even games.

Needing to save the rubber, Wyatt gambled and put South Africa in to bat on a perfect wicket at the Oval in the last Test. After putting on a century opening partnership with Siedle, Mitchell went on to 128 with support from Nourse and Viljoen. The last four South African wickets brought the score up to 476 with a century from Dalton and 73 from number ten, Langton. Hammond and Leyland came together and set a new record for the fourth wicket of 151 runs in 100 minutes. Leyland went on to another record partnership of 155 with Ames and made his highest Test score of 161. Ames scored 148 not out and Wyatt declared at 534 for six, a lead of 58. The South Africans batted out time. 55 000 people watched the three days in which 1 297 runs were scored for the loss of 22 wickets.

South African skipper Herbie Wade pulls a ball past wicketkeeper Ames in the first Test at Nottingham. Mitchell-Innes is at slip and Hammond in the gully. Wade was the first South African to lead his country to a Test match and series victory in England.

The South African team in England in 1935. Back: AD Nourse, EL Dalton, DS Tomlinson, RJ Crisp, ABC Langton, KG Viljoen, RJ Williams; middle: AJ Bell, CL Vincent, HF Wade (capt), SJ Snooke (manager), HB Cameron, IJ Seidle, B Mitchell; front: X Balaskas, EA Rowan.

Sir Julian Cahn put together a scratch side, including Morkel, the South African Test player now living in England. The rain-affected match was drawn. Rain again interfered with the start of the match against Kent but, when play started, the batsmen played delightful cricket. No-one could cope with Vincent, and Crisp became the first South African to take 100 wickets on tour.

A scratch England XI proved no opposition to the all-round strength of the South Africans at Folkstone and were defeated by an innings in two days. Another holiday game was played at Skegness against Minor Counties for whom Edrich scored 79. At the Scarborough Festival the South Africans were asked to follow on, for only the second time, in the match against HDG Leveson-Gower's XI. Then Cameron scored 160 in 140 minutes with a glorious display of hard hitting to end a very successful tour.

Having played 39 matches, of which only two were lost and 15 drawn, this South African touring team was by far the most successful ever. Although England was going through a bad patch and had lost the previous Test rubbers to Australia and West Indies,

South Africa's winning of the Test rubber was a great achievement.

They played attractive cricket and won the support of the huge crowds. In addition they made a handsome profit of £12 000 from the tour compared with the previous best of £1 400.

Eight batsmen scored over 1 000 runs; Rowan scored nearly 2 000 runs in a light-hearted manner. Mitchell and Siedle formed a good opening partnership and Viljoen scored runs when needed. Cameron thrilled everyone with his big hitting and his wicket-keeping was of a very high standard. Langton and Crisp took over 100 wickets and Vincent 92, while Bell and Tomlinson both took over 50 wickets. But it was the evenness of the team which made it so successful, even when injuries struck so many of the players.

The only sad part of the tour was the fact that Jock Cameron contracted typhoid fever on his voyage home and died shortly afterwards at the age of 30.

At the end of the tour South African cricket was riding the crest of a wave, but it was to be submerged on their return home when the Australians visited.

113

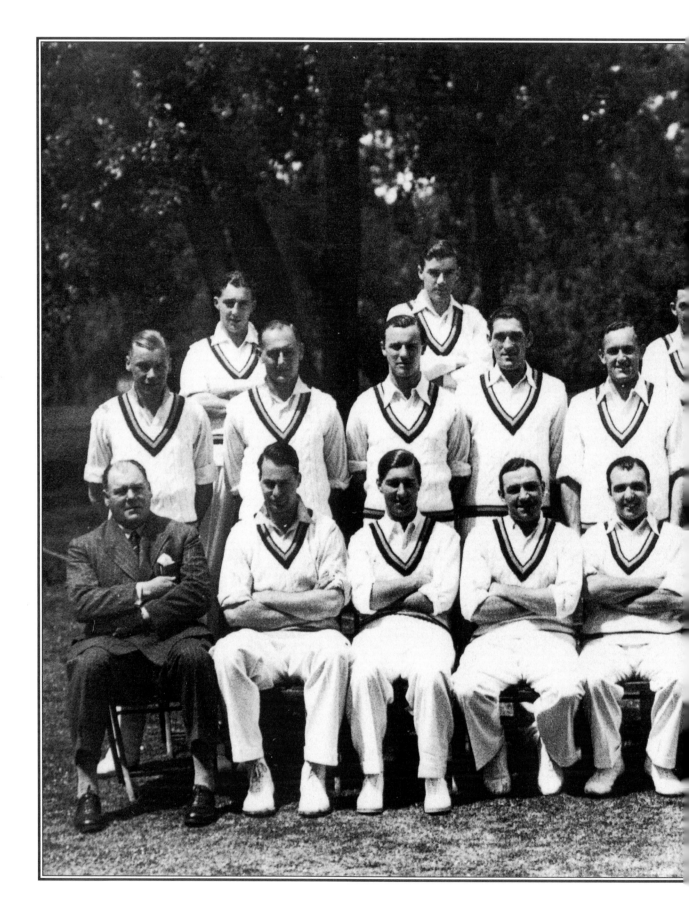

CHAPTER 20

1938/39

SEVENTH MCC TOUR OF SOUTH AFRICA

Captain: WR Hammond

A strong MCC side narrowly won the series by one game to nil. Overprepared turf wickets resulted in large scores and hardship for the bowlers. The series is best remembered for the drawn 'Timeless Test', the longest in history.

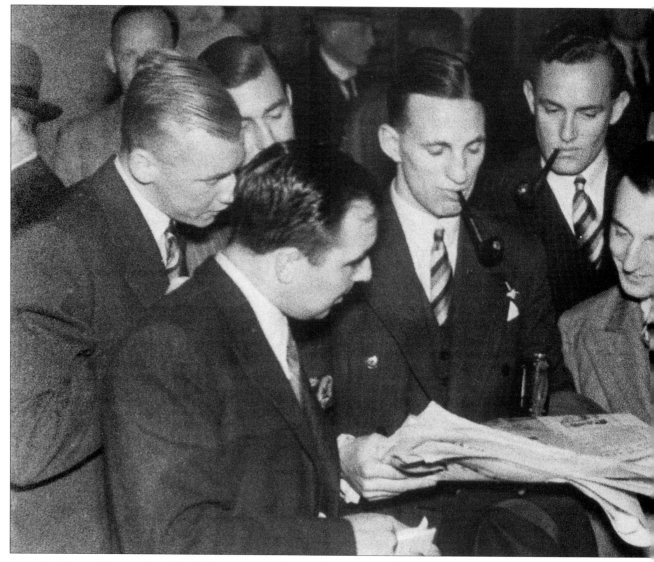

Len Hutton and other members of the MCC touring team on their arrival in Cape Town find out what the local newspapers have to say about their prospects in South Africa.

Wally Hammond had changed his status from professional to 'amateur' in order to captain England against Australia, and was a natural choice to captain the tourists. MCC sent the strongest team available with the exception of Denis Compton, who was under contract to play football for Arsenal.

Eighteen matches were to be played including five Tests. Eight-ball overs, as used in Australia, had been tried in the Currie Cup the previous season and this experiment was continued in matches against the visitors.

The team sailed on the *Athlone Castle* on 21 October 1938 and in the rough seas crossing the Bay of Biscay, Norman Yardley fell, cracked a rib and was unable to play in the first few games. The side quickly acclimatized themselves to conditions and mammoth scores were made against Cape, Free State and Natal sides. Eddie Paynter,

TOURING SIDE	
AMATEURS	PROFESSIONALS
WR Hammond (captain) (Glouc)	L Hutton (Yorkshire)
PA Gibb (Yorkshire)	H Verity (Yorkshire)
NWD Yardley (Yorkshire)	TW Goddard (Gloucestershire)
K Farnes (Kent)	WJ Edrich (Middlesex)
HT Bartlett (Sussex)	E Paynter (Lancashire)
BH Valentine (Kent)	LL Wilkinson (Lancashire)
LEG Ames (Kent)	DVP Wright (Kent)
RTD Perks (Worcestershire)	

Manager: Flight-Lieutenant AJ Holmes
Scorer and baggage-master: W Ferguson

second century of the match. Hammond declared at 291 for four, but the South African batsmen had no trouble playing out time to reach 108 for one as the Test ended in a draw.

The teams went to Cape Town for the second Test and another run feast. Rain interfered with the start but the wicket proved easy and England were able to declare at 559 for nine when Hammond, 181, and Ames, 115, put up a record fourth-wicket partnership of 197. Valentine added another 112. Dudley Nourse was the only South African batsman to impress and scored 120 out of 286. Hedley Verity took five for 70. In the

English left arm spinner Hedley Verity, who along with team-mate Ken Farnes was to lose his life in the Second World War.

Hammond and Hutton were particularly effective and the bowling of Ken Farnes and Hedley Verity was too much for the locals.

It was a different story against Transvaal where the South African batsmen found few problems with the MCC bowlers. Mitchell, Viljoen and Langton helped post a score of 428 for eight before declaring. Rain prevented a result. Hutton was struck on the head by a ball from Davies in the first over and was unable to play in the first Test. The Yorkshire amateur Paul Gibb replaced Hutton in the England side for the Test and South Africa included six new caps.

Gibb and Valentine narrowly missed their centuries and with Paynter scoring 117, the England first innings closed on 422. South Africa were 160 for two when Tom Goddard took a hat-trick, but a seventh-wicket stand between Dalton, with 102, and Viljoen 50, together with a ninth-wicket stand between Dalton and Langton, produced a total of 390, a deficit of only 32. Gibb scored a century to add to his 93 in the first innings, and Paynter notched up his

Players from both teams take a close look at the pitch at the Wanderers before the fourth Test. Rain before the match made for a soggy start and further poor weather during it meant that the game was eventually drawn.

follow-on Eric Rowan, with 89*, and Pieter van der Bijl, with 87, added 147 and a draw was assured at 201 for two.

In the matches that followed, Hutton scored a double century against Eastern Province in an innings victory and Border were also thrashed before the third Test at Durban.

Hammond hit his second successive century and Paynter made 243, the highest Test score in South Africa at that time, and only surpassed by Graeme Pollock's 274, 31 years later. England declared at 469 for four and a draw looked likely, but Farnes broke through and dismissed South Africa for 103. In the follow-on, Bruce Mitchell scored 109 and, despite support from Rowan and Viljoen, South Africa was unable to avoid an innings defeat although they did manage to make

a respectable second innings total of 353.

Combined Transvaal managed to draw their match before the tourists went to Rhodesia where Tom Goddard took his second hat-trick of the tour.

The fourth Test was played at Johannesburg and it was the last Test to be played at the old Wanderers ground. Hammond won the toss for the eighth successive time in rainy conditions. Langton bowled particularly well to take five for 58, but Hutton scored 92 in an innings of 215. Alan Melville and Van der Bijl put on a great opening stand of 108 on a rain-affected wicket and Mitchell, with 63, enabled South Africa to declare at 349 for eight. England batted again and were 203 for four when rain prevented any more play so that the match was drawn.

Natal scored 295 thanks to 110 from Dalton and 67 from Dudley

118

England faced a seemingly impossible task of scoring 696 to win. The match had been in progress for seven days but rain had fallen at the right time and the pitch was still perfect. Hutton and Gibb opened with 78 then Gibb and Edrich put on 280, a record partnership for the second wicket. Gibb scored 120 and Edrich went on to 219, which made his place in the England side secure following poor results previously. Hammond and Paynter continued until Paynter was out with the score on 611 and rain threatened to end the match, whereupon the Englishmen started to hit out. Hammond was stumped for 140. Rain stopped play after tea on the thirteenth day and the tourists reluctantly had to leave in order to catch the *Athlone Castle*.

The longest match in history was left drawn with England on 654 for five, still needing 42 to win. England had won the series by one game to nil.

All the matches, except the ones in Rhodesia, had been played on turf wickets which perhaps had been over-prepared. This resulted in a huge number of runs for the batsmen but suffering for the bowlers. Mitchell, Nourse, Melville, Van der Bijl, Rowan, Viljoen and Dalton all batted well, but only Gordon and Langton performed well with the ball. The fielding was outstanding and Grieveson proved a worthy successor to Cameron behind the stumps.

The forthcoming tour to the United Kingdom in 1940 was eagerly anticipated but that was not to be. Once more war interfered with cricket throughout the world. Chud Langton and Dooley Briscoe, along with Ken Farnes and Hedley Verity, were among those who were killed and it was to be a further eight years before South Africa would take to the field again.

England captain Walter Hammond, who scored three centuries in the Test series and led the tourists to victory in the rubber.

Nourse, but Edrich with 150, and Ames 62, brought the MCC score to 407. Doug Wright took six for 55 in Natal's second innings of 219 and Hutton again scored a fine 53 not out to win the game by nine wickets.

The final Test was to be played to a finish. South Africa won the toss and batted patiently for two-and-a-half days on a perfect wicket at Durban. Van der Bijl opened with 125, Dudley Nourse ground out 103, while Melville and wicket-keeper Grieveson scored in the 70s and Dalton scored 57 to post a massive total of 530. England fared poorly on the fourth day and were all out for 316 but, rather than enforcing the follow-on with a lead of 214, Melville decided to bat again. Van der Bijl and Mitchell had an opening stand of 191 before Van der Bijl was out, three runs short of his second century of the match. Mitchell was out hit wicket on 89 and Melville batted beautifully for his 103. Viljoen added 74 and the innings closed at 481.

1947

NINTH SOUTH AFRICA TOUR OF THE UNITED KINGDOM

Captain: A Melville

The 'Terrible Twins' dominated a record-breaking season, including spectacular success against the South Africans. Enormous post-war crowds appreciated the attractive South Africans. Although they lost the Test series three-nil, the popular side was better than the score suggests.

The South African tourists who played in the first post-war series in the United Kingdom in 1947. Back: TA Harris, DM Ovenstone, DW Begbie, VI Smith, L Tuckett, JB Plimsoll, LW Payne, JD Lindsay, GM Fullerton; front: OC Dawson, DV Dyer, B Mitchell, A Melville (capt), AS Frames (manager), AD Nourse, KG Viljoen, MBF Mann, AMB Rowan.

Once more, a war had interrupted the development of cricket throughout the world. The scheduled tour by South Africa to the United Kingdom during 1940 had naturally been cancelled because of the hostilities.

Australian and New Zealand Service teams had toured England in 1945 and the Indians had toured in 1946, but little top-class cricket had been played in South Africa.

England had sent a team to Australia the previous year and was on the road to recovery, but an eight-year absence from top-class cricket was sure to affect South Africa's untested youngsters and the average age of those selected was high. Dave Nourse had returned from the Middle East in poor health but recovered to lead a strong Natal side to victory in the 1947/48 Currie Cup competition.

Criticism was levelled at the non-selection of R Phillips of Border and Eric Rowan.

The team left Cape Town on 5 April and arrived in Southampton on 18 April 1947. It was snowing when the tourists arrived in Worcester for the opening match and the field had suffered the worst flooding in history. Continual bad weather affected the team in the first few matches.

The tourists were housed in HMS *Indefatigable* at Portsmouth for the traditional match against Combined Services and the sailors were surprised to find a South African cricketer's shoes left outside the cabin door waiting to be cleaned!

In the first Test, at Nottingham, Melville and Nourse produced a wonderful partnership of 319 – a third-wicket record for any Test and the highest for any South African wicket. Melville scored 189 and Nourse 149. The South African first innings ended on the highest score by a South African Test team at 533. Tufty Mann started his Test career to the 'Terrible Twins', Compton and Edrich, with eight successive maiden overs but they then put on a century partnership. Tuckett took the second new ball and eight England wickets fell for 54 before lunch, the last five wickets adding just 10 runs. Following on 325 runs behind, Hutton was again out early, but Washbrook and Edrich put on 96 before Edrich was out for 50. Yardley joined Compton and they went on to a partnership of 237

TOURING SIDE	
A Melville (captain) (Tvl)	
DV Dyer (Natal)	B Mitchell (Tvl)
AD Nourse (Natal)	KG Viljoen (Tvl)
LW Payne (Natal)	TA Harris (Tvl)
OC Dawson (Natal)	AMB Rowan (Tvl)
VI Smith (Natal)	DW Begbie (Tvl)
JB Plimsoll (W Province)	GM Fullerton (Tvl)
DM Ovenstone (W Province)	JD Lindsay (NE Tvl)
MBF Mann (E Province)	L Tuckett (OFS)
Manager: AS Frames	

before Compton fell with 163 to his name. Evans joined Yardley and, when Yardley was out for 99, carried on hitting for a score of 74. The last pair added 51 off the tired bowlers and South Africa were faced with a total of 227 to win in 140 minutes, which they made no attempt to chase. Melville, although limping, scored his second century of the match in an unbroken partnership of 145 with Viljoen. The first Test, which South Africa had a good chance of winning, was drawn.

The gates were closed before the start of the second Test at Lord's when 30 600 were in the ground. Hutton and Washbrook were slowed by brilliant fielding but Edrich and Compton were having a glorious summer and thrilled the crowd with a record partnership of 391. This beat Melville and Nourse's efforts in the first Test. Edrich scored 189, his first Test century in England, and Compton, 208, his first double century. Big hitting by the other batsmen allowed Yardley to declare at 554 for eight. Mitchell and Melville found the bowling easy until Compton was brought on and he had Mitchell stumped on 95. Melville completed his fourth successive Test century, a unique achievement, but he was the only one to play Wright with confidence and the side folded for 327. Following on 227 behind, play was held up while the teams were presented to the King and Queen. Then Edrich flattened Melville and Viljoen's stumps and put Mitchell into his shell. He defended dourly and when Edrich shattered Nourse's wicket with the first ball of the day and then took a brilliant catch to dismiss Mitchell, it was only a question of time before South Africa were dismissed for 252 and defeated.

It was a delightful match and South Africa were not beaten as severely as the score suggested. In fact, the bowling and fielding were superior to that of England.

The wind was so strong in the third Test at Manchester that the sight-screen was blown over. South Africa started slowly against a moderate attack and only Nourse showed any aggression. Dyer scored 62 and Mitchell a slow 80 before being run out, Viljoen was struck several times in his 93 and the innings closed on 339. On a drying pitch, Washbrook decided on attack and struck Tuckett for three fours off one over before leaving with Hutton. Compton and Edrich came together and once more dominated the game on a difficult wicket. Compton was out for 115 and Edrich carried on to 191 with three sixes and 22 fours. The partnership yielded 228 and England were all out for 478, a lead of 138. Dyer was out early and Mitchell went at 42, but Nourse then played the innings of the tour, Melville went for a good 59 but Viljoen joined Nourse and put on 121 together. Nourse was bowled for 115 and the rest collapsed for a total of 267, leaving England to get 129 to win in two-and-a-half hours. Washbrook scored 40 quickly before the effects of the roller wore off and Edrich closed off the innings for England to win by seven wickets.

Except for 25 minutes, Edrich had been on the field for the whole

time, had scored over 200 runs and taken eight wickets in 57 overs.

Hutton was again on form before his home crowd of over 30 000 at Headingley in Leeds in the fourth Test. Melville won the toss but the South African batting was disappointing. Mitchell and Nourse added 90 after a poor start but the last six wickets fell for 50 and South Africa were all out for 175, the lowest total of the series and scored at only 37 an hour. Rain fell over the weekend making the wicket suitable for spin and Rowan, Mann, Smith and Tuckett made the English batsmen fight for their runs. Hutton and

Ken Viljoen of Transvaal smacks the ball away during the final Test at the Oval. The wicketkeeper is Godfrey Evans.

'The Terrible Twins', Edrich and Compton, who both scored over 3 500 runs in the season – 2 000 of them against the South Africans.

Washbrook could not be separated until Washbrook was out for 75 at a score of 141. Hutton scored a century before being run out and Edrich, Compton and Yardley all played well on a drying wicket so that Yardley was able to declare at 317 for seven. South Africa again batted poorly and Dyer and Mitchell left early. Nourse tried to knock the bowlers off their length but South Africa were all out for 184 to lose by ten wickets.

The heat seemed to affect all the players in the last Test at the Oval and slow scoring was the result. All the England batsmen scored in a first innings total of 427, with Mann sending down 35 overs for only 33 runs. Bruce Mitchell was off the field for only 15 minutes in the match when he scored 120 in the first innings, being eighth man out and then batting through the second innings to score 189 not out.

South Africa's 302 meant a deficit of 125 and England's second innings was the most attractive of the match. Hutton and Washbrook fell forcing the pace and then Compton scored a lovely 113 out of 178 in an hour and three quarters. Yardley declared at 325 for six, leaving South Africa to get 451 to win. Mitchell's innings started slowly but the score built up and Nourse just missed his century. With an hour to go South Africa still needed 111 to win. Runs came fast and Mitchell, with Mann, scored 46 in the last half hour but it was too late and South Africa finished on 423 for seven, just 28 runs short of victory. Some 77 000 watched the four days and gate receipts were £14 103.

South Africa had lost three and drawn two of the Tests.

With the pressure of the Tests behind them, a series of holiday matches was played. South of England provided a powerful side for the match at Hastings but the public was more interested in Compton's achievement of scoring a record 17th century of the season, his sixth against the South Africans. The game was held up for five minutes when he reached his century and then he was out

Athol Rowan of Transvaal surprisingly dropped at slip by Edrich during the third Test of the series at Old Trafford. England went on to win the match by seven wickets, with Edrich scoring over 200 runs and taking eight wickets.

124

The England team walking onto the field at Headingley, led by their captain, Yardley. The English proceeded to bowl the South Africans out for 175, setting themselves up for a 10-wicket victory and an unbeatable three-nil lead in the series.

the very next ball. Mitchell scored an attractive 145 and Dawson 166 in festival mood to reach 510 for eight declared. South of England declared at 341 for nine, and Melville countered with an attacking declaration at 31 for one, leaving the South of England to score 201 runs to win. Athol Rowan and 'Tufty' Mann took all 19 wickets to fall in the match, to bowl the South of England out two runs short of the target.

The 1947 English season belonged to the 'Terrible Twins' Edrich and Compton. They both scored over 3 500 runs in the season, and both scored over 700 runs in seven successive innings for Middlesex and England. Compton scored six of his 17 centuries against the tourists, with three out of his four Test centuries coming in successive innings.

Of the 33 matches played, the South Africans won 16, lost five and drew nine. The losses were against England, MCC and Worcestershire. The South Africans were not as inferior to England as the final scores suggested, and a little more aggression could have changed the series.

Melville, Nourse, Mitchell and Viljoen carried the main responsibility but the superb South African fielding gave England a lesson and the youngsters in the South African side learned a lot. Once more the South Africans were a popular side and always played in the right spirit. The tour made a profit of £10 000 and half the gate money in matches against Surrey and Lancashire was donated to help rebuild their war-damaged grounds.

CHAPTER 22

1948/49

EIGHTH MCC TOUR OF SOUTH AFRICA

Captain: FG Mann

Despite some close and exciting finishes, England remained undefeated and won the series two-nil. Compton had a particularly good tour with his 300 runs in Benoni a highlight. South Africa depended too much on established players and were cautious compared to England's flair.

Denis Compton draws a crowd at the nets in Cape Town. The highlight of a prolific tour for the English batsman was his 300 in only 181 minutes against a North-Eastern Transvaal side.

Most of the established English players had declined the invitation to tour the West Indies the previous year and the tour had been a disaster. The MCC selection committee therefore declared that it would only be responsible for future tours provided they had the support of the counties, that professional players were sufficiently remunerated for the loss of their winter earnings, and that host countries guaranteed the MCC against any losses.

The strongest side available was selected to tour South Africa with the exception of two amateurs, the England captain, Yardley, and Edrich. George Mann, son of Frank Mann who had captained the MCC tour in 1922, was chosen to captain the side. Twenty-three matches were to be played, including five Tests.

The team sailed aboard the *Durban Castle* on 7 October 1948 and played the first match against Western Province on 29 October 1948. Owen Wynne scored the first century by a Western Province player against a touring side since 1913 in an even first innings. Cheetham declared, leaving MCC to score 118 in 55 minutes.

TOURING SIDE	
AMATEURS	PROFESSIONALS
FG Mann (captain) (Middx)	DSC Compton (Middx)
CH Palmer (Worcester)	JA Young (Middx)
RT Simpson (Notts)	RO Jenkins (Worc)
SC Griffith (Sussex)	JF Crapp (Glouc)
	TG Evans (Kent)
	C Gladwin (Derby)
	MF Tremlett (Somerset)
	L Hutton (Yorkshire)
	J Watkins (Glamorgan)
	DVP Wright (Kent)
	AV Bedser (Surrey)
	C Washbrook (Lancashire)

Manager: Brigadier MA Green
Baggage-master and scorer: W Ferguson

Washbrook, Hutton and Compton knocked off the runs in 97 deliveries with nine minutes to spare.

At Benoni, against a weak North-Eastern Transvaal side, Compton gave a demonstration of scoring unsurpassed anywhere by hitting 300 out of 399 in 181 minutes. Compton hit five sixes and 42 fours, 198 runs from boundaries, in an incredible display, assisted by Simpson who gave him the bowling as much as possible. Jenkins took 11 wickets but it was Compton's match.

Hutton, Washbrook, Compton, Crapp and Simpson flogged the South African bowlers in high-scoring matches. Jenkins took his fiftieth wicket of the tour and Wright was proving dangerous. South African batsmen also scored well. Owen Wynne scored two successive centuries against the tourists and Begbie scored 154 for Transvaal in a drawn game.

Melville, with a broken wrist, withdrew from the Test side in Durban in what was to be one of the closest Test match finishes to date. England fielded magnificently on the first day and South Africa struggled against the bowling of Bedser and Gladwin to be all out for 161. Bad light and rain interfered with the England innings but Hutton and Washbrook started well and were within 17 of South Africa's total when the spinners took over. Mann, with Rowan, changed the game and only a grim innings from Compton with 72 allowed England a first-innings lead of 92. Four South African batsmen were out for 90 but Begbie and Wade put on 85 and England were faced with a target of 127 which, under the conditions, was by no means certain. With two-and-a-quarter hours to play, Washbrook was dropped on the boundary off the first ball of the innings and Hutton left early. Mann promoted himself but was also dropped on the boundary. Mitchell took a great catch at slip and McCarthy had a good spell of six for 33 in ten overs, but Compton and Jenkins added 45 for the seventh wicket. With three balls to go, any one of four results could have been achieved – a win for either side, a tie or a draw.

Bedser brought the scores level with the sixth ball of the last over and Gladwin swung, the ball hit his pad and they ran a leg bye off the last ball. England had won by two wickets.

In another extraordinary finish, MCC won off the last ball in the two-day match against Natal Country Districts. Needing to score 56 in 25 minutes, MCC lost four wickets, including two run outs, before Bedser scored a run off the last ball to win the exciting match.

The second Test was played for the first time at Ellis Park in Johannesburg and the pitch proved to be a batsman's delight.

Some 1 193 runs were scored and various records established before a crowd of 35 000. Hutton with 158 and Washbrook with 195 set up a record partnership of 359 before Compton with 114 and Crapp put on another 150. The last seven wickets fell for 89 and England finished on 608 all out. Wynne and Eric Rowan were out early but Mitchell with 86 and Wade with 85 brought about a

recovery and South Africa were all out for 315. In the follow-on, Eric Rowan scored a wonderful 156 not out and Mitchell, with Nourse, played out time on 270 for two.

Ironically the team for the third Test was announced during Rowan's wonderful innings and he was dropped by the selectors.

The Newlands pitch proved awkward on the first day of the third Test but the South African bowlers failed to take advantage. Hutton and Washbrook tried to knock the bowlers off their length but a slip by Hutton, resulting in a run out, broke the partnership at 88. Crapp continued with Washbrook to 149 before England lost four men at 152. Athol Rowan bowled well and England were all out for 308. The pitch dried out over the weekend but South Africa batted so cautiously that Mitchell and Wynne took over three hours to make 110. Mitchell took 45 minutes to score the seven runs required for his century. He went on to 120

Len Hutton of Yorkshire and Cyril Washbrook of Lancashire, the English opening pair who put on 359 for the first wicket in Johannesburg.

129

The South African team in 1948/49. Back: CN McCarthy, OC Dawson, LA Markham, DW Begbie, EL Dalton (manager), WW Wade, NBF Mann, JE Cheetham, L Tuckett; front: AMB Rowan, B Mitchell, AD Nourse (capt), KG Viljoen, EAB Rowan; insets: A Melville, OE Wynne, TA Harris.

and, with Nourse, put on 190. Compton, with his slow left arm spin, caused a collapse, seven wickets fell for 58 and South Africa had a lead of only 48. Hutton and Crapp had a second-wicket stand of 134 and then Compton and Watkins hit out to allow Mann to declare at 276 for three, a lead of 228 with 125 minutes remaining. Melville and Wynne started out brightly but Nourse and Mitchell shut up shop when Jenkins threatened to break through with four quick wickets and the match was drawn with South Africa on 142 for four.

The February rainy season in Rhodesia once more ruined matches against the tourists.

A more competitive wicket had been prepared for the fourth Test at Johannesburg and McCarthy with Tuckett bowled with a lively pace. Hutton left early but Washbrook and Crapp had a stand of 120, with Washbrook narrowly missing his century. Watkins batted well with support from the lower order batsmen and England were all out for 379. Mitchell gave a catch in the first over, Viljoen was run out with the score on four and then Eric Rowan was also run out with the score on 19. Wade and Nourse once again had to retrieve the situation and put on 106 before Wade was out. Nourse played a great innings of 129 which enabled the South Africans to avoid the follow-on and then surprised everyone by declaring while 122 runs

behind. Any hopes of an England collapse disappeared when Hutton and Washbrook put on 77 and Hutton went on to a delightful 123. Athol Rowan bowled well for three-and-a-half hours and worried the English batsmen. Mann declared at 253 for seven leaving South Africa to score 376 in four-and-a-half hours. Eric Rowan, who had been dropped following his success in the previous Johannesburg Test, scored 86 not out and Viljoen 63, but no attempt was made to go for the target and the game ended in a tame draw.

At Pietermaritzburg a Natal XI scored 288 thanks to Nourse's third century in successive matches. Nourse scored another 76 in the second innings and declared leaving MCC to score 270 in just over two hours. Compton went for the runs and scored 141 in 99 minutes before being caught on the boundary.

This innings brought his seventh century of the tour and beat the record aggregate previously held by Hobbs. The run chase failed by ten runs in an exciting finish.

In a second match, Nourse had the first pair of ducks in his career following his success in all the other matches against the tourists.

England won the fifth Test at Port Elizabeth with one minute to play when Crapp hit ten from three balls. South Africa started badly, losing two wickets for 13 runs but Mitchell took six hours 37 minutes for his 99 and only 219 runs were scored on the first day for the loss of three wickets, many of the runs coming in the last hour. Nourse scored 73, Wade made his first Test century with

Ellis Park, the headquarters of the Transvaal Rugby Union, which hosted the second Test of the 1948/49 series and saw five more Tests between then and 1954, when matches were moved to the new Wanderers ground.

125, Viljoen scored 73 and the South African innings, which lasted for over nine hours, closed on 379. Five England wickets fell for 168 with Athol Rowan bowling on a crumbling pitch but Mann and Jenkins retrieved the situation and the last five wickets put on 227 for an England total of 395. Mann made 136 not out.

Once more South Africa batted cautiously and it came as a surprise when Nourse declared at 187 for three, leaving England to get 172 to win. Hutton hit the first ball for four and Washbrook hit his first ball for six and the chase was on. Some 57 runs were scored in the opening partnership in 27 minutes and 100 in 53 minutes when Compton joined Washbrook. Five were down for 125 and then Gladwin and Griffith were out in three balls for seven wickets down. Crapp settled the issue to win with one minute to spare.

A final game was played in Cape Town against Combined Universities. Compton and Washbrook hit 159 in 87 minutes. For the Universities, B Crews scored a century, the only one against the tourists by a non-Test player.

Two extremely narrow Test victories decided the rubber and the MCC team was undefeated, but the South African teams showed little enterprise compared to the Englishmen.

Melville was unavailable for much of the tour and the selectors again relied on the established players so that no youngsters came to the fore.

The South Africans rarely had a good start to the innings and five times Nourse, at number four, had to come in with the score at under 50. Athol Rowan bowled well and 19-year-old McCarthy showed promise.

By contrast, the English batsmen, Hutton, Washbrook and Compton, often gave their side a good start and they were well backed up by Crapp, Simpson, Mann and Jenkins. Compton broke a lot of records with a total of 1 781 runs and eight centuries, but he was less successful in the Tests. Of the bowlers, Bedser and Jenkins came out of the tour with enhanced reputations but Wright struggled to find form.

Griffith was preferred to Evans as England wicket-keeper in the last two Tests and thus broke Evans' record of 22 consecutive Test appearances.

It was a happy tour and the team was popular wherever it went. Gate receipts were over £90 000.

The team sailed from Cape Town on the *Stirling Castle* and arrived home on 1 April 1949.

The MCC team for the successful tour in 1948/49.
Back: JA Young, RO Jenkins, JF Crapp, J Watkins, W Ferguson (scorer); middle: TG Evans, DVP Wright, C Gladwin, AV Bedser, MF Tremlett, RT Simpson, CH Palmer; front: Brig. MA Green (manager), C Washbrook, SC Griffith, FG Mann (capt), L Hutton, DCS Compton, DJ Meintjes (South African manager).

CHAPTER 23

1951

TENTH SOUTH AFRICA TOUR OF THE UNITED KINGDOM

Captain: AD Nourse

A popular young South African side faced terrible weather conditions and an early injury to Dudley Nourse spoiled the balance of the side. Cautious play was the result, but they were unlucky not to square the series.

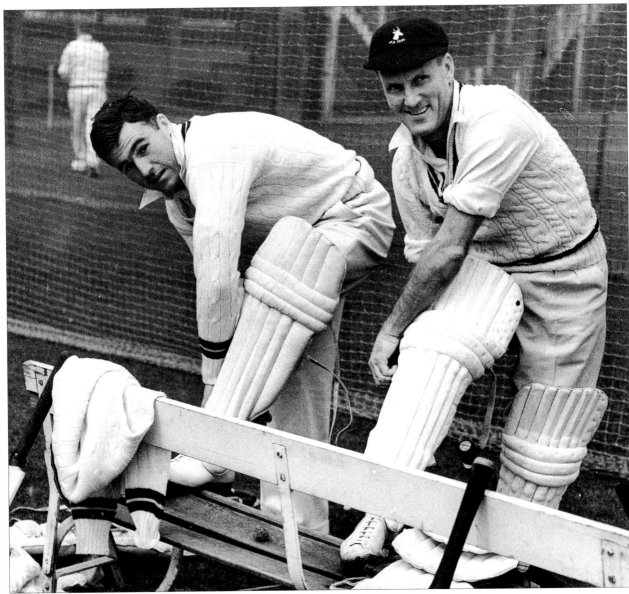

Russell Endean and Eric Rowan, both of Transvaal, pad up for net practice at Lords. Rowan took over as captain of the South Africans after the first Test when Dudley Nourse was forced to retire from the tour with an injury.

Only Dudley Nourse, the Rowan brothers, Tufty Mann and George Fullerton had toured abroad previously, so it was an inexperienced side chosen for the tour (although van Ryneveld had played for Oxford University). McGlew, McLean and Waite had no experience of international cricket. Tayfield was not selected originally, but flew out later to strengthen a side weakened by injuries.

Thirty-four matches were scheduled, including five Test matches. The match at Luton on 28 April was abandoned due to snow.

The opening first-class match was played against Worcestershire and it was again dismal, with showers and thunderstorms continually interrupting play. The weather at Bradford was even worse and the temperature was just above freezing with no play on the first day.

TOURING SIDE	
AD Nourse (captain) (Natal)	
EAB Rowan (Tvl)	CN McCarthy (Natal)
AMB Rowan (Tvl)	RA McLean (Natal)
GM Fullerton (Tvl)	DJ McGlew (Natal)
MG Melle (Tvl)	JE Cheetham (W Province)
GWA Chubb (Tvl)	CB van Ryneveld (W Province)
WR Endean (Tvl)	MBF Mann (E Province)
PNF Mansell (Rhodesia)	JHB Waite (E Province)
Manager: SJ Pegler	

Eric Rowan with Johnnie Waite at Headingley. Rowan scored 236, at the time the highest Test score by a South African.

Nourse fractured his thumb while stopping a drive from Tom Graveney in the match against Gloucestershire and had an operation the same evening. Injuries hit the South Africans; at one point there were four substitutes on the field.

The King was introduced to both the teams during the match against MCC at Lord's which was played in bitterly cold weather. Compton scored his fourth century in six innings with 147 but he was dropped four times off Chubb after he reached his century. Only 25 minutes of play were possible on the last day and the match was to end in a draw.

Nourse returned with a guard over his damaged thumb in the match against Surrey. The South Africans used this last match before the Test for batting practice. South Africa had not won in 28 Tests against England and Australia before the first Test at Nottingham.

Nourse was the hero with a score of 208 not out, the highest South African score against England, made with a broken thumb. South Africa batted for two days and only three wickets fell on the first day for 239. Waite and McGlew supported their captain and Fullerton joined Nourse in a stand of 121. At 410 for five, Bedser

and Bailey took the fourth new ball and broke through. Nourse was ninth to leave on 483 for nine declared and took no further part in the match on medical advice.

Chubb took Ikin's wicket with his second ball in Test cricket but Simpson and Hutton put on 124. Simpson went on to score 137. Compton was missed off Chubb at 45 but he and Watson added 141 and Compton completed his century. Freddie Brown declared 64 runs behind on 419 for nine. On a difficult pitch, Bedser had eight men close to the bat and within two hours five South African wickets were down for 99 runs. On the last day the remaining four wickets fell for only 26 runs, Bedser taking six for 37. England needed 186 to win in over five hours. Eric Rowan attacked and only 25 runs were scored before lunch. The rain-affected pitch suited Athol Rowan and Mann and only desperate hitting by Wardle made a respectable score. England were all out shortly after four o'clock for 114. The South Africans had won their first Test in 16 years, in front of 100 000 people. Gate money was £11 361.

Slow play was a feature of the game against Lancashire. Only 81 were scored in the two hours before lunch and Rowan, with Waite, went on to the first century opening stand of the tour in four hours and forty minutes. Rowan and Waite responded to the slow hand-clapping by sitting down on the pitch.

The second Test was played at Lord's and the conditions this time favoured England, particularly when Brown won the toss for the only time in the series. With the weather being uncertain, England forced the pace against good bowling and fielding by the South Africans. Hutton left early, but Simpson and Ikin scored steadily, then Compton and Watson had a stand of 122 for the fourth wicket. Both were dismissed for 79 and the England tail fell before the bowling of Chubb and McCarthy so that the England first innings ended on 311.

Rain appeared during the night and Brown soon called on his spinners, Tattersall and Wardle. Tattersall bowled to brilliant close-in fielding from Ikin, Hutton, Watson and Brown, who all took great catches. Eric Rowan was the only one trying to punish any stray deliveries and, when he went at 47 and Nourse followed at lunch, South Africa were 78 for four. The last six wickets fell for 37 in an hour and South Africa lost another four wickets for 57 before the close of play in the follow-on. Of the 14 wickets to fall on the day, Tattersall had taken nine for 88. Cheetham and Fullerton steadied the side and had a partnership of 94, but when they left, the South Africans were dismissed for 211 before lunch on the third day and England went on to win by ten wickets.

A short, time limit game was played on the Saturday afternoon to give the crowd some entertainment. Some 80 151 people attended the three days of play, including Princess Elizabeth, who was introduced to the teams on the second day.

The South African tour captain, Dudley Nourse. He scored an unbeaten double century in the first Test playing with a broken thumb.

Once more the South Africans went to Portsmouth and played a Combined Services side. They scored at 80 runs an hour on the first day and amassed 499 runs. 19-year-old Aircraftsman Jim Parks scored 51 and 20-year-old Signalman Brian Close made his highest score to date, 135 not out.

The pitch for the third Test at Manchester was affected by rain and Bedser troubled all the batsmen. He had Eric Rowan out off the fourth ball of the innings and ended the innings with seven wickets for 58 out of a total of 158. The second day was rained off and the wicket became even more spiteful when England were batting. Hutton was hit four times off good length balls in the first over. A captain's innings from Brown, combined with a stand of 53 by Bedser and Laker, allowed England to take a first innings lead of 53. With the exception of Chubb, the South African bowlers failed to take advantage of the pitch. Statham bowled Waite with the third ball of the innings and Laker bowled van Ryneveld with his first ball on 19. Nourse suffered further damage to his thumb but Cheetham and Eric Rowan had a partnership of 89 and then Bedser dismissed the last five batsmen for 11 runs in 32 deliveries for the innings to close on 191, giving England a lead of 138. Rain again interrupted the game and when play resumed, the batsmen had a hard time. Both Hutton and Ikin were hit

several times but Hutton survived and scored 98 of the runs required to win by nine wickets.

Freddie Brown lost the toss for the 11th time in 14 Tests and South Africa batted on a dead wicket in the fourth Test at Leeds. Eric Rowan and Van Ryneveld put on a record second wicket stand against England of 198. Rowan went on to 236, his first Test century in England and the highest Test score by a South African. McLean, with 67, and Mansell with 90, attacked the tiring bowlers and the South African innings ended on 538, a new record. Hutton and his Yorkshire partner Lowson put on 99 runs before Peter May, also in his Test début, scored 138 to add to Hutton's century. An injured Bailey was the only one to stay for a gallant 95 and his last wicket partnership with Hilton, who scored nine, produced 60 runs. England ended up only 33 runs behind the South African total with 505. In the second innings Rowan was again in great form but rain robbed him of the possibility of a century to add to his double century of the first innings and the match ended as a draw with his score on 60 not out.

The first innings was tied in the match against Glamorgan and the South Africans seemed to have the game won when the score stood at 54 without loss at tea on the last day. All ten wickets fell in the next 45 minutes for only 29 runs with McConnon taking a hat-trick, and Glamorgan had become the only county to beat the tourists. At the end Wooller was carried off the field shoulder high to the strains of the Welsh national anthem and a collection was taken for the victors.

The fifth and last Test was played at the Oval. Waite and Mann were unfit so Melle and Endean were brought into the South African side. Only 66 runs were scored by the South Africans before lunch on the first morning. Thereafter, Brown and Laker took six wickets while the score moved from 106 for one to 146 for seven. The Rowan brothers scored 96 of South Africa's 202 and nine wickets had fallen in two hours.

Lowson went early on but Hutton and May batted well until Hutton was out at 51. Compton stayed and batted through for 73 to bring the score to 194 with good bowling from Chubb, Athol Rowan and McCarthy. Bedser and Laker bowled well but the fielding was poor, Hutton dropped four catches, then Laker and Brown broke through and the last seven batsmen could score only 86 to finish the innings on 154, a lead of only 162.

Hutton and Lowson started well and then Hutton received a ball that hit his glove and spun into the air. Hutton thought that it would hit the stumps and flicked at it with his bat. Although he did not hit the ball, he was adjudged to have obstructed the wicket-keeper and given out obstructing the field. Athol Rowan had May's wicket the next ball and, with four wickets down, England still needed 73 to win. Brown chanced his luck: in his first three singles he offered three chances, but went on to make 40, the highest score of the innings. Together with Watson they took England out of trouble

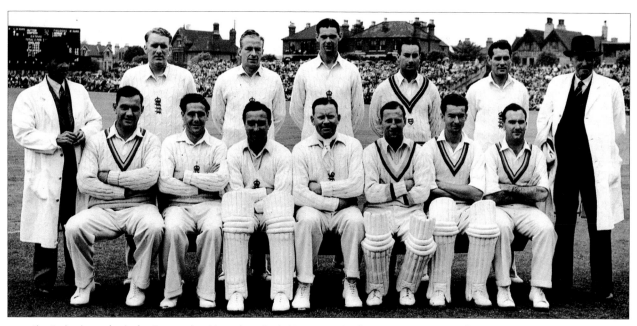

The England team for the first Test match in Nottingham. Back: Umpire, JH Wardle, W Watson, R Tattersall, D Kenyon (12th man), JT Ikin, Umpire; front: AV Bedser, TE Bailey, DCS Compton, FR Brown (capt), L Hutton, RT Simpson, TG Evans.

and won the series by three games to one. But it could so easily have been two Tests all.

The Hastings Festival saw big hitting by Compton for an England XI with three sixes and eight fours in his innings of 84. McLean outshone Compton with 88, made in 65 minutes, and with McGlew, added 126 in just over an hour.

A two-day match was played against the Minor Counties at Norwich. Cheetham scored an attractive 114 not out and Eric Rowan became the only tourist to complete 2 000 runs, repeating his performance on the 1935 tour.

Scarborough Festival saw the last match of the tour against TN Pearce's XI. Hutton scored a delightful 91 in front of his home crowd and needing 255 to win on the last day, Bedser finished the game by clean bowling Chubb and Melle to win the match by nine runs. 30 000 people watched the match.

A short tour of Holland followed in which the South Africans beat a Dutch side by an innings.

The prolonged injury to Dudley Nourse affected the team considerably and forced changes to tactics. Eric Rowan became the sheet anchor and batsmen adopted a defensive approach. Consequently the bowlers were forced to follow suit. Eric Rowan headed the Test batting for both sides with an average of 57.

Regrettably, as a result of the incident at Manchester when he sat down as a result of the barracking, and his behaviour towards a spectator, Eric Rowan received a letter from the South African Cricket Association on his return home informing him that his services would no longer be required.

Chubb, then 40 years old, bowled consistently and was most successful, but McCarthy was erratic and, although English umpires thought his action suspect, there were no incidents. Athol Rowan was always dangerous. Mann was missed in the last Test when he was unfit and broke a sequence of 19 consecutive Test appearances. Tayfield was flown in to reinforce the party but did not perform up to expectations. The fielding was of a high standard and superior to that of England. The poor weather at the start of the season shook the team and their best performances were kept for the Test matches where they were unfortunate not to have saved the series.

Out of 30 first-class matches played, 20 were drawn, five won and five lost. But the team was popular and 900 000 people watched their matches, producing a record profit of £17 500.

Eric Rowan skies one on his way to his massive score of 236 at Headingley in the fourth Test.

CHAPTER 24

1955

ELEVENTH SOUTH AFRICA TOUR OF THE UNITED KINGDOM

Captain: JE Cheetham

*'Cheetham's Babes', after a successful tour of
Australia, lost only one first-class match but lost
the narrow Test series by three games to two.
McGlew, Goddard and McLean scored well
and Tayfield was the outstanding bowler.
It was another popular side.*

Captains Jack Cheetham of South Africa and Peter May of England toss at the start of the fifth and decisive Test of the series at the Oval. May's team went on to win the match and the series by three games to two.

TOURING SIDE

JE Cheetham (captain) (W Province)	DJ McGlew (Natal)
ERH Fuller (W Province)	HJ Keith (Natal)
NAT Adcock (Tvl)	HJ Tayfield (Natal)
JHB Waite (Tvl)	RE McLean (Natal)
WR Endean (Tvl)	VI Smith (Natal)
PL Winslow (Tvl)	TL Goddard (Natal)
PNF Mansell (Rhodesia)	ARA Murray (E Province)
CAR Duckworth (Rhodesia)	PS Heine (OFS)

Manager: KG Viljoen

Scorer and baggage-master: M McLennan

Jack Cheetham had taken a young side of 'no hopers' to Australia and New Zealand in 1952/53, beaten the Australians twice and taken the series against New Zealand, both away and at home. So a strong side was selected to tour the United Kingdom. Van Ryneveld was not available but ten of the Australian party were included and Cheetham, with Viljoen, formed a good combination. England had just concluded a tour of Australia and dismissed New Zealand for the lowest Test score ever, 26, thus relieving South Africa from occupying that unenviable position.

The team was the first side to fly to the United Kingdom for a tour and arrived on 24 April, leaving themselves two weeks to become acclimatized to the bitterly cold weather.

The tour started badly when Worcestershire again beat the tourists in the opening match, but a strong MCC side, captained by Len Hutton, was beaten at Lord's. Hutton was unable to continue in the match because of lumbago. He had been chosen as England's captain for all the Tests, but was unable to take part and his place was taken by May for the match at Nottingham.

England opened, on a sodden pitch, with a partnership of 91 between the new openers, Kenyon and Graveney. Adcock, Goddard and Fuller caused the batsmen problems but Kenyon and May added 75 before Kenyon was out for 87. Brilliant fielding kept Compton quiet and England were all out for a very slow 334 made in over nine hours. Tyson and Statham broke through the South African batting and they were 55 for five. McGlew and Cheetham were the only ones to offer resistance and the South Africans were all out for 181. McGlew again played well for 51 in the follow-on, but Tyson again broke through and in one spell had taken five wickets for five runs. South Africa were out for 148 and lost the match by an innings and five runs with a day to spare. Slow play was a feature of the game and the crowds stayed away.

Heine played his way into the Test team with his performance against Somerset. Tyson and Appleyard were unfit for the second Test and their places were taken by Trueman, who had done well against the Indians, and Titmus, making his début. May won the toss and elected to bat on a green wicket. Heine caused the ball to

lift and no one looked comfortable. Goddard was hit for two sixes by Wardle but England were all out for 133. Heine took five wickets and Goddard four. McGlew and Goddard both snicked the ball to Evans without scoring and South Africa were in trouble. Cheetham and Endean added 44 then Endean and McLean added 50 for the fourth wicket to pass the England score. McLean went on to a sparkling 142 and the South Africans made 304, a lead of 171. Kenyon was bowled for nine but then things changed. Graveney and May carried the score to 141. Graveney scored 60 while May went on to 112, Compton scored 69 and the innings ended on 353, a lead of 182. Statham sent back McGlew and Goddard. McGlew, incidentally, faced only three balls in the match without scoring a run. Then Trueman hit Cheetham on the elbow and fractured it so South Africa were effectively three down for 17. No one was playing Statham confidently and he sent back McLean, Endean, Waite and Keith for 17 runs. His seven for 39 was his best ever analysis. The innings ended on 111 and South Africa had lost the exciting match by 71 runs. 103 000 watched the game.

Wicket-keeper Duckworth opened the innings and scored 158 in the drawn Northamptonshire match. Yorkshire, without Hutton, Appleyard and Trueman, were beaten comfortably.

The third Test was played at Manchester on a lively pitch in glorious sunshine for the whole match. For the first time ever, there was not a single Yorkshireman or Lancastrian in the England team. May won the toss and England were soon in trouble, with Heine and Adcock having two wickets down for 22. May left for 34 and Cowdrey for one, and four wickets were down for 75. Compton got into his stride after giving chances off his first two scoring shots and scored 158, so the innings closed on 284. McGlew and Goddard started with 147. Goddard was out for 62 then McGlew was hit on the hand and had to retire. Dropped catches helped Waite and Winslow to score centuries, Winslow reaching his with a drive over

The South African side being introduced to Queen Elizabeth II during the match against Surrey at the Oval.

Popular South African skipper Jack Cheetham led the most successful tour from his country to date.

the sight screen. McGlew returned and took his score from 77 to 104 not out and South Africa ended on 521 for eight declared, a lead of 237 and only 17 short of their best ever Test score. Kenyon and Graveney were both out with the score on two then May and Compton had a glorious stand of 124 in 105 minutes.

May made 117 and support came from Cowdrey. Bailey and Lock tried to save the game and Evans, with a damaged thumb, added 48 for the last wicket but England were all out for 381. Needing 145 to win in two and a quarter hours, South Africa went for the runs. McGlew and McLean hit 72 in 50 minutes with McLean scoring one six and seven fours. South Africa made the runs in the penultimate over and kept the series open. One interesting factor was the number of injuries sustained in the match. Evans broke a finger in two places, his substitute Graveney also hurt his thumb, Compton, May, Cowdrey, McGlew, Tayfield and Waite damaged their hands, while Bailey, Tyson, Heine and Keith suffered strains.

The Queen was introduced to the teams during the match at the Oval. McLean was in sparkling form and scored 151

while Tayfield took 13 wickets to beat Surrey.

The fourth Test was played at Leeds in glorious weather for the whole five days. Cheetham was still injured so McGlew captained the side and won the toss. Loader and Bailey had South Africa reeling at 37 for four at lunch. Then Waite was run out to make it 38 for five. McLean hit out for 41 and Endean played a determined innings for 41 but South Africa were all out for 171. Lowson and Bailey were out early, but an injury to Adcock left McLean with only three bowlers, which meant setting a defensive field. May stayed for 47, Compton scored 61 and the three bowlers, Goddard, Heine and Tayfield bowled South Africa out of trouble by restricting England to a lead of only 20. McGlew and Goddard looked for runs and scored 176 before being parted. Goddard made 74 and McGlew 133. Keith stayed for 73 then Endean came in and scored 116. He had partnerships with Waite, Tayfield, Heine and even Adcock who came in with a runner. South Africa scored 500 and had a lead of 480. Lowson was bowled by Goddard for a duck and Graveney was out to a good catch by McLean for eight. May went on to 97 before being LBW to Tayfield. Tayfield and Goddard took the last six wickets in two hours and England were all out for 256 to lose by 224 runs. Goddard bowled throughout the last day and Mansell allowed Tayfield to rest until the final burst.

South Africa deserved their win and the rubber now depended on the final Test. Attendance over the five days was a record 113 500 and receipts were £31 032.

Glamorgan could not repeat their previous successes against the South Africans and Warwickshire were also beaten. Leicestershire provided another innings victory by the tourists before the final Test at The Oval.

England chose five left-handed batsmen to counter Goddard's leg theory bowling, but the plan misfired. May won the vital toss and elected to bat. There was rain around and Heine, with Fuller, caused problems for the batsmen with aggressive bowling. May, Close and Ikin were out for 70 when rain interrupted play and a soft pitch suited the spinners. Goddard finished with five for 31 and England were all out for 151. Lock and Laker also found the pitch suited them and the South Africans were dismissed for 112. The pitch became docile when England batted again. Ikin and Close went early but May and Graveney had the biggest stand of the match with 65. Compton was limping with a knee injury but added 62 with May. When Compton left, four wickets fell quickly and England were all out for 204 with May not out on 89. South Africa needed 244 to win and the openers saw off the fast bowlers but the game changed when the spinners came on. South Africa lost four wickets in 18 balls. Waite stayed for 60 but no one else could cope with Lock and Laker on their own pitch. South Africa were all out for 151 and lost the match by 92 runs and the exciting series by three games to two. Laker and Lock had taken 15 of the 18 wickets falling to bowlers. It was a magnificent Test series in that each match produced a result, with

Godfrey Evans watches from behind the stumps as Hugh Tayfield of Natal is bowled by Fred Titmus in the Lord's Test match.

the rubber undecided until the final Test.

The serious matches having been completed, a series of holiday matches concluded the tour. Hampshire fast bowler Shackleton drove three sixes in one over from Tayfield who got his own back by taking 14 wickets in the match which was won by the South Africans. In Canterbury the South Africans scored at 80 runs an hour in their first innings of 467 for eight declared.

McGlew hit 161, his highest score of the tour, while Cheetham scored his only century of the tour.

The tourists' last appearance at Lord's was against Middlesex when Smith and Tayfield bowled Middlesex out. At the Hastings Festival, the South Africans batted only moderately, but drew against an England XI. Durham were outplayed by the South Africans when 621 runs were scored on the first day's play. Winslow scored 133 with seven sixes and 13 fours. Mansell hit 148 with a six and 18 fours.

The South Africans entered into the spirit with a total of 354 at the Scarborough Festival. Endean hit two sixes and twenty fours in an innings of 138 not out. Graveney played brilliantly for 159, which brought his Festival figures to 460 runs with one dismissal in six innings. Needing 211 to win in two hours and twenty minutes, Cheetham and Waite hit 20 off an over by Close, then Cheetham hit the winning runs off the penultimate ball.

Although they did not win the rubber, the South Africans did better than any previous South African side in winning two Tests in England. Having started disappointingly with early defeats, the side improved as the weather improved and became an attractive side to watch. The fielding was again outstanding and the hard work and team spirit, for which Cheetham and Viljoen were largely responsible, was the reason for their success.

McGlew was by far the most consistent batsman and headed the averages in both the Tests and all matches. His fielding at cover point was a delight. Goddard proved to be a valuable ally and scored over a thousand runs in addition to taking 60 wickets.

McLean was the most attractive batsman with several brilliant innings to his credit. Waite kept wicket well and could be excused for his lack of form with the bat. The strength of the tourists was in the attack and the support in the field. Tayfield was outstanding and took 143 wickets at an average of under 16. Together with newcomers Heine and Goddard, they took 72 of the 90 wickets to fall to bowlers in the Tests. Heine could be hostile and had a great tour but Adcock was erratic and disappointing.

The team was popular wherever they went and they returned home having made many friends. Apart from the loss of the Test rubber, only one first-class match resulted in a defeat.

The profit from the tour was £35 000 and the total attendance exceeded 930 000.

CHAPTER 25

1956/57

NINTH MCC TOUR OF SOUTH AFRICA

Captain: PBH May

Peter May's very strong MCC side faced a lacklustre opposition. Slow scoring was a feature of the season and the bowling was firmly on top. Tayfield was outstanding for South Africa and a controversial final Test squared a nondescript series.

England touring captain Peter May with the man appointed to captain South Africa in the series, Jackie McGlew. In the end McGlew was only fit to play in the second Test match at Newlands. May had a poor Test series but was outstanding in other matches.

England's cricket was strong: they had just completed a successful series against Australia and hammered the West Indies, so it was a compliment to South African cricket that a full-strength side was sent on tour. The only notable omissions were Trueman and Graveney. The South Africans had chosen to travel by air for the previous tour, but the MCC squad sailed to South Africa on the *Edinburgh Castle*. Twenty-two matches were to be played, including five Tests.

Having played one match against Western Province, Parks complained of eye problems and flew home once the side reached Johannesburg. He attempted to return following treatment but collapsed on the plane at London airport and was forced to abandon the attempt. Such was the strength of the touring side that they elected to carry on with the tour without calling for a replacement.

Both Western Province and Eastern Province were soundly beaten, with Wardle and Lock bowling well. MCC captain Peter May started the tour with a perfect 162 against Western Province and 118 against Eastern Province.

TOURING SIDE

PBH May (captain) (Surrey)	DJ Insole (Essex)
PJ Loader (Surrey)	TE Bailey (Essex)
GAR Lock (Surrey)	B Taylor (Essex)
JC Laker (Surrey)	MC Cowdrey (Kent)
PE Richardson (Worcestershire)	TG Evans (Kent)
ASM Oakman (Sussex)	DCS Compton (Middlesex)
JM Parks (Sussex)	JH Wardle (Yorkshire)
JB Statham (Lancashire)	FH Tyson (Northamptonshire)

Manager: FR Brown
Scorer: G Duckworth
Masseur: H Dalton

Following a 22-hour rail journey, the side arrived in Bloemfontein, where Cowdrey scored 173 and Oakman 150, adding a record 318 in 220 minutes.

The pattern of winning by an innings continued in the two

matches in Rhodesia where 18-year-old Colin Bland showed promise. The first five matches had all been won by an innings and Peter May had scored 678 runs for an average of 170.

Transvaal provided the first shock of the tour on their new home ground at Wanderers. MCC, needing only 64 to win in two-and-a-half hours, seemed comfortable, but Heine and Adcock bowled superbly and six wickets fell for 36 runs. In the end MCC won by three wickets with ten minutes to spare.

A South African XI played the tourists at Pretoria. The new pitch, which had only been laid for three months, started to break up on the first day. The spinners had a field day and MCC lost their first match outside a Test in South Africa since 1913/14.

The first Test was played at the new Wanderers ground and a record crowd of 100 000 watched the five days, despite the fact that through the match runs were scored at an average of 28 an hour. On the evening before the match, McGlew announced that he was not fit and Watkins arrived from Durban as replacement an hour before play started. Van Ryneveld took over as captain.

Richardson achieved the dubious distinction of scoring the slowest Test century ever, in eight hours and eight minutes. Cowdrey stayed around, scoring 59, but England were all out for 268 with Adcock, Goddard and Heine taking the wickets. South Africa started well, with 91 on the board for one wicket down. Tyson then went down with tonsillitis and could take no further part in the match. Bailey took over and broke through, dismissing South Africa for 215, 53 runs behind. Evans's score of 30 was the only bright spot in England's second innings of 150 and South Africa were left to score 204 with plenty of time. Bailey and Statham bowled well and South Africa were 40 for seven with one day to play. The next day they were all out for 72, the lowest score at home since 1889. Good bowling and brilliant fielding were the only redeeming features of a slow-scoring match.

The second Test followed immediately in Cape Town and McGlew declared himself fit. Richardson and Bailey put on 76 for the first wicket then Compton scored 58 and Cowdrey a slow century. Evans joined in with 62 and the innings closed on 369. South Africa were soon in trouble and only 42 from McLean and 49 from Waite took the score over 200. South Africa were not asked to follow on. As Richardson and Bailey built a partnership of 74, Adcock went off the field with a sore toe. Van Ryneveld was also unable to bowl because of a broken finger and the score mounted to 220 for six declared, with a better innings from Compton of 64 and a brighter one from Cowdrey of 61.

Set to score 385 to win on a turning pitch, Wardle took the wickets of McGlew and Keith and four wickets fell with the score on 67. During the innings Endean padded up to a ball outside his off stump and deflected the ball with his hand when it threatened to fall onto his wicket. The English appealed and he was given out 'handled ball'.

School teacher and fast bowler Frank 'Typhoon' Tyson signs autographs for schoolboys in Cape Town.

In the end South Africa folded completely, with the final eight wickets falling for 31 runs and they were all out for 72 – equalling their disastrous score in the first Test. They lost the match by 312 runs, with Wardle taking seven for 36 to add to his five wicket haul in the first innings, his best ever Test performance.

For the third Test in Durban, Funston was brought back for Watkins while Pithey made his début in place of McGlew. May won the toss for the third time in the series and for the eleventh time in 13 Tests. Richardson and Bailey opened with the brightest start of the series and a partnership of 115. Compton and May left early along with Cowdrey, and England went into their shell, scoring slowly but losing the last six wickets for 34 to be all out for 218. In South Africa's reply, Pithey and Goddard started well with a stand of 65, Keith and Endean failed, and then Goddard and McLean added 64 and South Africa went ahead with five wickets standing. McLean hit the first century against the

Peter May undertakes another of his many duties as tour captain as he plants an oak tree at Paarl Cricket Ground.

The return match against Transvaal was spoiled by rain, but the wicket for the fourth Test in Johannesburg was unaffected and proved to be a beautiful track for batting. Winning the toss for the first time on a beautiful batting wicket South Africa soon lost Pithey, but Goddard and Waite put on the first century stand of the series against the tourists. At 234 for four South Africa lost two quick wickets but McLean carried on to 93 and South Africa achieved their highest score of the summer with 340, the first score of 300 against the MCC. England started shakily with both openers out for 40, but Insole continued his good form with 47 and May at last found his Test form with 61. Compton had a scratchy innings of 42 and the tail wagged for a final score of 251, a lead for South Africa of 89. A slow start of 62 by Pithey and Goddard forced the others to go for quick runs and they lost five wickets for 48. South Africa were all out for 142, leaving England needing 232 to win on the last day. Richardson and Insole scored 55 and England were 147 for two, needing only 85 to win. May and Compton could manage only one between them, but a stand between Cowdrey and Wardle put the game within England's reach, leaving them with 46 required to win with four wickets in hand. The end came when Hugh Tayfield's brother, Arthur, fielding as a substitute, caught Loader of his brother's bowling. England were all out for 214 and South Africa had won by 17 runs. Tayfield was chaired off the field in triumph having taken a record nine wickets in an innings and a total of 13 in the match.

In the return match against Western Province May continued his non-Test form with a century. Going into the final Test South Africa had a chance of squaring the series, having been two down.

Port Elizabeth had imported soil from Durban to prepare a pitch only three months previously and it was thought that this was insufficient time to prepare a Test wicket. South Africa again won the toss and elected to bat. The pitch was dead but the ball kept low at one end, giving the fast bowlers a great advantage. Statham, however, was unavailable and Wardle required treatment for his cartilage.

Five South African wickets fell for 78 and then Endean, together with McLean and Van Ryneveld, managed to bring the total to 164, a satisfactory one under the circumstances. Adcock took the wickets of Richardson and Compton for ducks, but May managed 24. Bailey came out and hit the ball hard, playing one of the best innings of his career for 41, but England could score only 110.

The third day's play was the slowest in Test history with only 122 runs being scored. Goddard took a blow on the chin, retired and then came back to score 30, while to add to the injuries Compton had fallen in the hotel and hurt his back. Tayfield had knee trouble and Waite tore a muscle in his shoulder while diving in the field. Tyson bowled off a shortened run and took six wickets for 40, but South Africa managed to score 134, a lead of 188. Bailey and May stayed for a time but Tayfield took six for 78 and South Africa won a controversial match by 58 runs and squared the series two-all.

tourists but England restricted South Africa's lead to 65. Richardson and Bailey gave England another good start but Bailey received an awkward ball from Heine and broke a bone in his hand. Tayfield dismissed Compton and May in one over and Insole was beaten several times, but he settled down and scored a century.

On the last day, the England tail enders managed to bring the total to 254, a lead of 189. Tayfield had bowled beautifully and ended with eight for 69, the best by a South African in Tests. Needing 190 to win at a rate of 45 an hour, Pithey was out second ball and South Africa fell behind the clock against accurate bowling. Funston and Endean added 75 and gave South Africa a chance but once they left the remaining batsmen put up the shutters and the match was drawn with South Africa on 113 for six.

Insole, Bailey, Wardle and Statham flew home before the final match of the tour against Combined Universities in Cape Town and, as Tyson developed a cold before the match, Freddie Brown, the manager, was co-opted to make up the eleven.

Only one century partnership was taken off the MCC bowling in 22 matches and only two South Africans scored centuries. May had an outstanding tour to end with an average of 55 but his loss of form in the Tests – he scored only 153 runs in ten innings – was inexplicable. Insole improved as the tour went on and ended with the highest Test average and the second highest first-class average. Bailey proved reliable with both bat and ball. Cowdrey had a moderate tour but the biggest disappointment was the form of Compton. Following the operation to his knee, he was not the player he had been in previous years.

Wardle took over a hundred wickets on the tour and stood out – his success kept Lock out of the side until the last Test. Laker, on the other hand, was nowhere as effective as Tayfield with his off-spinners. The fast attack of Statham, Loader and Tyson was always menacing on the favourable pitches while Evans was outstanding as wicket-keeper.

South Africa had shown great powers of recovery after being two down in the series to share the rubber for only the second time in their history. The injuries to McGlew were unfortunate, but Goddard proved himself world-class both with the bat and ball and McLean had several good innings, although he was inconsistent.

Van Ryneveld took over the South African captaincy with enthusiasm and one noticeable difference between the two teams was in the superb ground fielding of the South Africans. Tayfield was the outstanding bowler, although Adcock stood out as a fast bowler, notwithstanding Heine's ability to bowl the unplayable ball.

The bowling from both sides dominated the batting and slow scoring rate resulted in all the Tests. For the first time, the MCC had insisted on taking a share of the profits from a tour, and came away with £26 500.

Clive van Ryneveld leads out the Western Province team at Newlands in the second of their two games played against the MCC.

CHAPTER 26

1960

TWELFTH SOUTH AFRICA TOUR OF THE UNITED KINGDOM

Captain: DJ McGlew

Griffin's no-balling controversy overshadowed everything else on the tour and only Adcock and McLean performed well. South Africa lost the series by three matches to nil. Television and poor weather kept spectators away and the disappointing tour lost money.

South African captain Jackie McGlew (second right) and his squad, immaculately dressed prior to a practice at the home of cricket, Lord's. They were to go down to a heavy defeat at the ground in the second Test.

Anti-apartheid demonstrators had threatened to disrupt the tour and the MCC gave the South African Cricket authorities the option of withdrawing. However it was decided to carry on. A small crowd of demonstrators was at the airport when they landed and at most of the grounds.

Seven of those selected had been on tour previously and O'Linn had played for Kent, while Fellows-Smith had played for Oxford University and Northamptonshire. A surprising omission from the team was Winslow, who had been off form.

The team flew in to London on 17 April 1960 and played their first warm-up game on 30 April against the Duke of Norfolk's XI at Arundel Castle. In their opening first class fixture the tourists

TOURING SIDE	
DJ McGlew (captain) (Natal)	
TL Goddard (Natal)	NAT Adcock (Tvl)
RA McLean (Natal)	S O'Linn (Tvl)
GM Griffin (Natal)	HJ Tayfield (Tvl)
C Wesley (Natal)	PR Carlstein (Tvl)
AJ Pithey (Rhodesia)	JP Fellows-Smith (Tvl)
CAR Duckworth (Rhodesia)	JHB Waite (Tvl)
JE Pothecary (W Province)	AH McKinnon (E Province)

Manager: AD Nourse

Baggage-master: M McLennan

it was McLean who sparkled with a glorious 180 to enable McGlew to declare at 461 for three. In the second innings McGlew decided to give the others batting practice and opened with Pithey and Duckworth but his plan misfired when he found himself going in at number ten with the score 94 for eight. He declared at 101 for eight and left Northamptonshire to score 165 in three hours and twenty minutes. Reynolds hit Tayfield for two sixes in his opening spell and Tyson hit out for 29 in 15 minutes so that three runs were needed off the last over. The fourth ball went through for four byes and the South Africans had lost their first match of the tour.

Griffin was 'no balled' eight times for throwing, and seven times for dragging, in the match against Nottinghamshire. At the end of the match it was announced that he would go to Alf Gover's Cricket School to try to eradicate the problem. He played in the match against Glamorgan but bowled only six overs. McGlew and Goddard then took part in a magnificent opening stand of 256.

England had five county captains in their side for the first Test at Edgbaston. Fellows-Smith, Griffin and O'Linn made their débuts for South Africa. Griffin was given a short spell at each end and was not called for throwing but was erratic, while Adcock bowled too short. Dexter, Subba Row and Mike Smith scored fifties but Pullar broke a bone in his hand off a ball from Adcock. Seven wickets fell for 117 runs through the sustained bowling of Tayfield and Adcock, and England were all out for 292. Trueman and Statham bowled aggressively and the first five South African wickets were down for 91. O'Linn joined Waite to rescue the situation and managed to avoid the follow-on, but South Africa were all out for 186, 106 runs behind. Cowdrey was out second ball but Dexter hit out for 26 and the tail-enders Walker, Trueman and Statham brought the score to 203, a lead of 309. McGlew and Goddard fell to Statham for five runs but Pithey and McLean stayed for another 53 runs before Pithey was out. Next ball, newcomer Waite played onto his stumps but the bail did not fall. McLean played a good innings of 68, and with Waite put on 62 before close of play. Next morning McLean was out second ball to Trueman and then seven wickets fell in two hours for South Africa to be all out for 209, and to lose the Test by 100 runs.

There was big hitting in the match against Hampshire. Griffin hit three sixes and three fours in his 65 but was no-balled for throwing twice in the first innings and four times in the second.

Griffin again caused sensation in the second Test at Lord's where he became not only the first man ever to be no-balled for throwing in a Test in England, but also the first to take a hat-trick in a Test at Lord's.

Subba Row and Mike Smith narrowly missed their centuries in England's first innings of 362 for 8 declared. Smith was caught by Waite for 99 off the last ball of Griffin's over. Walker hit two sixes off Goddard, then Griffin bowled him off the first ball of his next over and bowled Trueman for a hat-trick.

met Worcestershire, who had not lost to the South Africans since the 1935 tour. Coming in with three wickets down for 28, McLean joined Pithey and scored an incredible 207 out of 288 in under four hours. In the second innings, McKinnon took seven wickets for 42 and Worcestershire were all out for 141 to lose by 133 runs.

Derbyshire was the scene of the first 'no balling' problem that was to cloud the rest of the tour. Strangely it did not concern Griffin, who had a suspect action, but Rhodes, the Derbyshire bowler, who was called six times for throwing by Paul Gibb the umpire. Gibb called Griffin three times but it was for dragging over the line. Griffin's problems started in the drawn match against MCC at Lord's when both umpires called him for throwing.

There was an exciting match against Northamptonshire in which Goddard batted through the South Africans' innings for 186 but

Statham bowled magnificently on a difficult pitch and took six for 63 to bundle South Africa out for 152. He followed this up with five wickets in the second innings to become the first fast bowler since the war to take more than ten wickets in a Test. South Africa were again bundled out for 137 to lose by an innings and 73 runs. Wesley, with 35, was the top scorer in either South African innings. Griffin was no-balled 11 times in the Test by umpire Frank Lee at square leg. Because the match was finished early, an exhibition match of twenty overs was arranged to be played. In one over, Griffin was no-balled four times for throwing by umpire Buller. He finished the eleven-ball over bowling underarm and was again no-balled by the other umpire, Frank Lee, for failing to inform the batsman of his change in action. This effectively ruined Griffin's career and the balance of South Africa's attack in future games.

The Queen and Duke of Edinburgh watched the exhibition match, during which Trueman smashed the ball onto the roof of the stand at Lord's.

The South Africans were 43 runs ahead with nine wickets in hand when the second day's play started against Gloucestershire. Sixteen wickets then fell for 128 runs with only one caught in front of the wicket. Nine South African wickets fell for 41 runs for a total of 49, the lowest to date.

Pothecary replaced Griffin for the third Test at Trent Bridge. South Africa did well to restrict England to 242 for seven on the first day but the tail-enders took the final score to 287. Adcock, Goddard and Tayfield bowled well. The England side took seven hours for their score but then South Africa were all out in two hours and fifty minutes for 88, the lowest score since the 30 achieved in 1924. Statham and Trueman caused the damage. Goddard, Fellows-Smith and McLean were out for 34 in the follow-on, but McGlew came to form with a good 45 before being run out in a curious incident. McGlew collided with bowler Moss in taking a quick single and Statham threw the wicket down. McGlew was given out by the umpire and walked, but the crowd objected. Cowdrey called McGlew back three times and appealed to the umpire to change his decision but the umpire was adamant that the collision was accidental and the decision stood. Wesley had the distinction of making a 'king pair,' being dismissed first ball in each innings. O'Linn played pluckily and batted through for 98 with good support from Waite, who had injured a finger while keeping wicket. Waite made 60 but the total of 247 was only sufficient to make England bat again and the 49 runs required were scored for the loss of two wickets enabling England to win the match by eight wickets. This also gave them the rubber.

Rain prevented any play in the first two days of the fourth Test at Manchester. Pithey replaced Fellows-Smith which left South Africa with only four bowlers. Cowdrey won the toss for the ninth time in succession and England batted. England scored quickly but only Barrington was able to put a reasonable score together with 76 and they were all out for 260. Adcock, Pothecary and Goddard shared the wickets. Statham and Trueman broke through and the South African score became 92 for five, but O'Linn joined McLean and they added 102 with McLean responsible for 86 of the runs. He went on to a magnificent 109 before being bowled by off-spinner Allen, who took four of the last five wickets, and South Africa's innings closed on 229, 31 behind. Subba Row had injured his finger while fielding and was not able to bat. Cowdrey hit Adcock for six and was out two balls later for 25 and wickets fell so that England

Geoff Griffin's arm with the splint specially designed to help cure the action that saw him constantly no-balled for throwing on the tour.

were 71 for five. Barrington used a runner because of a pulled thigh muscle but played slowly to ensure a draw. Cowdrey declared at 153 for seven, leaving South Africa to score 185 at over 100 runs an hour. South Africa batted out time without losing a wicket.

For the last Test at the Oval, South Africa brought in Fellows-Smith and gave McKinnon his début in place of Pithey and Wesley. Yet again, Cowdrey won the toss and batted in damp conditions. Eight wickets fell for 131 and England were all out for 155. Pullar scored 59 and Adcock took six for 65. Pothecary gave good support with four for 58. McGlew scored 22 in an opening partnership of 44 and Goddard went on to 99 before being caught off Statham by Cowdrey in the slips. Fellows-Smith and McLean were out from consecutive balls off Dexter but Waite and O'Linn brought the score to 330 for seven and the third new ball brought the wicket of O'Linn. Tayfield and McKinnon hit out and the total reached 419 all out, a first-innings lead of 264.

12 500 spectators saw England play some sparkling cricket in the second innings. Cowdrey scored 155 and Pullar 175 in a brilliant opening partnership of 290. Nothing could stop the run rate and all the bowlers were punished. The other English batsmen did not take advantage of this start and Cowdrey declared on 479 for nine leaving South Africa to score 216 in three hours. Three wickets fell for 66 but rain prevented a conclusion and the match was drawn.

AER Gilligan supplied the side at the Hastings Festival. McLean hit the fastest century of the season in 76 minutes. The final match of the tour was at the Scarborough Festival against a strong TN Pearce XI. Barrington conceded 94 runs in 15 overs in a farcical ending to the tour.

It was a disappointing tour, full of controversy. The throwing incidents overshadowed the team's efforts and left an unbalanced attack. McGlew and Goddard did not live up to their expectations in the Tests and young players did not perform.

Adcock and McLean were the exceptions and both featured in Wisden's five Players of the Year, but too much depended on them. Tayfield took 123 wickets on the tour but his Test performance was disappointing. O'Linn showed character in his Test debut, Wesley and Carlstein had their moments but did not have consistency. Waite was a competent wicket-keeper with 63 victims and headed the Test batting averages. The ground fielding was not as good as in previous years.

The weather and television kept spectators away from the matches and the gates did not cover the tour expenses of approximately £35 000. The results were actually comparable with previous tours, with 30 matches played of which 14 were won, five lost and 11 drawn. However, the Test results of five played, three lost and two drawn were what counted.

McGlew and his players, particularly Griffin, behaved impeccably throughout, in the face of much controversy, and once more were a popular side which made many friendships.

Hugh 'Toey' Tayfield, the Transvaal and South African off-spinner who took 123 wickets on tour.

CHAPTER 27

1960/61

FIRST WOMEN'S CRICKET TOUR OF SOUTH AFRICA

Captain: H Sharpe

TOURING SIDE

H Sharpe (captain)

R Westbrook (vice-captain)	A Ratcliffe
A Sanders	R Heyhoe
K Smith	M Hunt
S Plant	A Jago
M Rutherford	E Irwin
B Pont	O Marshall

The South African Women's Cricket team which played against the English tourists in 1960. Back: D Wood, B Cairncross, E Lambert, Y van Mentz, J Gove, L Ward, M Payne, J McNaughton; front: T Wilson, E Hurley, E Kelly , M Robison, J Irwin (capt), P Hollet, E Rowan.

The South African and Rhodesian Women's Cricket Association was formed in 1952 and an invitation was issued to an English side to play in 13 matches throughout the Republic including four Tests. Only those players capable of financing themselves for the fares, equipment and pocket money were selected.

In the first Test, which appropriately took place at Port Elizabeth, South Africa had the advantage after the first innings, thanks to an unbeaten 96 from Eileen Hurley, but the match ended up in a draw.

The second Test at the Wanderers was also drawn with the South Africans hanging on long enough to be saved by rain. B Lang scored 51 in the second innings when South Africa were on 140 for eight needing 217 to avoid an innings defeat.

South Africa were dismissed for 151 in the third Test at Durban and England went on to 269 for eight declared, with Helen Sharpe scoring 126 for England and Jean McNaughton taking six of the wickets for 39 runs. The South African second innings could produce only 166 and England knocked off the required 49 runs for the loss of two wickets. This was the last Test to be played on the old Kingsmead ground and Helen Sharpe and Jean McNaughton were invited to plant trees to commemorate their feats. The trees were later transplanted to the new ground.

The final Test in Cape Town was drawn after Yvonne van Mentz scored the first Test century for South Africa. South Africa took a substantial lead on the first innings but England recovered in the second innings before declaring on 236 for four.

The English team was undefeated in the tour and won the Test series with their victory in Durban.

TOURING SIDE

RA McLean (captain) (Natal)

CG de V Burger (Natal)   RA Gripper (Rhodesia)

MK Elgie (Natal)   JT Botten (NE Tvl)

L Morby-Smith (Natal)   DT Lindsay (NE Tvl)

GS Bunyard (Tvl)   PL van der Merwe (W Province)

EJ Barlow (Tvl)   CG Rushmere (W Province)

KC Bland (Rhodesia)   PM Pollock (E Province)

Manager: CO Medworth

CHAPTER 28

1961

SOUTH AFRICAN FEZELA TOUR OF THE UNITED KINGDOM

Captain: RA McLean

The Fezela team of 1961. Back: L Morby-Smith, EJ Barlow, DT Lindsay, GS Bunyard, KC Bland, PM Pollock, CG Rushmere, RA Gripper, JT Botten, I Fullerton (replacement), WJ Lott (baggage master); front: PL van der Merwe, CO Medworth (manager), RA McLean (capt), ES Murphy (sponsor), MK Elgie (vice-capt), Dr A Stevenson (medical doctor), CGdeV Burger.

Mr E Stanley Murphy, a retired sugar planter from Durban, put up the £10 000 required for a tour of the United Kingdom by a squad of young South African cricketers. The name *Fezela*, meaning the sting of a scorpion, was chosen for the side. The Fezelas were to play 21 fixtures on their tour, including three matches against first-class opposition.

The strength of the South African side was severely underestimated by all their opposition, with the result that weak sides were selected. The Fezelas went through the 21-match tour without defeat, including comfortable wins in their three first-class matches. Over 6 000 runs were scored in total, including 80 sixes and almost 1 000 fours.

Kim Elgie, who also played rugby for Scotland, was the most successful batsman for the team with 879 runs, followed by Eddie Barlow, Ray Gripper and Roy McLean. Jackie Botten claimed over 70 wickets with his medium-fast deliveries and the fielding was superb. Denis Lindsay kept wicket well and was responsible for some hurricane hitting including, on one occasion, five consecutive fours in one over.

The tour proved to be very pleasant socially, and provided some valuable experience in English conditions for the young cricketers who were to become the mainstay of successful South African sides in the future.

CHAPTER 29

1964/65

TENTH MCC TOUR OF SOUTH AFRICA

Captain: MJK Smith

Some brilliant young South Africans were coming through the system following a successful tour of Australia and this tour blooded them in Test cricket at home. Mike Smith's MCC side did well to hold onto a one-nil lead in the Test series. The future of South African cricket looked promising.

The South African team for the final Test in the series at Port Elizabeth. Back: MJ Macaulay, DT Lindsay, KC Bland, PM Pollock, RG Pollock, HD Bromfield, AH McKinnon, EJ Barlow; front: JHB Waite, TL Goddard (capt), EB Norton (manager), PL van der Merwe, AJ Pithey.

Ted Dexter had captained the England side in the previous series against Australia but decided to become a candidate in the forthcoming general election for Parliament and was therefore unavailable for the post of captain. In the event he was not elected to Parliament and joined the touring party later as vice-captain. Mike Smith of Warwickshire captained a side very strong in batting although without Cowdrey, Russell, Graveney and Stewart. On the other hand it was thought to be weak in bowling against a South African side which had performed well in Australia.

MCC had not won a series overseas for five years.

The team travelled to South Africa by air for the first time and played the first match in Rhodesia on 21/22 October 1964.

South African Colts scored 398 at Benoni, with the last-wicket partnership of 108 from Macaulay and Botten, made at two runs per minute, stealing the show. MCC were bowled out for 267 and then the Colts put on another 62 before illness struck the team and only nine men could bat. At one point in the MCC innings, the Colts had six substitutes on the field and Van der Merwe had only two bowlers at his disposal.

TOURING SIDE	
MJK Smith (captain) (Warwickshire)	KF Barrington (Surrey)
RW Barber (Warwickshire)	G Boycott (Yorkshire)
TW Cartwright (Warwickshire)	JM Parks (Sussex)
DJ Brown (Warwickshire)	NI Thompson (Sussex)
PH Parfitt (Middlesex)	RNS Hobbs (Essex)
JT Murray (Middlesex)	DA Allen (Gloucestershire)
FJ Titmus (Middlesex)	ER Dexter (Sussex)
JSE Price (Middlesex)	JM Brearley (Middlesex)

Team manager: DB Carr
Baggage-master: M McLennan

by an innings and 104 runs with a day and a half to spare.

Smith won the toss in the second Test at Johannesburg. Barber and Dexter added 136 for the second wicket, Barber scored 97 and Dexter went on to 172 then Barrington added 121 in his second successive century. England were all out for a massive 531 with Peter Pollock taking 5 for 129 and his brother Graeme 2 for 50. Goddard with 40 and Barlow with 85 got off to a good start with an opening partnership of 78, then Pithey added 85 but no one was comfortable against Allen and Titmus and the innings closed on 317. In the follow-on, Goddard scored 50 and Pollock 55 while Bland stayed for 144 not out in an innings lasting four hours with two sixes and 16 fours. South Africa avoided defeat with a score of 336 for six and the match was drawn.

The third Test was played over the New Year in Cape Town and Goddard and Barlow got the South Africans off to a good start with a partnership of 80. Goddard was out for 40 and an appeal against Barlow with his score on 41 was turned down. The English players thought he should walk but Barlow stood his ground and went on to 138. The English players did not applaud his century but later apologized. He and Pithey put on 172 with Pithey scoring a slow 154 and the score at the end of the first day was 252 for one. Bland was run out for 78 and Goddard declared towards the end of the second day on 501 for seven. A record crowd of 21 000 watched the day's play. England went out to save the game and the

Geoff Boycott had not been making runs but the match against Eastern Province changed all that when he scored 193 not out. Smith scored 153 and had a partnership of 278 with Boycott after MCC had been 45 for four. Boycott scored another century against Western Province on a fast pitch and Barrington scored 169 not out so that the MCC totalled 441. MCC delayed their declaration at 228 for six, leaving WP to score 313 in four hours. Wickets fell and at one point only nine MCC players were fielding. The other two were moving the sightscreen ready for the next over. However Province held out at 158 for eight for a draw.

The first Test was played at Durban. Smith won the toss and elected to bat on a pitch short of grass. Boycott and Barber both scored in the seventies and had a partnership of 120, then Barrington scored 148 not out and put on 206 for the sixth wicket with Parks, who scored 108 not out. England declared at 485 for five. Goddard, Barlow and Pollock were out for 20 and South Africa were all out for 155 to follow on 330 behind. Only Bland with 68 featured in South Africa's second innings and they were all out for 226 to lose

Graeme Pollock tucks away a single on the leg side. The young Eastern Province batsman averaged over 50 in the series.

161

Colin Bland sweeps the ball past wicketkeeper Jim Parks during his 78 in the first innings of the Newlands Test match.

batsmen went into their shells. Barber scored 58, Dexter a slow 61, then Barrington tickled a ball to Lindsay but was given not out. He walked to add fuel to the previous incident. Smith added 121 and the England total went on to 442 in an innings lasting eleven-and a half hours. For South Africa Barlow scored 78 while Pollock, Bland and Lindsay all contributed but the innings lasted until half an hour before close of play on the last day and the match was drawn.

Goddard was asked to stand down as skipper for the remaining Tests but refused.

Smith won the toss and surprisingly asked South Africa to bat in the fourth Test at Johannesburg. John Waite, who had announced his retirement, was persuaded to return in place of Lindsay. Barlow scored 96 and Goddard 60 for a first-wicket partnership of 134. Then Bland scored 55 and Pithey with 95 put on 157 with Waite to allow Goddard to declare on 390 for six in a rain-interrupted innings. Waite missed two catches and a stumping to allow Barber, Parfitt and Barrington to help put on a total of 384. Barrington scored 93, Barber 61 and Parfitt 122 not out. Goddard scored his first Test century in 62 innings with 112, while Pollock scored 65 not out and Goddard declared at 307 for three, leaving England to score 314 runs at 78 runs an hour. Boycott stayed throughout the innings for a stubborn 76 not out to save the game for England and the match ended in a draw with England on 153 for six at the close.

A strong Invitation XI scored 437 against MCC in Cape Town with a second wicket partnership of 188 in two and a quarter hours from Gamsy and Bland. Gamsy scored 88 and Bland was run out for 116, having hit five sixes and nine fours. Geoff Boycott batted more fluently than usual for his 114 while a last wicket partnership between Cartwright and Hobbs put on 62 to bring MCC's total to a respectable 326. Gamsy, with 55, Bland 67, Pollock 91 and Muzzell with 52 allowed a declaration at 316 for seven, a lead of 427. Seven MCC wickets fell for 100 then Smith with 78 not out and Cartwright with 42 not out batted for the last three hours to save the game and MCC's unbeaten record.

Port Elizabeth was the venue for the fifth and final Test on a perfect wicket. The MCC side had a problem with injuries, to the extent that Smith had been using Boycott as a medium-pace change bowler, and they called on Ken Palmer, a medium-pace bowler for Somerset, who was coaching in South Africa, to play in the match. Goddard and Barlow both scored in the sixties and put on 114 for the first wicket, Bland with 48 and Pollock with a sparkling 137 kept the score moving and Van der Merwe added 66 to bring the first-innings score to a massive 502. A typically dour century from Boycott set the pattern for England's reply and Barrington played an equally dour 72 so that England achieved a good score, at tea on the fourth day, of 435, 67 in arrears. Tight bowling restricted the South

162

England captain Mike Smith is given out LBW in the match against a South African Invitation XI at Newlands. The successful bowler is Clive Halse and the batsman at the non-striker's end Geoff Boycott, who scored a century in the match.

African batting to a run a minute but then Graeme Pollock cut loose with 77 not out to allow a declaration on 178 for four, leaving England to score 246 at 65 runs an hour. Boycott left early but showers prevented a conclusion to the match, which meant that England won the series by one game to nil, with four draws, and remained undefeated on the tour.

Mike Smith's team confounded the critics who said that it would have no chance against a revitalized South African side. They proved too good for the Currie Cup sides and most were beaten by an innings. In the Test matches, the first two were decisive and England hung on to their lead in spite of injuries to his bowlers.

Barrington headed both the batting and bowling averages in all the first-class matches and all of the batsmen came good at the right time. Brearley was the exception and had a disappointing tour.

The MCC bowlers suffered and not one of them was outstanding. The South African batsmen often got off to a good start, Goddard having a particularly good season, while Colin Bland and 20-year-old Graeme Pollock played wonderful scoring shots and exciting cricket.

The bowlers on both sides struggled. Peter Pollock and Joe Partridge did not live up to the reputation which they deserved following the Australian tour and Goddard was below form. Following the last Test, Goddard announced his retirement along with John Waite who had completed 50 Test appearances.

CHAPTER 30

1965

THIRTEENTH SOUTH AFRICA TOUR OF THE UNITED KINGDOM

Captain: PL van der Merwe

The Pollock brothers and Colin Bland took England by storm in a season during which the South Africans lost only two first-class matches and took the Test series. Peter van der Merwe's side played attractive cricket in front of large crowds.

Peter van der Merwe, popular captain of one of the most attractive sides to visit England, puts one away for four. Wicketkeeper Jim Parks and Colin Cowdrey at slip look on.

The International Cricket Council decided that the English season should be shared between New Zealand and South Africa with each side playing three Tests against England. New Zealand toured for the first half of the season and proceeded to lose all three Tests and approximately £4 000 on the English portion of the tour.

Peter van der Merwe was selected as captain of the South African team and a young squad was chosen to travel.

Six of the side had toured England with the Fezela side. Coming into the English season half-way through, the team was at a disadvantage and required a few matches to acclimatize.

Only the first day's play was possible in the game against Gloucestershire and this was dominated by two South Africans, who happened to be playing for Gloucestershire. Teenagers Mike Procter and Barry Richards from Natal were on a season's trial with the county and shone in a partnership of 116 for the fifth wicket against their countrymen.

The 100th Test between the countries took place at Lord's and it was a thriller. South Africa got off to a shaky start. Three wickets fell for 75 due to brilliant catches and then Pollock with 56 and Bland with 39 recovered the situation to 155 for four. More wickets fell until the last three wickets put on 102 for South Africa to end the first innings on 280. Little play was possible on the next day but Boycott and Barber put on 82 for the first wicket in front of a crowd

166

TOURING SIDE	
PL van der Merwe (captain) (W Province)	
HD Bromfield (W Province)	RG Pollock (E Province)
A Bacher (Tvl)	EJ Barlow (E Province)
HR Lance (Tvl)	P Pollock (E Province)
AH McKinnon (Tvl)	DT Lindsay (NE Tvl)
R Dumbrill (Natal)	JT Botten (NE Tvl)
D Gamsy (Natal)	MJ Macaulay (OFS)
NS Crookes (Natal)	KC Bland (Rhodesia)

Manager: JB Plimsoll

Baggage-master and scorer: M McLennan

of 26 000. Barrington scored 91, then Bland hit his wicket direct from a wonderful piece of fielding, and followed it up with another to dismiss Parks. Titmus helped bring the score to 338, a lead of 58. Barlow made 46 of the 55 scored for the first wicket, but South Africa were in trouble at 120 for four when Bland was out for 70. Bacher and Van der Merwe brought about a recovery to 248 all out, a lead of only 190 and under four hours to play. Pollock bowled aggressively and England fell behind the clock so that seven wickets had fallen for 145 when stumps were drawn. The fielding of Colin Bland was the feature of the match which was watched by over 100 000 spectators.

Graeme Pollock scored a wonderful double century against Kent at Canterbury. His first century came in three hours, and the second in one hour, with five sixes and 28 fours. In the next match Peter Pollock took five for 28 and had Essex reeling at 74 all out in the first innings, then Macaulay finished off Essex's second innings of 144 with a hat-trick for a victory by an innings and 147 runs.

The second Test was played at Trent Bridge in Nottingham and it was to be the Pollock family's match. Cartwright had his only game of the series and took six for 94 before breaking his finger, having the South Africans in trouble at 80 for five in a total of 269. Graeme Pollock hit 125 out of 160 in 140 minutes. At one point he had hit 91 out of 102. Peter Pollock took two vital wickets on the first day but Cowdrey with 105, and Smith, recovered until Pollock and Botten cleaned up the tail with the new ball and England were all out for 240. Barlow, batting with a bruised toe, scored 76, Boycott bowled 19 overs for 25 runs, and South Africa had scored 219 for four when Snow and Larter took the new ball. Six wickets fell for 70 runs and South Africa had scored 289, a lead of 318. Graeme Pollock was sixth out for a good 59. South Africa again took two wickets before close of play and three wickets were down for only 10 runs. Boycott scored 16 in two hours and twenty minutes and England struggled to 127 for seven at tea, Parfitt having taken 160 minutes over 40 runs. Then Parfitt and Parks flayed the bowling and added 80 in one hour until Parfitt was out for 86 and England were dismissed for 224. South Africa had won the

match by 94 runs with a day to spare.

It was England's first defeat in 15 matches under Smith's captaincy and South Africa's first win in England for 10 years. It was a well deserved triumph for the South Africans, abetted by good captaincy and brilliant fielding by Van der Merwe and Bland. Graeme Pollock scored 184 runs in his two innings, held a good slip catch and then took a wicket on the final day. Peter Pollock took five wickets in each innings and ended the match with 10 for 87 runs.

Against Hampshire, Graeme Pollock launched an onslaught with 94 in 66 minutes with three sixes and 15 fours. He was caught on the boundary going for the fastest century of the season with 36 minutes to spare. He added 87 in 36 minutes with Van der Merwe who scored eight of them.

Graeme Pollock also carried on in the same vein against Sussex when he scored a century in one-and-three-quarter hours, with two sixes and 17 fours.

Colin Bland in typically dynamic form in the covers. On this tour he was hailed as the greatest outfielder the game had seen.

Colin Bland stumped by Parks for a duck as Cowdrey appeals. In addition to his fielding, Bland was a big-hitting middle-order batsman who frequently made significant contributions for South Africa.

England made a lot of changes for the third Test at the Oval. Statham was recalled to the England side at the age of 35 and Higgs played his first game for England. The two fast bowlers took nine South African wickets in an innings of 208. Only Lance, with 69, played reasonably after South Africa had been sent in to bat. Cowdrey took almost four hours for 58, Barber over two hours for 40, and Barrington an hour-and-a-half for 18. Peter Pollock took five wickets for a third successive time, and England were all out for a deficit of six runs. Bacher scored a good 70 and Bland hit 16 fours in his 127, made in four-and-a-half hours. South Africa were all out for 392 with seven hours remaining for play. England started going for the runs, Russell and Parfitt scored 99 for the second wicket then Barrington and Cowdrey scored 135 and England needed 109 in 85 minutes at tea.

Rain stopped any further progress and the match was left drawn with England on 308 for four.

South Africa had won the series for the second time in history.

Higgs took three South African wickets in his first spell for Lancashire. Graeme Pollock took 20 runs off Lloyd's first over and hit 10 fours in his 75.

The Scarborough Festival match against TN Pearce's XI was played in a light-hearted fashion. Bacher and Pollock sparkled and 164 runs were scored in two hours before lunch. In the second innings, the South Africans lived even more dangerously and Dumbrill took 18 off each of two overs from Titmus to make 64 in 37 minutes. The tourists were all out for 224 and the Pearce's XI needed 191 to win with plenty of time to spare. Parfitt with 87 and Cowdrey with 39 saw the side to a victory in two days for the

The Pollock brothers, Peter and Graeme. Named along with Colin Bland as three of the five Wisden Cricketers of the Year, both the brothers were instrumental in South Africa's series victory. In the decisive second Test Graeme scored 125 and 59 while Peter took five for 53 and five for 34.

loss of only two wickets. As the previous game was concluded with a day to spare, a 40-over match was arranged which the South Africans took more seriously. Only one over throughout the game was a maiden and the match was enjoyed by a healthy holiday crowd of 5 000.

Of the 18 first-class games, 11 were drawn and five won. The Test series was won by one game to nil with two drawn.

Graeme and Peter Pollock, together with Colin Bland, were the stars of the side. In addition to his hitting, the fielding of Colin Bland was a revelation. He was asked to appear on BBC Television and knock down three stumps with three balls, which he did successfully. The three South Africans were named Wisden Cricketers of the Year.

Barlow could not find a regular opening partner to match his skill but Lance and Lindsay played well lower in the order. Bacher joined Pollock in scoring 1 000 runs during the tour.

Botten, Dumbrill and Macaulay backed up Peter Pollock with their seamers while McKinnon added his spin. Peter van der Merwe proved to be an astute and popular captain and it was a happy squad with good team spirit. Largely they were not affected by the small crowds of anti-apartheid demonstrators which appeared at some of their matches around the country.

Peter van der Merwe's side were one of the most attractive to tour England. They played positive cricket and won the hearts of the spectators so that large crowds flocked to their matches.

CHAPTER 31

1966

FIRST WILFRED ISAACS TOUR OF THE UNITED KINGDOM

Captain: W Isaacs

TOURING SIDE	
W Isaacs (captain)	
RA McLean (vice-captain)	A Bruyns
J Cole	J Ferrandi
KJ Funston	P Henwood
G Hall	L Irvine
D Mackay-Coghill	DJ McGlew
M Procter	B Richards
HJ Tayfield	G Watson
C Wesley	NAT Adcock
Manager: R Eriksen	

A young Mike Procter bats in the nets at Lord's while the man behind the 1966 tour of the United Kingdom, Wilf Isaacs, looks on.

Following the success of the South African Fezela team five years previously, South African businessman and cricket enthusiast Wilf Isaacs sponsored a team which combined experienced players and promising youngsters for a short tour of the United Kingdom. Seventeen games were to be played, against reasonably strong opposition.

The inclusion of former Test players McLean, McGlew, Tayfield, Adcock and Funston formed a solid base to the side, while up-and-coming youngsters such as Richards, Procter, Bruyns, Irvine and Mackay-Coghill were able to draw on the experience of the older players and provide some exciting cricket.

Games were played against strong club sides or Invitation XIs, which included Test players such as Richie Benaud, Dennis Compton, Jim Laker, Richard Hutton and Peter Richardson. The side was too strong for the opposition and the top batsmen usually made sufficient runs without needing the help of the lower order. Runs were scored quickly and attractively with Barry Richards and Mike Procter featuring strongly. Mackay-Coghill, Funston, Irvine and Andre Bruyns also all had a successful tour with the bat. The bowling was led by the veterans Tayfield, Adcock, Cole and Hall, but there were outstanding performances from youngsters Procter, Henwood and Watson. Ferrandi, Irvine and Bruyns were all capable wicket-keepers.

The side was unbeaten throughout the tour and once more the strength of the developing South African youngsters had been underestimated. Wilf Isaacs had provided a useful taste of touring to some players of considerable talent who were likely to provide the core of South African cricket in the future.

TOURING SIDE	
MC Cowdrey (captain) (Kent)	
APE Knott (Kent)	KF Barrington (Surrey)
DL Underwood (Kent)	JH Edrich (Surrey)
DJ Brown (Warwickshire)	PI Pocock (Surrey)
TW Cartwright (Warwickshire)	G Boycott (Yorkshire)
RMH Cottam (Hants)	TW Graveney (Gloucestershire)
JT Murray (Middlesex)	RM Prideaux (Northants)
JA Snow (Sussex)	KWR Fletcher (Essex)

CHAPTER 32

1968/69

PROPOSED MCC TOUR OF SOUTH AFRICA

Cancelled

For some time there had been trouble brewing in the cricket world, but the first intimation of the difficulties immediately ahead came in the summer of 1968 when Rhodesian passport holder Colin Bland was refused permission to participate in a World XI which was to play England.

Later that year the MCC was due to send a team to South Africa. After the MCC touring party had been announced, Cartwright was pronounced unfit and Basil d'Oliveira was chosen in his place – a decision which sparked one of the most unfortunate incidents in the sport's history.

D'Oliveira, classified by the South African government as a Coloured, was born in Cape Town and, frustrated by the government's refusal to allow sport between the race groups, had emigrated to England to play cricket. His success with Worcestershire led to his selection for England in 1966 and a tour of the West Indies in 1966/67. He was in and out of England's Test side against Australia, and was picked as a replacement for the injured Prideaux for the final Test. On the day he scored a magnificent 158 the touring team was chosen, but he was not selected and the selectors gave sound reasons for their decision.

The possibility of non-white players being eligible to play for England had been discussed at length by the South African cricket authorities but the government's policy was not clear. MCC had made their position clear to the South African government, that 'any team to tour South Africa would be chosen on merit and ... if any player chosen were to be rejected by the host country ... the projected tour would be abandoned.'

The then South African prime minister, BJ Vorster, stated his government's position by saying that visiting teams of mixed race would be able to tour South Africa if they were from countries with which South Africa had 'traditional sporting ties' and 'if no political capital was made out of the situation'.

MCC wrote to the South African Cricket Association asking for assurances that no pre-conditions would apply to their choice of team but received no firm answer.

With the announcement of the team the country and MCC was split into factions. The 'D'Oliveira affair' became uglier by the

Basil d'Oliveira, the only person to come out of the affair with dignity.

day, with the selectors' integrity being questioned and special meetings of the MCC called. Politicians and activists on both sides entered the fray and sport in general became a target.

The *News of the World* newspaper announced that they had commissioned D'Oliveira to go to South Africa to report on the matches, which created suspicion in South Africa that political motives were behind the move. This view was reinforced when D'Oliviera was subsequently announced as Cartwright's replacement.

Vorster announced that he was not prepared to accept a team that had been forced upon the people 'with certain political aims.' MCC formally cancelled the tour and quickly organized a tour to Ceylon, India and Pakistan. In the end the MCC team returned early after India refused the necessary exchange guarantee of £20 000 and riots ruined the tour of Pakistan.

A special general meeting of MCC failed to resolve the South African question, but the affair had been a sorry episode and the cancellation of the tour essentially signalled the end of formal cricketing relations between the two countries for over two decades.

CHAPTER 33

1969

SECOND WILFRED ISAACS TOUR OF THE UNITED KINGDOM

Captain: W Isaacs

TOURING SIDE	
W Isaacs (captain)	JHB Waite (vice-captain) (Tvl)
IR Tayfield (Natal)	E Chatterton (Tvl)
RR Collins (Natal)	WR Kerr (Tvl)
PP Henwood (Natal)	JPD Flanagan (Tvl)
MJ Smithyman (Natal)	D Mackay-Coghill (Tvl)
MM Harvey (Natal)	CI Day (NE Tvl)
VAP van der Bijl (Natal)	N Rosendorff (OFS)
RG Pollock (E Province)	A Bruyns (W Province)

Manager: R Eriksen
Assistant manager: T Mortimer

Graeme Pollock bowled at Lord's. Well known in the United Kingdom from the 1965 tour, Pollock's batting was again inspired and elegant.

Wealthy South African businessman Wilf Isaacs once again took a team which included promising young cricketers on tour to England and Ireland. Most of the matches were against club sides but four, against Essex, Oxford University, Surrey and Ireland, were initially regarded as first-class. Strangely, these games were later reclassified. Anti-apartheid demonstrators followed the team and attempted to interrupt most of the games.

Graeme Pollock was dropped off the first ball he received when he went to the crease at 19 for three in the match against Oxford University. He then thrashed the bowling, making the highest score of the season at The Parks, 231 not out, in a total of 351 for seven declared. University captain Goldstein, who dropped Pollock, was out twice to poor shots and the students' batting was poor. At one point, demonstrators sat down on the wicket and had to be removed.

Despite the almost constant threat of interruptions from demonstrators the tour was again a success both on and off the field, and finished with a record of nine wins and one loss. Van der Bijl and Mackay-Coghill were a strong pair of opening bowlers, and Henwood was very successful with his left-arm spinners. There was great depth to the batting and the fielding was keen.

Vintcent van der Bijl, another of the talented young South Africans who was to be denied full international cricket in the years ahead.

TOURING SIDE

A Bacher (captain) (Tvl)	EJ Barlow (W Province)
BL Irvine (Tvl)	GA Chevalier (W Province)
HR Lance (Tvl)	MJ Procter (W Province)
GLG Watson (Tvl)	PM Pollock (E Province)
BA Richards (Natal)	RG Pollock (E Province)
AM Short (Natal)	D Lindsay (NE Tvl)
PHB Trimborn (Natal)	AJ Traicos (Rhodesia)

Manager: JB Plimsoll

CHAPTER 34

1970

PROPOSED SOUTH AFRICA TOUR OF THE UNITED KINGDOM

Cancelled

In the wake of the cancelled tour in 1968, the question of whether the projected tour of the United Kingdom by South African cricketers scheduled for 1970 would go ahead was understandably a much-discussed issue in both England and South Africa.

The Springbok rugby tour of the United Kingdom in 1969 had been almost continuously disrupted by demonstrators and the cost of police protection was high, both in financial terms and in injuries sustained by policemen. The South African Cricket Association was adamant that the tour go ahead, a tour itinerary was agreed upon and a squad chosen to travel.

The MCC asked counties to consult the police in order to assess the security aspects for the games and estimates varied between £7 000 and £10 000 per game, which would have wiped out any anticipated profit due to the counties from the tour.

The rows escalated to debates in the Houses of Parliament and the country was split into 'pro' and 'anti'. Buckingham Palace announced that the Queen would not attend the matches. On 18 May the Cricket Council announced that the tour would take place as planned. The anti-tour faction was outraged and plans to disrupt the tour escalated. British Prime Minister James Callaghan then stepped in and called on the Cricket Council to cancel the tour. In view of this directive from the government, the Council had no choice and the 1970 tour of England by South Africa was cancelled.

A hastily arranged progamme of five 'Tests' against the 'Rest of the World' was arranged as an alternative. The counties called on the government to reimburse them for losses resulting from the cancelled tour, but without success. Formal tours to the United Kingdom had reached an end and South Africa now had to start relying on other means of keeping cricket alive.

Anti-apartheid demonstrators outside Lord's during the 1965 tour. An escalation in such protests was anticipated for the 1970 tour.

CHAPTER 35

1973

FIRST DERRICK ROBINS XI TOUR OF SOUTH AFRICA

Captain: DJ Brown

TOURING SIDE	
DJ Brown (capt) (Warwicks)	
J T Murray (vice-captain) (Middx)	CT Radley (Middlesex)
P Willey (Northants)	MJ Smith (Middlesex)
FC Hayes (Lancashire)	A Long (Surrey)
DP Hughes (Lancashire)	RD Jackman (Surrey)
JH Hampshire (Yorkshire)	DR Turner (Hants)
RDV Knight (Gloucestershire)	RNS Hobbs (Essex)
AS Brown (Gloucestershire)	JK Lever (Essex)
RGD Willis (Warwickshire)	PJ Lewington (Warwickshire)

Manager: JD Bannister
Physiotherapist: J Jennings
Press officer: Brian Johnston

The first Derrick Robins XI to tour South Africa. Back: JK Lever, DP Hughes, DR Turner, RNS Hobbs, CT Radley, MJ Smith; middle: A Brown, A Long, FC Hayes, RGD Willis, RDV Knight, PJ Lewington, B Johnston (press officer); front: JH Hampshire, DJ Brown (capt), D Robins, JD Bannister, JT Murray.

A tour by Bill Lawry's Australians in 1970 displayed the strength of South African cricket when South Africa won all four Tests. Now the future of cricket in the country was in crisis following the isolation of all South African sport.

A side was selected to go to Australia in 1971/72 but this was a meaningless exercise as there was no chance of the tour taking place.

Richards, Procter, Barlow, Peter and Graeme Pollock had all taken part in five hurriedly organized Tests for a 'Rest of the World' side against England, in lieu of the cancelled South African tour.

Several South Africans were playing for the counties, but the standard of cricket in South Africa was in danger of falling without overseas competition. The lack of prospects for promising youngsters was a great concern.

Derrick Robins, a cricket and soccer enthusiast who had played for Warwickshire, was invited by the Transvaal Cricket Union, with

the approval of the South African Cricket Association, to put together an unofficial team of county standard to tour South Africa. Several one-day matches along Gillette Cup rules were scheduled, which promised some exciting cricket for the crowds eager for a taste of international cricket.

David Brown, Murray, Hobbs, Hampshire and Willis had represented England and several of the others were on the fringe of the England side.

The tour started badly with defeats by Eastern Province and Western Province, where Eddie Barlow hit the first century before lunch ever recorded at Newlands. Injuries to Knight and Willey caused Robins to send for Tony Brown of Gloucestershire to join the tourists.

The tourists played better in Johannesburg but Transvaal held out for a draw. Ali Bacher scored a good 147. His partnership of 145 with 19-year-old Jimmy Cook took 99 minutes, with Cook unbeaten on 64. Radley reached his second century of the tour.

An exciting match developed against Natal at Kingsmead when the tourists were left a target of 158 in two hours. Sixty runs were scored in the first hour, leaving a target of 98 in the second. The next 14 overs added 65 runs and with two overs to go, 14 runs were needed. Seven runs were needed off the last over and only a single was possible off the first four balls. Hayes hit a four off the penultimate ball and required two off the last ball. Hayes opened his shoulders and hit a four for a sensational victory which reminded everyone of the famous England Test result on the same ground when Gladwin scored off the last ball.

A Combined B Section XI played at Pretoria but a promising match faded into a draw.

The injury-hit Robins side called on Jackman to add spice to the attack for the game against an invitation side at Johannesburg. Some 6 500 watched Barry Richards hit a century in full flight. Irvine scored 53 in a partnership of 127 with Richards, then Procter was caught just when he appeared to be taking the bowling to pieces. Bruyns and young Kenny McEwen came together in a partnership of 111. Bruyns went on to 97 in a total of 387 for nine. Procter had both openers out with the score on seven and the only partnership of note was between Hampshire and Hayes for 46. The procession ended with the score on 118. Bacher enforced the follow-on and the carnage continued in the worst batting of the tour. The Robins side were dismissed for 152 to lose by an innings and 117 runs with over a day to spare. 16 639 spectators watched the match on the Saturday and were treated to superb fast bowling and excellent fielding. To fill the extra day, a 60-over match was played which the invitation side also won.

The experimental Robins tour was a success in spite of the lack of warm-up matches. The cricket public flocked to watch and the South African cricketers proved their worth.

The following Robins tours were eagerly awaited.

CHAPTER 36

1973

SECOND DERRICK ROBINS TOUR OF SOUTH AFRICA

Captain: DB Close

Enormous excitement was generated in South Africa by the inclusion of 'non-white' players in the touring team, with government approval. Efforts were made through the tourists to extend the game into other areas, but local cricket administration remained divided.

Wicket-keeper Murray returns to the pavilion as John Lever walks out to face the South African Invitation XI. In the the series of unofficial 'Tests' the South African team beat the Robins XI by one match to nil.

The side chosen for Robins' second tour was surprising, given the fact that two non-white players, Younis Ahmed of Pakistan and John Shepherd of West Indies, were included. Both risked life suspension from their National Boards of Control.

South African government sanctions had been required for their presence, as had the presence of Pakistani Test stars Mushtaq Mohammad and Intikhab Alam, together with Gary Sobers, for a Datsun double-wicket competition earlier in the season.

However, Hassan Howa, spokesman for the non-white cricket community, was not granted permission to leave the country to state the views of his community.

The segregation of spectators by race groups at grounds had

TOURING SIDE	
DB Close (captain) (Somerset)	BC Francis (Australia)
RE East (Essex)	JW Gleeson (Australia)
JK Lever (Essex)	JN Shepherd (Kent/West Indies)
JH Edrich (Surrey)	Younis Ahmed (Surrey/Pakistan)
GRJ Roope (Surrey)	GW Johnson (Kent)
P Lee (Lancashire)	RA Woolmer (Kent)
JA Snow (Sussex)	MJ Smith (Middlesex)
RW Tolchard (Leicestershire)	JT Murray (Middlesex)
Manager: LEG Ames	

ended but this was no indication that the integration of South African cricket was assured.

Unlike the previous tour, the itinerary included several warm-up matches before meeting the major sides.

The side flew from London on 15 October 1973.

For the first time ever, a touring side played at the Moroka-Jabatu Stadium in Soweto, near Johannesburg, against a SA African XI. Both Roope and Edrich scored centuries in the Robins' score of 359 and the African side were beaten comfortably. Orange Free State and Griqualand West were both beaten in matches played under Gillette Cup rules. All the warm-up matches had been won convincingly by the tourists.

The first first-class match was played against Western Province at Cape Town. Ackerman hit three sixes and 27 fours in a magnificent 179 not out. Western Province declared on 286 for four. Then the Province bowlers had a torrid time. Francis went on to 194 and Edrich joined him with a partnership of 202. Edrich scored 118 and the Robins Eleven declared on 375 for four, a lead of 89. Three hours were lost to rain but this made no difference to the result which was obviously heading for a draw.

An important aspect of the series of Derrick Robins tours was to promote the game itself, and an interest in the game, in disadvantaged areas.

The South African Invitation XI which played the Derrick Robins XI at Kingsmead. Back: AJS Smith , PD Swart, VAP van der Bijl, RW Hanley, HM Ackerman, AL Biggs; front: JH du Preez, BA Richards, EJ Barlow (capt), GB Payn (manager), RG Pollock, MJ Procter, BL Irvine.

Close had his best innings of the tour with 72 and Gleeson took five wickets in beating Border in a 60-overs match.

The government had to give permission for play on Sunday, but rain washed out the first day of the match against Natal. In spite of declarations by both Close and Richards, the match fizzled out into a draw.

Irvine, Mackay-Coghill, Muzzell and Rice were not playing for Transvaal against the tourists. No-one was outstanding in the Transvaal's innings but when Younis Ahmed came to the crease he hit a scintillating 123. Then Shepherd pulverized the bowling. His partnership of 50 with Tolchard took 19 minutes with Tolchard scoring only a single. Transvaal were beaten by eight wickets.

Eastern Province were also beaten by eight wickets. Pollock scored nine and two, while Gleeson and Snow took 13 wickets.

The first of three 'Mini Tests' was played at Newlands against a South African Invitation XI. Bacher had announced his retirement and Barlow took his place as captain. Richards and Barlow got the side off to a good start with a partnership of 98, and the Invitation

XI went on to 278 with 76 from Ackerman. Johnson and Edrich were out early, but Francis and Roope withstood the Procter onslaught so that the South African score was passed with the loss of only six wickets. The Robins XI scored 329 in their first innings. Richards with 81, and Barlow with 54, again got the side off to a good start with a century partnership. Ackerman scored 56 and Barlow declared at 287 for eight with a lead of 237. Francis, Johnson and Younis lost their wickets and with rain interrupting play, Close abandoned any hope of forcing a win.

Kingsmead was the scene of the second 'Mini Test' with an unchanged Invitation XI. Surprisingly, Tich Smith kept wicket in lieu of Irvine. Gleeson broke down in the previous match and was replaced by Lee in the Robins XI. Edrich played a very patient innings of 170, outliving eight partners. Close and Murray scored 50s and Close declared at 383 for nine. Barlow and Richards put on 90 for the first wicket. Richards went on to 180 but the Invitation XI trailed by 42 runs when last man Van der Bijl joined Smith. The last wicket put on 113 with 81 from Smith. Van der Bijl scored his highest

first-class total and his first 50. The South Africans' 454 all out was sufficient to ensure a drawn match.

Smith was dropped and Irvine restored to the wicket-keeping position for the third 'Mini Test' at Johannesburg. Hanley came into the side as a fast bowler and Henwood replaced Du Preez. Gleeson was still injured and there was sensation when Robins announced that Snow had been dropped 'for disciplinary reasons'.

Barlow won the toss and asked the Robins XI to bat on a pitch which suited his bowlers. Swart took three of the first four wickets, then Roope and Close steadied the side. But it was Shepherd again, with two sixes and five fours, who scored 42 of the 43 runs in a ninth-wicket partnership for a declaration at 227 for nine. Once more, the South Africans got off to a good start with 59 from Richards in a partnership of 115, then Irvine joined Barlow in a stand of 146 in two hours. Irvine scored 125 and Procter 54, but Barlow went on to 211, one short of his highest ever score, having been dropped on five. The Invitation XI's massive 528 for eight was too much for the Robins XI and they were bowled out for 218 to lose by an innings and 83 runs with a day to spare. Rain unfortunately prevented any play in a scheduled one-day match in New Brighton, outside Port Elizabeth, against an African XI.

The tour did not display a true reflection of the strength of South African cricket, but the loss of form by Pollock and Procter was surprising. Van der Bijl was the exception, and looked the only one to have international pretensions. The opening partnerships between Richards and Barlow were first class.

Andre Bruyns turns the ball down the leg side batting for the South African Invitation XI against the Derrick Robins XI at the Wanderers.

181

FOURTH TOURING SIDE

D Lloyd (captain) (Lancashire)	GA Cope (Yorkshire)
PG Lee (Lancashire)	P Carrick (Yorkshire)
FC Hayes (Lancashire)	DW Randall (Nottinghamshire)
PA Slocombe (Somerset)	RW Tolchard (Leicestershire)
DS Steele (Northhants)	GP Howarth (Surrey)
M Hendrick (Derby)	TM Chappell (Australia)
GB Troup (New Zealand)	JR Douglas (Australia)
FJ Titmus (Middlesex)	DF Whatmore (Australia)

Manager: KF Barrington

THIRD TOURING SIDE

B Close (captain) (Somerset)	
C Radley (Middlesex)	J Lyon (Lancashire)
S Turner (Essex)	F Hayes (Lancashire)
B Francis (Essex)	T Greig (Sussex)
S Rouse (Warwickshire)	J Shepherd (Kent)
E Hemmings (Warwickshire)	Younis Ahmed (Surrey)
RW Tolchard (Leicestershire)	M Walker (Australia)
J Hampshire (Yorkshire)	T Jenner (Australia)

Manager: KF Barrington

The Third Derrick Robins Team to visit South Africa, in 1975. Back: Y Ahmed, C Radley, S Turner, A Greig, M Walker, S Rouse, B Francis, F Hayes, R Tolchard; middle: T Jenner, D Bennet (assistant manager), B Close (capt), DH Robins, K Barrington (manager), J Hampshire, J Shepherd; front: E Hemmings, J Lyon.

CHAPTER 37

1975/76

THIRD AND FOURTH
DERRICK ROBINS XI TOURS
OF SOUTH AFRICA
Captains: DB Close and D Lloyd

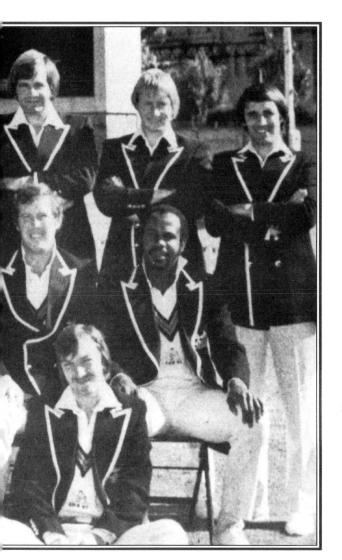

Derrick Robins brought a side to South Africa in 1975, but with such players as Max Walker and Younis Ahmed the team was moving away from being a side representing the English counties and taking on a more international flavour. Robins then took a side to the West Indies, where two of the governments there banned his participation because of his South African connection. Nevertheless, he organized and went ahead with a fourth tour to South Africa.

The original intention was to include only those players who were under 25 years of age, but this proved impractical and the side included several players who were on the fringe of international sides. Titmus joined the party when both Hendrick and Cope dropped out through injury.

Although not to be compared with official tours, Derrick Robins provided the South African public with international cricket at a time when it was much needed.

In a return to the origins of touring, entrepreneurs saw possibilities in South Africa's isolation and tours began to be organized from all quarters. It was to be only a few weeks before another side arrived in South Africa, this time known as the International Wanderers.

Cricketers became intent on making money out of the game, a motivation soon to be aggravated by the Packer 'Revolution'.

CHAPTER 38

1977

THE PACKER
AFFAIR

*The Australian television entrepreneur Kerry
Packer revolutionized cricket throughout the
world, both in the way the game was
promoted and played, and in the way cricketers
were paid. The MCC lost its traditional grip
over the organization of the game for the first
time since 1903.*

Tony Greig, right, celebrating an England victory with his successor as captain, Mike Brearley, left. South African-born Greig led the break from English cricket to Kerry Packer's World Series, and also used his connections to recruit players from South Africa.

Although the revolution against the cricketing establishment created by Kerry Packer was primarily concerned with Australia, it quickly spread around the world and had a profound effect on the game everywhere, including South Africa and England.

A Cricketers' Association was formed in England in 1968 to look after the interests of professional cricketers as well as to further the development of the game. It was supported by virtually every county cricketer playing in England and provided them with a voice when dealing with the establishment.

The historic divide between professional and amateur cricketers had ended and now the majority of English cricketers depended on the game for their livelihood. Sponsorship was growing and the cricketers looked with envy on the fortunes being made by other sportsmen such as golfers and tennis players.

Kerry Packer took over the reins of his father's newspaper and television empire in 1974, and tried to negotiate exclusive rights for televising the Centenary Tests to be held in Australia in 1977. He failed, and decided to organize his own competition outside the jurisdiction of the Australian Board of Control.

Working with a sports agency, JP Sport, Packer secretly signed-up 35 international players for a three-year contract to play matches in what was to be called the World Series. The

first hint that this had occurred was in the South African *Sunday Times* on 24 April 1977, when it was announced that Eddie Barlow, Denys Hobson, Graeme Pollock, Mike Procter and Barry Richards had all signed contracts to play.

When the official announcement was made on 9 May, the squad included 18 Australians, five South Africans, four Englishmen, four West Indians and four Pakistanis. The England captain, South African-born Tony Greig, was to lead the World XI, while Australian captain Greg Chappell would lead the Australian side in five 'Tests', six one-day matches and six three-day matches.

Talks begun between the ICC and Packer broke down and threats that players would be punished were challenged in court. It was pointed out that cricketers' earnings were low. Greig earned under £10 000 per annum, Mike Procter £7 500, and Jon Snow £4 000. Allan Knott expected to earn £11 500 from cricket in 1977, and had been forced to sign on as unemployed following the cancellation of the South African tour. The England team's Test match appearance money was even increased from £210 to £1 000 as a result of Packer's challenge, but this was still felt to be insufficient.

Packer's proposals, on the other hand, were offering substantial rewards to cricketers. The court challenge ended with the threats to the players being held to amount to an unreasonable restraint of trade and the decision went in favour the players. Packer's plans escalated and 50 players signed contracts.

For the World Series, cricket's laws, which were copyright of the MCC, were to be changed and matches would be played under floodlights. As regular cricket grounds were unavailable, matches were to be played on rugby and football grounds with pitches pre-fabricated in greenhouses on concrete bases and inserted by cranes. Following one settling-down season, the World Series circus proved successful and became a significant influence on the way cricket was played and organized.

Steps were taken to bring the two sides together. Packer was given exclusive rights to televise Australian matches and the Packer disruption appeared to be at an end. A month later, the Australian Cricket Board announced a 10-year contract between themselves and a Packer subsidiary, PBL Sports Pty Limited. The board agreed to the use of grounds and would be responsible for choosing Australian teams, but promotion of Australian cricket would be the responsibility of PBL.

Cigarette manufacturers Benson and Hedges came in to provide sponsorship for a World Series Cup, which was to be played between two overseas teams and Australia. Substantial prize money was made available, and coloured clothing and a 30-yard fielding circle were to be introduced as an experiment for one-day matches.

The ICC accepted the Australian board's proposals but the English Test and County Cricket Board, concerned about the dan-

Garth le Roux of Western Province, who shot to superstardom in the World Series, winning the first Man of the Series award.

ger to Test matches, objected and stated that no 'abnormal conditions' such as coloured clothing would be acceptable, and that the 'Ashes' would not be at stake. The Australians treated the latter announcement with derision.

One-day games, providing instant results and aimed at a new breed of cricket followers through television, proliferated. They attracted huge crowds at the expense of the traditional games, and brought in substantial funds to the clubs. Soon, one-day cricket became a means of subsidizing the traditional game. Control over the marketing of cricket also passed out of the hands of the establishment for the first time since the MCC took over the role in 1903. Throughout the world cricket would not be the same again.

South Africans took to the one-day and day-night limited-overs matches immediately, and amateur South African cricketers and administrators realized there was money to be made out of the sport. Western Province played several matches at the football stadium in Green Point before it became obvious that this was unsatisfactory and floodlights were installed at all the major grounds. On the field defensive bowling combined with superb fielding and unorthodox shots to change the pattern of the game, but exciting finishes became the order of the day, and cricket had entered a new era.

Kerry Packer and Tony Greig arrive to begin their battle over players' contracts at the High Court in London in September 1977.

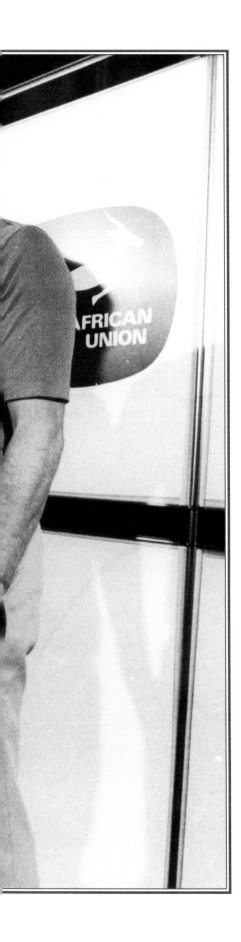

CHAPTER 39

1981/82

SAB TOUR TO SOUTH AFRICA

Captain: GA Gooch

Cricket throughout the world was affected by politicians and attitudes towards the South African government. Cheque-book diplomacy started to have an influence and in spite of the threat of bans, rebel tours started to make their way to South Africa.

Graham Gooch, the Essex and England opener who agreed to lead the SAB team to South Africa. The team, which contained most of the official English squad which had toured India, did not live up to expectations. Gooch was by far the team's most effective batsman.

TOURING SIDE	
GA Gooch (captain) (Essex)	G Boycott (Yorkshire)
JK Lever (Essex)	CM Old (Yorkshire)
JE Emburey (Middlesex)	DL Underwood (Kent)
DL Amiss (Warwickshire)	APE Knott (Kent)
M Hendrick (Derby)	W Larkins (Northhants)
LB Taylor (Leicestershire)	P Willey (Northhants)

They were joined by three players already in South Africa:
GW Humpage (Warwickshire)   RA Woolmer (Kent)
A Sidebottom (Yorkshire)

Vintcent van der Bijl, though nearing the end of his career, was still a force in both English county cricket and in the series against the SAB XI.

World-wide reaction against the apartheid policy of the South African government led to a sports boycott which affected cricket throughout the world. Frustrated South African cricketers left South Africa to play in other countries and became the backbone of many overseas teams. During the 1980 season in England, 23 South Africans and Zimbabweans played first-class cricket. South Africans Alan Lamb, Kepler Wessels and Peter Kirsten headed the English batting averages and Vintcent van der Bijl headed the bowling averages. Over the years a number of players, such as Lamb, the Greig brothers, the Smith brothers and Wessels, left South Africa and qualified to play for their adopted countries.

All teams containing players with South African connections were banned from touring. The MCC's West Indies tour in 1981 was interrupted when Robin Jackman, who had played in South Africa, was refused entry to some of the West Indian islands. The difficulties implementing such policies was shown later when, in 1984, the West Indies threatened to cancel their tour of England if any players with South African connections were chosen to play against them. It was pointed out that this involved 82 players and that literally every side had players who had played or coached in South Africa, and the threat was dropped.

The three main South African cricket factions, the multi-racial South African Cricket Union (SACU), the South African Control Board (SAACB), and the predominantly Indian and Coloured South African Control Board (SACB),were unable to unite as one body. Ludicrous situations arose whereby black sides were admitted to the Gillette Cup competition for the first round only. This was permitted on condition that they played against Natal in the first round but were not allowed to progress further in the competition, whatever the result! South African cricketers walked off the field in protest against the situation but the government's attitude did not change.

Repeated attempts by South Africa in the 1970s and early 1980s to obtain readmission to the ICC proved unsuccessful. The South African Cricket Union responded by stating that if this was the case it would be compelled to use 'cheque-book diplomacy' to ensure the future of South African cricket.

This led to the formation of rebel sides consisting of players who were prepared to play anywhere for cash and felt that they had little to lose. The popularity of the one-day, instant-result matches attracted the attentions of sponsors and television producers, who were prepared to offer incentives to those prepared to risk official cricket censure.

It was in this atmosphere that the South African Breweries agreed to sponsor a tour of South Africa by a rebel side consisting of most of the official English team. The English side had completed an unsatisfactory tour of India, during which the Indian government threatened to cancel the tour if Boycott and Cook, who had played

Barry Richards, so starved of international cricket during the prime of his career, was unable to show the SAB tourists the full force of his talents.

Mike Procter, who captained the South Africans at the start of the 'Test' series against Gooch's team, but was later injured.

in South Africa, were included. Boycott left India early complaining of stomach cramps.

Four days after returning home, most of the MCC side were on the plane to Johannesburg. The team, led by Graham Gooch, tried to recruit Alvin Kallicharran, who was under contract to Transvaal, but this move failed. The strength of the team was such that only the absence of Botham and Willis prevented the side from being regarded as a full England squad. The South African Cricket Union declared that the matches played against the tourists would be regarded as full Tests and that caps would be awarded to the South Africans taking part.

As soon as the announcement of the rebels' departure for South Africa had been made, the Indian government threatened to cancel their team's forthcoming tour to the United Kingdom if any of the rebels involved were chosen to play for England. Officials from English county Northamptonshire demanded the withdrawal of the rebels' county registrations. The British government were asked to condemn the tour and the touring party, but they refused to do so.

The first warm-up match was played against a South African Under-25 side in Pretoria. Adrian Kuiper took five for 22 in the SAB XI's first innings but the game petered out into a draw. Gooch scored the first century of the tour with 117, and Amiss scored 71 not out, in a total of 240 for five in a 50-overs match against South Africa at Newlands in Cape Town. South Africa knocked off the runs in 47,2 overs with 82 from Cook, 62 from Richards, and 57 not out from Pollock.

The opening first-class fixture was against Western Province. Kuiper scored 90 in a first innings score of 263 for eight declared, and the SAB XI batted reasonably in reply with 50s from Amiss and Gooch but could only make 219. Jefferies and Hobson took the wickets. Jefferies went in early to force the pace and scored a quick 45, while Peter Kirsten's 67 allowed a declaration at 204 for seven, leaving a target of 249. Boycott was run out for 95, but the match was left drawn with the visitors on 225 for eight. Lever injured himself in the match and could not bat, while Emburey broke his thumb and could take no further part in the tour, a blow which considerably weakened the English team's attack.

The first 'Test' match was played in Johannesburg. Mike Procter won the toss and decided to bat. Richards with 66 and Cook with 114 put on 117 for the first wicket, then Kirsten added 88 for the score to bring it to 278 for two. Pollock added 64 but the others collapsed and a declaration came at 400 for seven. Only Amiss with 66 and Gooch with 30 reached double figures in the SAB XI's innings of 150 as Van der Bijl took five for 25. In the follow on Gooch and Boycott put on 119 before Boycott was out for 36. Gooch went on to 109, but no-one could stay with him and the side were all out for 283, Van der Bijl taking another five wickets to finish the match with 10 for 104. South Africa lost Richards and Cook in knocking off the 37 runs to win by eight wickets.

A 50-overs match was played against South Africa in Durban, but the SAB XI were easily beaten with Van der Bijl taking three for 19. Rain allowed only three hours play on the first day in the four-day match against South Africa at Cape Town. Once more Gooch was top scorer, but he received little support. Van der Bijl and Jefferies each took three wickets and Alan Kourie four for 52. Kirsten hit a glorious century for South Africa but no-one supported him and South Africa were bowled out for 253 by Lever with six wickets and Taylor with three. In the SAB XI's second innings Boycott failed again, but Gooch added 68 to his first innings 83 and his partnership with Larkins put on 104. Larkins went on to his century and Gooch declared at 249 for three. Kuiper and Jennings opened and the match was called off with the score on 38 without loss for a draw.

The final four-day match was played at Durban and Gooch put South Africa in to bat on a green wicket. Richards scored 41 but no-one else did much until Kourie hit 50 not out and the South Africans declared on 181 for nine. Gooch and Boycott gave the tourists a reasonable start, before Amiss scored 50 and Woolmer 100 to allow Gooch to declare on 311 for eight. Rain interfered with play with the South Africans on 143 for two when the match was called off as a draw.

Unfortunately for the South African public, the cricket did not live up to expectations and the crowds did not support the matches. The England players did not play to their capabilities and only Gooch was prominent. South African cricket showed that it could hold its own but cracks were beginning to appear.

Procter eventually withdrew from the series with injury, while Pollock and Richards were shadows of their former selves. Kirsten,

Cook, Jefferies, Kourie and Van der Bijl were impressive.

Before the tour was concluded, the Test and County Cricket Board announced that the participants of the tour would be banned from Test cricket for three years, which was to affect English cricket profoundly in that time. The rebel players were paid on a sliding scale ranging from £10 000 to £40 000 each for their participation in the one-month tour.

South African authorities announced that, in future, two overseas players would be allowed in each Castle Currie Cup side so that several players in the rebel squad could return to join South African sides in the near future.

Meanwhile, two more hastily arranged rebel tours were announced, by Sri Lankan and West Indian sides.

Gooch found the pressures of leading the rebel team high as they provided a focus for heated debate surrounding the sports boycott of South Africa.

CHAPTER 40

ENGLISH XI TOUR OF
SOUTH AFRICA

Captain: MW Gatting

*Further attempts by the South African cricket
authorities to rejoin the ICC were unsuccessful
and controversial rebel tours by an English
team under Mike Gatting were announced.
The South African government's announcement
of startling changes in early 1990 led to the
eventual abandonment of the tours.*

The English XI under Mike Gatting faced a barrage of demonstrators and disruptions wherever they travelled in South Africa. Here the staff of the Sandton Sun Hotel in Johannesburg protest against the team's presence at the hotel.

There was no tour during the 1988-89 season in South Africa and attention was focused on the Currie Cup and the Test Centenary celebrations. A new pavilion was built at St George's Park, the site of the first Test, and hundreds of influential administrators from all over the world were invited to see the progress being made in developing cricket among disadvantaged race groups.

South African Cricket Union President Geoff Dakin, former President Joe Pamensky and Chief Executive Ali Bacher went to England in June 1989 with a request that they be allowed to attend the meeting of the ICC, but it was again denied.

TOURING SIDE	
MW Gatting (captain) (Middlesex)	GR Dilley (Worcestershire)
BC Broad (Nottinghamshire)	CS Cowdrey (Kent)
RT Robinson (Nottinghamshire)	CWJ Athey (Gloucestershire)
KJ Barnett (Derby)	MP Maynard (Glamorgan)
JE Emburey (Middlesex)	BN French (Nottinghamshire)
NA Foster (Essex)	RM Ellison (Kent)
PW Jarvis (Yorkshire)	DA Graveney (Gloucestershire)

The ICC announced the automatic ban for defined periods, depending on the age of the culprits, on any cricketer contracting for future tours of South Africa. Dr Ali Bacher was, however, allowed to address the gathering at the annual *Wisden* dinner and spoke of the rapid developments taking place in South Africa. He warned those present that 'If South Africa was not to be granted tours through the front door it would be forced to use the back door.' He also promised that 'Out of Africa will come something new. It will be dazzling, it will be strong and it will be good.'

Mike Gatting, the England captain, had been named in allegations of impropriety during a Test match and deprived of the captaincy of the England team. Ironically, the position was given to Graham Gooch, who had been banned for leading the previous side to South Africa. Gatting was also fined £5 000 for publishing a book that had not been sanctioned by the Test and County Cricket Board and he asked not to be considered for the remaining Tests in England, nor for the coming tour of India.

In the event, the tour of India was cancelled when the Indian government refused to grant visas to the eight players who had appeared in South Africa. It was in this atmosphere that a contract for two tours to South Africa by English cricketers, to be led by Gatting, was announced. The announcement was made immediately before the deadline required by the English selectors on players' availability for a tour of the West Indies.

All the players in Gatting's line-up, except Graveney, had played Test cricket. Five county captains were included. The initial side included Butcher and De Freitas, but they asked to be released from their contracts when political pressure was placed on them. Their place was taken by Greg Thomas, who was playing for Eastern Province, and Alan Wells of Sussex. Wells headed the batting averages in England at the time, followed by five southern Africans and Mike Gatting.

The announcement caused major problems for the English selectors, faced with choosing a side for the West Indies tour, and outrage from the anti-tour faction both inside and outside South Africa.

The first match was played at the De Beers Country Club from 26–28 January against a Combined Bowl XI. The visitors soon showed their strength. as Graveney and Emburey took 18 of the 20 wickets to fall and the Bowl side were easily beaten.

At Springbok Park in Bloemfontein, Hansie Cronje, captain of the Universities XI, scored a century, while Terence Lazard scored 87 in the first innings, but rain intervened and saved the tourists when they were in trouble.

Batsmen dominated the match against a South African Invitation XI at Pietermaritzburg. Mark Rushmere achieved the distinction of being the only South African to score 150 without being dismissed in both innings. He was on the field throughout the match. Rain again prevented a result – the Invitation XI had scored

The South African team which played the English XI in 1990. Back: BM McMillan, AA Donald, RF Pienaar, DB Rundle, KC Wessels, RP Snell, RK McGlashan (12th man), T Boven (physio); front: RV Jennings, AP Kuiper, NAT Adcock (manager), SJ Cook (capt), PN Kirsten, H Fotheringham.

Jimmy Cook, captain of the South African team at the time of the tour, and a prolific batsman for both Transvaal and Somerset.

at Durban. However it was Barnett, along with Emburey, who bowled economically and troubled the South Africans. Rice and Madsen put on 76 together as the South African total reached 219. Athey and Barnett gave the visitors a good start with 94 in 30 overs then Kuiper and Rice put the brakes on. The innings ran out of steam and French, with Thomas, surprisingly made no attempt to go for the 14 runs required off the last over. Barnett with three for 33 and 76 was man of the match.

Adrian Kuiper then played one of the most remarkable innings ever seen in the match at Springbok Park, Bloemfontein. Cook scored 73, and Kirsten 40, to give the South Africans a good start. Kuiper came in next, took one over to settle down, then hit 19 off Ellison and 20 off Greg Thomas. He eventually scored 117, with his century coming off 49 balls with eight sixes and seven fours. Suffering from exhaustion, his last 17 came with only one four in 17 balls. Following the onslaught, Allan Donald and Fanie de Villiers soon had the England XI struggling on 23 for four. Rice, Shaw, and then Kuiper with two wickets, had them reeling at 63 for nine. Athey and Ellison lived dangerously scoring 31 for the last wicket but the English XI lost by a massive 207 runs. Adrian Kuiper was the obvious man of the match.

a total of 620 for the loss of only four wickets, and a total of 1 110 runs were scored in the match for the loss of 14 wickets.

The pitch at the Wanderers for the first 'Test' came in for criticism when Donald and Snell demolished the tourists for 156 in their first innings. Fotheringham, Wessels and Kirsten were out early, quickly followed by Cook and McMillan, leaving South Africa on 77 for five. Kuiper was dropped with his score on nine, as he went on to 84 in a beautiful innings and with support from Jennings and Rundle brought the score to 203.

Donald had Broad for no score, McMillan had Athey and Robinson out cheaply, then Kuiper clean-bowled Gatting for a duck and the tourists found themselves in trouble. They were all out for 122, with a lead of only 75 runs. Cook and Fotheringham saw off most of the deficit, Wessels failed for the second time in the match but Kuiper came in to see South Africa to victory by seven wickets inside three days.

A series of one-day internationals followed, with the first at Centurion Park, Verwoerdburg. Fanie de Villiers and Richard Snell bowled well but the English XI made a reasonable 217 in their 50 overs. Cook and Pienaar added 60 in 17 overs before Kuiper hit out for 37, leaving Rice and Madsen to finish off the match and seal a comfortable victory.

Injuries struck the Englishmen, causing Gatting to bat lower in the order, while Barnett suffered cramps in the second international

Adrian Kuiper, perhaps the most explosive cricketer in South Africa, who played some astonishing cricket against the English XI.

Mike Gatting flanked by tour organisers Geoff Dakin (left) and Ali Bacher on his team's arrival in South Africa. Three weeks into the controversial tour major changes were announced in South Africa, and the English cricketers eventually returned home before the scheduled tour was finished.

After suffering such an embarrassing defeat in the previous match, the English XI pulled themselves together in the final match at the Wanderers. Barnett took 15 off Fanie de Villiers' first over and 50 runs came off 8 overs. Barnett took only 34 balls for his first 50 then went on to a century off 105 balls. Bill Athey added 118 with Barnett and the England XI made a total of 296 in their 55 overs. In reply Fotheringham made 58 and Kirsten 52, but no-one else managed to get into double figures as Gatting brought himself on and bowled a wonderful spell of six for 26 in 6,2 overs. The South Africans were thoroughly beaten by 134 runs, but they had won the series fairly easily by three matches to one. Not surprisingly Kuiper was named man of the series.

The tour generated enormous pressures on the tourists. Demonstrators constantly made their presence known and Mike Gatting, in particular, became a target. He handled the pressures well and insisted that his democratic right was to seek employment wherever and whenever he chose.

On 2 February, two matches into the tour, President de Klerk had announced sweeping changes to the political scene that surprised the public and led to a surge of optimism for the future.

Eventually it was accepted that the continuation of the tour was likely to cause further embarrassment to the government, cricket administrators and the public. An announcement was made that the tour was to be curtailed and the proposed second tour, due to take place later in the season, was cancelled.

CHAPTER 41

1991

SOUTH AFRICA'S RETURN TO NORMAL CRICKET

The South African Cricket Board and the South African Cricket Union eventually settled their differences and came together under the banner of the United Cricket Board of South Africa on 29 June 1991.

A few days later, a delegation from the board, including Geoff Dakin, Krish Mackerdhuj, Ali Bacher and the African National Congress's Steve Tshwete, arrived in London to seek readmittance to the ICC as a full member. This was granted on 10 July 1991.

On 23 October 1991, Sir Colin Cowdrey announced that the International Cricket Conference had accepted the United Cricket Board of South Africa's application to participate in the World Cup, to be held in Australia and New Zealand in 1992.

Geoff Dakin, Krish Mackerdhuj, Percy Sonn and Ali Bacher went to Sri Lanka, Pakistan and India on a goodwill tour and to watch the Test series between India and Pakistan. When Pakistan cancelled the tour, South Africa was invited by India, previously a staunch opponent of South Africa's policies, to take Pakistan's place.

As one of the conditions attached to the amalgamation, it was agreed to drop the use of the term 'Springbok' and the use of the national flag. Instead, South African teams would play under the banner of the United Cricket Board of Control.

For the first time ever, the way was open for South Africans to play against every cricket-loving nation of the world. South African cricket had arrived at the most exciting period in its history.

CHAPTER 42

1993/94

ENGLAND 'A' SIDE TOUR OF SOUTH AFRICA

Captain: H Morris

The second-string England side exposed the lack of depth in South African cricket below the main Test squad. The tourists only lost one match against provincial sides and drew against a South African 'A' side.

Young Orange Free State batsman Rudi Steyn, who was one of the few South Africans to make a strong claim for future promotion during the England 'A' side tour. He scored 80 against the tourists playing for Orange Free State and 69 in the 'mini-Test' at Port Elizabeth.

While the full South African national side was in Australia, a team of young England 'hopefuls' made an extensive tour of South Africa and played a series of first-class matches against the provinces. One-day matches were also played in the disadvantaged areas of Alexandra, Zwide and Langa as part of the development programme, and against Western Transvaal, Eastern Transvaal and Griqualand West. The short tour concluded with a five-day match against a South African 'A' side in a 'mini-Test' at Port Elizabeth.

The side proved too strong for the provincial sides, somewhat weakened with their top players in Australia, beating Transvaal, Eastern Province, Western Province,

TOURING SIDE	
H Morris (captain) (Glamorgan)	AP Wells (vice-captain) (Sussex)
RDB Croft (Glamorgan)	JP Crawley (Lancashire)
A Dale (Glamorgan)	MP Bicknell (Surrey)
DG Cork (Derby)	D Gough (Yorkshire)
MC Ilott (Essex)	MN Lathwell (Somerset)
PM Such (Essex)	MB Loye (Northhants)
MJ McCague (Kent)	SJ Rhodes (Worcestershire)
Tour manager: Bob Bennett	
Team manager: PA Neale	

Northern Transvaal, Orange Free State and Border. The one match which they lost was against Natal, while the match against a South African 'A' side in Port Elizabeth was drawn.

A pedestrian first day, with South African runs coming at less

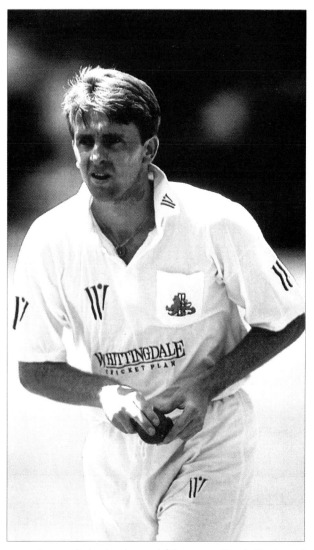

Dominic Cork, who along with fellow tourists Gough, Rhodes and Crawley, went on to make a significant impact in the full England side.

Hugh Morris, the experienced Glamorgan opener, captained an England 'A' side which contained an impressive range of talent.

than two per over, set the course of the Port Elizabeth match. Gerhardus Liebenberg made 79 and Eric Simons 88, but Crookes and Pringle brought the score up to 357. After losing two quick wickets, Wells and Loye shut out any chance of a breakthrough. Wells went on to 130 and the England 'A' side made 329. In the South African second innings Rudolph Steyn made 69 and Cook and Kuiper reached the 40s but wickets fell and South Africa 'A' could only set a target of 250 in 65 overs. Aubrey Martyn broke through but England 'A' shut up shop to force a draw and ended well short but safe on 120 for four.

The young side showed the depth of the English talent but no South Africans really enhanced their potential as a result of the visitors' tour. In spite of good performances by the visitors, the matches were poorly attended. The highlight of the tour was a record 286 by John Crawley against Eastern Province.

CHAPTER 43

1994

FOURTEENTH SOUTH AFRICA TOUR OF THE UNITED KINGDOM

Captain: KC Wessels

The South African team was much in demand around the world and a tired side left for the United Kingdom. After an emotional victory at Lord's and a draw in Leeds, the side collapsed at the Oval and lost the following one-day matches. It was a disappointing conclusion to a long-awaited tour.

Devon Malcolm, the Derbyshire and England fast bowler, during his dramatic spell of nine for 57 in the South African second innings at the Oval. It was the sixth-best return in Test cricket history.

TOURING SIDE

KC Wessels (E Province) (captain)	WJ Cronje (v-c) (OFS)
DJ Richardson (E Province)	AA Donald (OFS)
TG Shaw (E Province)	GFJ Liebenberg (OFS)
BM McMillan (W Province)	AC Hudson (Natal)
CR Matthews (W Province)	PL Symcox (Natal)
A Martyn (W Province)	JN Rhodes (Natal)
G Kirsten (W Province)	PS de Villiers (N Tvl)
PN Kirsten (Border)	R Snell (Tvl)

Manager: F Bing
Assistant manager: Mustapha Khan
Coach: MJ Procter
Physiotherapist: Craig Smith

Twenty-nine years after the successful tour by the side led by Peter van der Merwe, and on the 100th anniversary of the first tour, an official South African side departed for the United Kingdom. Democratic elections had taken place peacefully in South Africa in April 1994 and, for the first time, the side could truly claim to have the support of all South Africans. The country had a colourful new flag and the team sported a new emblem in the form of a King Protea.

The two youngsters, Gerhardus Liebenberg and Aubrey Martyn, promised hope for the future and two spinners in Tim Shaw and Pat Symcox were included in the squad. Unfortunately for Martyn, he had to return home without playing a match because of a troublesome back.

The side flew out on 17 June for a few days' practice at Lord's before a warm-up match against the Earl of Carnarvon's XI at Highclere, during which they were introduced to the Queen. Rain and lack of competition affected the team's build-up to the first Test at Lord's, with Kent beating the tourists in a rain-affected match following a contrived attempt at producing a result.

Against Sussex the South Africans had a field day. In reply to the county side's 358 Cronje scored 94, Wessels 77, Peter Kirsten 130, McMillan 132, Liebenberg 64 and Symcox a quick 37 in a total of 613 for eight declared. Symcox then took five wickets in quick succession but the match was drawn. The Hampshire match ended in another frustrating draw when the final morning was washed out. Gloucestershire did not attempt to go for a win and that match fizzled out into another unsatisfactory draw. Rain completely ruined the fixture against Scotland with only 31 balls being bowled. The Durham match was used as much needed batting practice by the tourists. Most of the recognized batsmen made runs, although both Cullinan and Hudson were unable to lift themselves from a run of bad form. Gary Kirsten scored his second consecutive century against Northamptonshire but yet again the match was drawn in spite of three declarations.

New Zealand had been in England for the first part of the season but had performed poorly against an improved England side. Anticipation at the arrival of the South Africans was heightened by the historical significance of the tour. Thus it was a very emotional day when the South Africans appeared at Lord's for the first time in 29 years.

Kepler Wessels won the toss and elected to bat in front of a capacity crowd. Hudson fell into a trap set by Atherton and was caught by Gooch at fine leg for six, then Cronje struggled to seven to leave South Africa on 35 for two, but Gary Kirsten and Wessels played well and built a partnership of 106. Kirsten made 72 and when Wessels was out in the final over of the day for 106, South Africa had reached 241 for six. McMillan, Richardson and Matthews played beautifully the next morning and brought the score to a good 357. The four-pronged fast-bowling attack of Donald, De Villiers, McMillan and Matthews blasted into the English batsmen and seven wickets were down with England still needing 17 runs to avoid the follow-on. England were all out for 180, leaving South Africa with a lead of 177. When South Africa batted again, Hudson once more failed but virtually everyone else scored before Wessels declared at 278 for eight with a massive overall lead of 455. Once more, the South African fast bowlers ran through the English line-up and dismissed them for only 99 in 45,5 overs. The emphatic and historic victory was by 356 runs and achieved with a day to spare.

It was South Africa's greatest ever win over England and one

South African skipper Kepler Wessels, who led his team's march to victory in the emotional Lord's Test match with a first-innings century.

Craig Matthews, one of South Africa's quintet of fast bowlers, celebrates a wicket during the Lord's Test match. In the second innings he took three for 25 in 14 overs to help bowl England out for 99.

England captain Mike Atherton is grilled by the press following allegations that he tampered with the ball during the Lord's Test match. Despite criticism and speculation in the media, Atherton retained the captaincy and went on to score 99 in his next innings at Leeds.

achieved by a wonderful team effort. To add to England's woes, their captain, Atherton, was accused of interfering with the condition of the ball during the second innings and fined £2 000 by the chairman of the selectors for not giving a satisfactory explanation to the match referee. Ironically, the South Africans were also fined, for failing to achieve the required over rate during the match.

Cronje took over the captaincy for the next match against a weak Nottinghamshire side. The South Africans had few problems and declared at 327 for six, then dismissed Notts for 218. Cullinan came into form in the second innings and Cronje declared at 164 for three, leaving Notts to score 274 off 64 overs. At 131 for three, with only 16 overs left, Symcox and Shaw managed to get the breakthrough and seven wickets fell for another eight runs in 59 balls. Symcox took eight for 100 in the match. The South Africans had won their first match against a county side and received a £2 000 bonus from the sponsors as a result.

The following game at Leicester was played on a very fast pitch. Wessels declared on 270 for eight then bowled Leicestershire out for 167. The South Africans again declared, at 163 for five, with 50s from Gary Kirsten and Hansie Cronje. Wessels received another nasty blow on the forearm from the first ball that he received and a fracture was suspected. The Leicestershire openers went for the runs but after Donald took two wickets in seven balls and Shaw dismissed half-century maker Whittaker, the light worsened and the game was called off as a draw with Leicestershire on 216 for seven.

England selected a spinner, Tufnell, for the Test at Headingley but South Africa kept the side that had been so successful at Lord's. England won the toss and batted first. For once the South African fast bowlers did not perform well and the English batsmen all made

runs. Atherton received moral support from the Yorkshire crowd and was unfortunate to just miss his century. Stewart made 89, Thorpe 72 and Rhodes was not out on 65 when the England first

South African batsman Peter Kirsten, who at the age of 39 and after 52 first-class hundreds, scored his maiden Test century at Leeds.

Kepler Wessels and the England team gather around Jonty Rhodes after he had been hit by a ball from Devon Malcolm during the South African first innings at the Oval. Rhodes retired hurt, and was only able to return at the fall of the seventh wicket in the second innings.

innings closed on 477 for nine. Brian McMillan took three wickets and three brilliant catches in the innings. In the reply Hudson again failed and Richardson came in as nightwatchman. The next morning, Gary Kirsten and Cronje were out off successive balls in the first over, and South Africa were in deep trouble at 31 for three and then 105 for five. In a tremendous fight-back, Richardson made 48, Jonty Rhodes 46 and Peter Kirsten made a magnificent 104, an emotional maiden Test century at the age of 39. The follow-on was avoided then McMillan, with 78, Matthews, with 62 not out, De Villiers and Donald quickly brought the score to within 30 of the English score. Donald was injured and England batted slowly in the second innings against a depleted attack. Hick scored a cen-

tury and Thorpe was run out for 73. England declared at lunch on the final day at 267 for five, with a lead of 297. Hudson failed once more but Gary Kirsten made 65 and South Africa batted out time to reach 116 for three and a comfortable draw.

The four fast bowlers who had played so well in the Test were rested for the match against Minor Counties at Torquay. Hudson's poor spell continued and it was left to Cronje and Cullinan to restore some respectability to the first innings of 249. However the Minor Counties hammered the second-string attack and they were on 153 for two with one day to play. The rain-interrupted match ended in a surprising manner when, following two declarations, the Minor Counties' last pair were at the crease when time was called.

Atherton showed his displeasure on being given out first ball of the English reply and England were soon on 33 for two. Hick, Thorpe and Stewart then played well and brought the score to 222 for seven. De Freitas and Gough came in and slammed the bowling in an incredible spell which changed the course of the series, putting on 70 in 50 minutes. The England innings closed on 304, 28 runs behind. In the South African second innings Devon Malcolm stormed in and produced one of the best bowling performances ever, taking nine for 57 with only Cullinan managing to score, reaching 94. South Africa were all out for 175, leaving England to score 204 for victory. Gooch and Atherton scored at five runs an over then Hick took over to knock off the runs in 33 overs. South Africa had failed to take advantage of a one–nil lead for the third Test series in a row and morale was low.

Two subsequent one-day Internationals did nothing to dispel the gloom. The tired and dispirited South Africans lost both matches comfortably and the only players to come out with credit were De Villiers and Cullinan. The rot continued in two matches against a President's XI at Scarborough. The tourists were easily beaten in the one-day match and the rain-affected three-day match fizzled out into a tame draw.

A tour which started with such promise had fallen apart and worse was to come when the South Africans were soundly beaten by Holland in a one-day match.

England played well to come back after the defeat at Lord's but the South African party showed signs of fatigue and depression. Brian McMillan and Craig Matthews enhanced their reputations but the loss of form of Cronje, Hudson and Donald was inexplicable.

A similar team played Glamorgan in Pontypridd and, again, the weak attack was hammered with Glamorgan declaring at 337 for five. Hudson and Kirsten were out with four runs on the board but nightwatchman Snell went on to score a career best 94 and Cronje made 78 so that Wessels was able to declare on 288 for six. Glamorgan lost four quick wickets at the start of their second innings but carried on to declare at 222 for nine, leaving the South Africans to score 272 to win. Hudson failed but Gary Kirsten batted out time for a draw on 142 for three.

Hudson's lack of form, 266 runs in 17 innings, led to his omission from the team for the final Test at the Oval. In the South African first innings Jonty Rhodes ducked into a flyer from Malcolm and was taken to hospital, but gutsy innings from McMillan with 93 and Richardson with 53 brought the score to 332.

South African vice-captain Hansie Cronje. Despite high expectations in England, he had a very disappointing Test series, averaging only 18.

RESULTS

RESULTS OF ALL TEST MATCHES PLAYED BETWEEN ENGLAND AND SOUTH AFRICA 1888–1994

ENGLISH TEAMS IN SOUTH AFRICA

1888/89

1ST TEST, 12–13 MARCH, PORT ELIZABETH.
South Africa 84 and 129; England 148 and 67 for two. England won by eight wickets.

2ND TEST, 25–26 MARCH, CAPE TOWN.
England 292; South Africa 47 and 43. England won by an innings and 202 runs.

1891/92

1ST TEST, 19–22 MARCH, CAPE TOWN.
South Africa 97 and 83; England 369. England won by an innings and 189 runs.

1895/96

1ST TEST, 13–14 FEBRUARY, PORT ELIZABETH.
England 185 and 286; South Africa 93 and 30. England won by 288 runs.

2ND TEST, 2–4 MARCH, JOHANNESBURG.
England 482; South Africa 151 and 134. England won by an innings and 197 runs.

3RD TEST, 21–23 MARCH, CAPE TOWN.
South Africa 115 and 117; England 265. England won by an innings and 33 runs.

1898/99

1ST TEST, 14–16 FEBRUARY, JOHANNESBURG.
England 145 and 237; South Africa 251 and 99. England won by 32 runs.

2ND TEST, 1–3 APRIL, CAPE TOWN.
England 92 and 330; South Africa 177 and 35. England won by 210 runs.

1905/06

1ST TEST, 2–4 JANUARY, JOHANNESBURG.
England 184 and 190; South Africa 91 and 287 for 9. South Africa won by one wicket.

2ND TEST, 6–8 MARCH, JOHANNESBURG.
England 148 and 160; South Africa 277 and 33 for one. South Africa won by nine wickets.

3RD TEST, 10–14 MARCH, JOHANNESBURG.
South Africa 385 and 349 for five declared; England 295 and 196. South Africa won by 243 runs.

4TH TEST, 24–27 MARCH, CAPE TOWN.
South Africa 216 and 136; England 198 and 160 for six. England won by four wickets.

5TH TEST, 30 MARCH–2 APRIL, CAPE TOWN.
England 187 and 130; South Africa 333. South Africa won by an innings and 16 runs.

1909/10

1ST TEST, 1–5 JANUARY, JOHANNESBURG.
South Africa 208 and 345; England 310 and 224. South Africa won by 19 runs.

2ND TEST, 21–26 JANUARY, DURBAN.
South Africa 199 and 347; England 199 and 252. South Africa won by 95 runs.

3RD TEST, 26 FEBRUARY–3 MARCH, JOHANNESBURG.
South Africa 305 and 237; England 322 and 221 for seven. England won by three wickets.

4TH TEST, 7–9 MARCH, CAPE TOWN.
England 203 and 178; South Africa 207 and 175 for six. South Africa won by four wickets.

5TH TEST, 11–14 MARCH, CAPE TOWN.
England 417 and 16 for one; South Africa 103 and 327. England won by nine wickets.

1913/14

1ST TEST, 13–17 DECEMBER, DURBAN.
South Africa 182 and 111; England 450. England won by an innings and 157 runs.

2ND TEST, 26–30 DECEMBER, JOHANNESBURG.
South Africa 160 and 231, England 403. England won by an innings and 12 runs.

3RD TEST, 1–5 JANUARY, JOHANNESBURG.
England 238 and 308; South Africa 151 and 304. England won by 91 runs.

4TH TEST, 14–18 FEBRUARY, DURBAN.
South Africa 170 and 305 for nine; England 163 and 154 for five. Match drawn.

5TH TEST, 27 FEBRUARY, 3 MARCH, PORT ELIZABETH.
South Africa 193 and 228; England 411 and 11 for no wicket. England won by 10 wickets.

1922/23

1ST TEST, 23–28 DECEMBER, JOHANNESBURG.
South Africa 148 and 420; England 182 and 218. South Africa won by 168 runs.

2ND TEST, 1–4 JANUARY, CAPE TOWN.
South Africa 113 and 242; England 183 and 173 for nine.
England won by one wicket.

3RD TEST, 18–22 JANUARY, DURBAN.
England 428 and 11 for one; South Africa 368. Match drawn.

4TH TEST, 9–13 FEBRUARY, JOHANNESBURG.
England 244 and 376 for six declared; South Africa 295 and 247 for four. Match drawn.

5TH TEST, 16–22 FEBRUARY, DURBAN.
England 281 and 241; South Africa 179 and 234. England won by 109 runs.

1924/25 (UNOFFICIAL)

1ST "TEST", 23–26 DECEMBER, JOHANNESBURG.
Joel's XI 198 and 149; South Africa 295 and 53 for one. South Africa won by nine wickets.

2ND "TEST", 1–5 JANUARY, DURBAN.
Joel's XI 285 and 174; South Africa 211 and 200. Joel's XI won by 48 runs.

3RD "TEST", 15–16 JANUARY, CAPE TOWN.
South Africa 113 and 150; Joel's XI 224 and 40 for no wicket.
Joel's XI won by 10 wickets.

4TH "TEST", 6–10 FEBRUARY, JOHANNESBURG.
Joel's XI 239 and 164; South Africa 193 and 16 for no wicket.
Match drawn.

5TH "TEST", 20–24 FEBRUARY, PORT ELIZABETH.
South Africa 183 and 200; Joel's XI 94 and 266. South Africa won by 21 runs.

1927/28

1ST TEST, 24–27 DECEMBER, JOHANNESBURG.
South Africa 196 and 170; England 313 and 57 for no wicket.
England won by 10 wickets.

2ND TEST, 31 DECEMBER–4 JANUARY, CAPE TOWN.
England 113 and 428; South Africa 250 and 224. England won by 67 runs.

3RD TEST, 21–25 JANUARY, DURBAN.
South Africa 248 and 464 for eight; England 430 and 132 for two.
Match drawn.

4TH TEST, 28 JANUARY–1 FEBRUARY, JOHANNESBURG.
England 265 and 215; South Africa 328 and 156 for six. South Africa won by four wickets.

5TH TEST, 4–8 FEBRUARY, DURBAN.
England 282 and 118; South Africa 332 for 7 declared and 69 for two. South Africa won by eight wickets.

1930/31

1ST TEST, 24–27 DECEMBER, JOHANNESBURG.
South Africa 126 and 306; England 193 and 211. South Africa won by 28 runs.

2ND TEST, 1–5 JANUARY, CAPE TOWN.
South Africa 513 for 8 declared; England 350 and 252. Match drawn.

3RD TEST, 16–20 JANUARY, DURBAN.
South Africa 177 and 145 for eight; England 223 for one declared.
Match drawn.

4TH TEST, 13–17 FEBRUARY, JOHANNESBURG.
England 442 and 169 for nine declared;
South Africa 295 and 280 for seven.
Match drawn.

5TH TEST, 21–25 FEBRUARY, DURBAN.
South Africa 252 and 219 for seven declared; England 230 and 72 for four.
Match drawn.

1938/39

1ST TEST, 24–28 DECEMBER, JOHANNESBURG.
England 422 and 291 for four; South Africa 390 and 108 for one.
Match drawn.

2ND TEST, 31 DECEMBER–4 JANUARY, CAPE TOWN.
England 559 for nine declared; South Africa 286 and 201 for 2.
Match drawn.

3RD TEST, 20–23 JANUARY, DURBAN.
England 469 for four declared; South Africa 103 and 353. England won by an innings and 13 runs.

4TH TEST, 18–22 FEBRUARY, JOHANNESBURG.
England 215 and 203 for four; South Africa 349 for eight declared.
Match drawn.

5TH TEST, 3–14 MARCH, DURBAN.
South Africa 530 and 461; England 316 and 654 for five.
Match drawn.

1948/49

1ST TEST, 16–20 DECEMBER, DURBAN.
South Africa 161 and 219; England 253 and 128 for eight.
England won by two wickets.

2ND TEST, 27–30 DECEMBER, JOHANNESBURG.
England 608; South Africa 315 and 270 for two. Match drawn.

3RD TEST, 1–5 JANUARY, CAPE TOWN.
England 308 and 276 for three declared; South Africa 356 and 142 for four. Match drawn.

4TH TEST, 13–16 FEBRUARY, JOHANNESBURG.
England 379 and 253 for seven declared; South Africa 257 for nine and 194 for four. Match drawn.

5TH TEST, 5–9 MARCH, PORT ELIZABETH.
South Africa 379 and 187 for three declared; England 395 and 174 for seven. England won by three wickets.

1956/57

1ST TEST, 24–29 DECEMBER, JOHANNESBURG.
England 268 and 150; South Africa 215 and 72. England won by 131 runs.

2ND TEST, 1–5 JANUARY, CAPE TOWN.
England 369 and 220 for six declared; South Africa 205 and 72.
England won by 312 runs.

3RD TEST, 25–30 JANUARY, DURBAN.
England 218 and 254; South Africa 283 and 142 for six.
Match drawn.

4TH TEST, 15–20 FEBRUARY, JOHANNESBURG.
South Africa 340 and 142; England 251 and 214. South Africa won by 17 runs.

5TH TEST, 1–5 MARCH, PORT ELIZABETH.
South Africa 164 and 134; England 110 and 130; South Africa won by 58 runs.

1964/65

1ST TEST, 4–8 DECEMBER, DURBAN.
England 485 for five declared; South Africa 155 and 226. England won by an innings and 104 runs.

2ND TEST, 23–29 DECEMBER, JOHANNESBURG.
England 531; South Africa 317 and 336 for six. Match drawn.

3RD TEST, 1–6 JANUARY, CAPE TOWN.
South Africa 501 for seven declared and 346; England 442 and 15 for no wicket. Match drawn.

4TH TEST, 22–27 JANUARY, JOHANNESBURG.
South Africa 390 for six declared and 307 for three declared; England 384 and 153 for six. Match drawn.

5TH TEST, 12–17 FEBRUARY, PORT ELIZABETH.
South Africa 502 and 178 for four declared; England 435 and 29 for one. Match drawn.

SOUTH AFRICAN TEAMS IN THE UNITED KINGDOM

1907

1ST TEST, 1–3 JULY, LORD'S.
England 428; South Africa 340 and 185 for three. Match drawn.

2ND TEST, 29–31 JULY, HEADINGLEY.
England 76 and 162; South Africa 110 and 75. England won by 53 runs.

3RD TEST, 19–21 AUGUST, THE OVAL.
England 295 and 138; South Africa 178 and 159 for five. Match drawn.

1912

1ST TEST, 10–12 JUNE, LORD'S.
South Africa 58 and 217; England 337. England won by an innings and 62 runs.

2ND TEST, 8–10 JULY, HEADINGLEY.
England 242 and 238; South Africa 147 and 159. England won by 174 runs.

3RD TEST, 12–13 AUGUST, THE OVAL.
South Africa 95 and 93; England 176 and 14 for no wicket. England won by 10 wickets.

1924

1ST TEST, 14–17 JUNE, EDGBASTON.
England 438; South Africa 30 and 390. England won by an innings and 18 runs.

2ND TEST, 28 JUNE–1 JULY, LORD'S.
South Africa 273 and 240; England 531 for two. England won by an innings and 18 runs.

3RD TEST, 12–15 JUNE, HEADINGLEY.
England 396 and 60 for one; South Africa 132 and 323. England won by nine wickets.

4TH TEST, 26–29 JULY, OLD TRAFFORD.
South Africa 116 for four. Match drawn.

5TH TEST, 16–19 AUGUST, THE OVAL.
South Africa 342; England 421 for eight. Match drawn.

1929

1ST TEST, 15–18 JUNE, EDGBASTON.
England 245 and 308 for four declared; South Africa 250 and 171 for one. Match drawn.

2ND TEST, 29 JUNE–2 JULY, LORD'S.
England 302 and 312 for eight declared; South Africa 322 and 90 for five. Match drawn.

3RD TEST, 13–16 JULY, HEADINGLEY.
South Africa 236 and 275; England 328 and 186 for five. England won by five wickets.

4TH TEST, 27–30 JULY, OLD TRAFFORD.
England 427 for 7 declared; South Africa 130 and 265. England won by an innings and 32 runs.

5TH TEST, 17–20 AUGUST, THE OVAL.
England 258 and 264 for one; South Africa 492 for eight declared. Match drawn.

1935

1ST TEST, 15–18 JUNE, TRENT BRIDGE.
England 384 for seven declared; South Africa 220 and 17 for one. Match drawn.

2ND TEST, 29 JUNE–2 JULY, LORD'S.
South Africa 228 and 278 for seven declared; England 198 and 151. South Africa won by 157 runs.

3RD TEST, 13–16 JULY, HEADINGLEY.
England 216 and 294 for seven declared; South Africa 171 and 194 for five. Match drawn.

4TH TEST, 27–30 JULY, OLD TRAFFORD.
England 357 and 231 for six declared; South Africa 318 and 169 for two. Match drawn.

5TH TEST, 17–20 AUG, THE OVAL.
South Africa 476 and 287 for six; England 534 for six declared.

1947

1ST TEST, 7–11 JUNE, TRENT BRIDGE.
South Africa 533 and 161 for one; England 208 and 551. Match drawn.

2ND TEST, 21–25 JUNE, LORD'S.
England 554 for eight declared and 28 for no wicket; South Africa 327 and 252. England won by 10 wickets.

3RD TEST, 5–9 JULY, OLD TRAFFORD.
South Africa 339 and 267. England 478 and 130 for three. England won by seven wickets.

4TH TEST, 26–29 JULY, HEADINGLEY.
South Africa 175 and 184; England 317 for seven declared and 47 for no wicket. England won by 10 wickets.

5TH TEST, 16–20 AUGUST, THE OVAL.
England 427 and 325 for six declared; South Africa 302 and 423 for seven. Match drawn.

1951

1ST TEST, 7–12 JUNE, TRENT BRIDGE.
South Africa 483 for nine declared and 121. England 419 for nine and 114. South Africa won by 71 runs.

2ND TEST, 21–23 JUNE, LORD'S.
England 311 and 16 for no wicket; South Africa 115 and 211. England won by 10 wickets.

3RD TEST, 5–10 JULY, OLD TRAFFORD.
South Africa 158 and 191; England 211 and 142 for one. England won by nine wickets.

4TH TEST, 26–31 JULY, HEADINGLEY.
South Africa 538 and 87 for no wicket; England 505. Match drawn.

5TH TEST, 16–18 JULY, THE OVAL.
South Africa 202 and 154; England 194 and 164 for six. England won by four wickets.

1955

1ST TEST, 9–13 JUNE, TRENT BRIDGE.
England 334; South Africa 181 and 148. England won by an innings and 5 runs.

2ND TEST, 23–27 JUNE, LORD'S.
England 133 and 353; South Africa 303 and 111. England won by 71 runs.

3RD TEST, 7–12 JULY, OLD TRAFFORD.
England 284 and 381; South Africa 521 for eight declared and 145 for seven. South Africa won by three wickets.

4TH TEST, 21–26 JULY, HEADINGLEY.
South Africa 171 and 500; England 191 and 256. South Africa won by 224 runs.

5TH TEST, 13–17 AUGUST, THE OVAL.
England 151 and 204; South Africa 112 and 151. England won by 92 runs.

1960

1ST TEST, 9–14 JUNE, EDGBASTON.
England 292 and 203; South Africa 186 and 209. England won by 100 runs.

2ND TEST, 23–27 JUNE, LORD'S.
England 362 for eight declared; South Africa 152 and 137. England won by an innings and 73 runs.

3RD TEST, 7–11 JULY, TRENT BRIDGE.
England 287 and 49 for two; South Africa 88 and 247. England won by eight wickets.

4TH TEST, 21–26 JULY, OLD TRAFFORD.
England 250 and 153 for seven; South Africa 229 and 46 for no wicket. Match drawn.

5TH TEST, 18–23 AUGUST, THE OVAL.
England 155 and 479 for nine declared; South Africa 419 and 97 for four. Match drawn.

1965

1ST TEST, 22–27 JULY, LORD'S.
South Africa 280 and 248; England 338 and 145 for seven. Match drawn.

2ND TEST, 5–9 AUGUST, TRENT BRIDGE.
South Africa 269 and 289; England 240 and 224. South Africa won by 94 runs.

3RD TEST, 26–31 AUGUST, THE OVAL.
South Africa 208 and 392; England 202 and 308 for four. Match drawn.

1994

1ST TEST, 21–24 JULY, LORD'S.
South Africa 357 and 278 for eight declared. England 180 and 99. South Africa won by 356 runs.

2ND TEST, 4–8 AUGUST, HEADINGLEY.
England 477 for nine declared and 267 for five declared; South Africa 447 and 116 for three. Match drawn.

3RD TEST, 18–21 AUGUST, THE OVAL.
South Africa 332 and 175; England 304 and 205 for two. England won by eight wickets.

ENGLISH TEAMS IN SOUTH AFRICA

Date	Non 1st class				1st class					Tests			
	P	W	D	L	P	W	D	L	T	P	W	D	L
1888/89	17	11	2	4	-	-	-	-	-	2	2	-	-
1891/92	20	13	7	-	-	-	-	-	-	1	1	-	-
1895/96	14	4	7	3	1	-	1	-	-	3	3	-	-
1898/99	12	1	2	-	3	3	-	-	-	2	2	-	-
1905/06	14	1	4	-	7	6	-	1	-	5	1	-	4
1909/10	5	3	2	-	8	5	2	1	-	5	2	-	3
1913/14	4	3	1	-	13	5	7	1	-	5	4	1	-
1922/23	8	4	4	-	9	8	1	-	-	5	2	2	1
1924/25	7	3	4	-	9	3	6	-	-	*5	2	1	2
1927/28	3	1	2	-	11	5	6	-	-	5	2	1	2
1930/31	4	2	2	-	11	5	6	-	-	5	-	4	1
1938/39	1	1	-	-	12	7	5	-	-	5	1	4	-
1948/49	3	2	1	-	15	7	8	-	-	5	2	3	-
1956/57	2	2	-	-	15	9	5	1	-	5	2	1	2
1964/65	1	1	-	-	12	9	3	-	-	5	1	4	-
TOTALS	115	7	38	7	126	72	5	4	-	63	27	21	15

*Unofficial

SOUTH AFRICAN TEAMS IN THE UNITED KINGDOM

Date	Non 1st class				1st class					Tests			
	P	W	D	L	P	W	D	L	T	P	W	D	L
1894	24	12	7	5	-	-	-	-	-	-	-	-	-
1901	1	8	2	-	15	5	-	9	1	-	-	-	-
1904	4	3	-	1	22	10	9	2	1	-	-	-	-
1907	4	4	-	-	24	17	4	3	-	3	-	2	1
1912	-	-	-	-	34	13	16	5	-	3	-	-	3
1924	3	-	3	-	3	8	16	6	-	5	-	2	3
1929	5	2	3	-	29	9	15	5	-	5	-	3	2
1935	10	5	5	-	26	16	8	2	-	5	1	4	-
1947	6	2	3	1	23	14	7	2	-	5	-	2	3
1951	7	3	#4	-	25	4	19	2	-	5	1	1	3
1955	3	1	2	-	23	13	9	1	-	5	2	-	3
1960	1	1	-	-	26	14	#10	2	-	5	-	2	3
1965	2	-	#1	1	15	4	9	2	-	3	1	2	-
1994	3	1	1	1	11	1	8	2	-	3	1	1	1
TOTALS	82	42	31	9	300	125	130	43	2	47	6	19	22

#One match abandoned due to snow or rain

PHOTOGRAPHIC CREDITS

Allsport: 202; 205 left; 205 right
Anne Laing/Action Shots: 204
Argus: 132; 134; 137 top; 138; 140; 142; 143; 146; 147;
148; 149; 150; 152; 154; 162; 163
Beeld: 190
Central Press Photos: 141; 168
The Cricketer magazine: 187 bottom
Dave Munden/Sportsline/Action Shots: all cover shots;
4—5; 198 top; 206; 208; 210; 211 top; 211 bottom
Die Burger: 176; 193; 209; 213
Hulton Deutsch: 144
International Press Agency (INPRA): 8—9; 10 bottom;
120; 123; 123; 124 bottom; 196; 199
Julian Herbert/INPRA: 212
Ken Oosterbroek/INPRA: 200
Lord's: 12; 18; 22; 26; 30; 36; 44; 46; 50; 52; 56; 68; 80;
90; 102; 113; 131 bottom
Museum Africa: 77; 78; 79 / Times Media courtesy
Museum Africa: 178; 179; 180
SA Cricket Almanac 1949/50: 128; 130
SA Cricketer magazine: 172 right; 186; 192 left; 192 right
SA Cricket Annuals:
1961: 157
1973: 174
1974: 181
1975: 182
1978: 187 top
1979: 191
1990: 194; 197; 198 bottom
South African Library (Heesom Collection): 100; 105;
114; 126; 171
Sport and General: 10 top; 108; 135; 136; 137 bottom;
155; 158; 161; 166; 167; 169; 170; 172 left; 173; 184
The Star: 164
Sunday Times/ Times Media: 188

The Publishers would like to thank the
following people and organisations for their
help in producing this book:
Dougie Ettlinger; Maureen Payne;
South African Library, UCBSA, WPCA, WPCC.

In addition, material was sourced from the following
books:

Arlott, J *Rothman's Jubilee History of Cricket 1890—1965*.
Arthur Baker Ltd: 60; 66
Bassano, B (1979) *South Africa in International Cricket
1888—1970*. Chameleon Books, East London:
15 left; 17 top; 21 right; 25 left; 25 right; 32; 39 left;
40; 48; 54 right; 59 top; 64; 67; 74; 76; 83; 86; 88;
89; 92; 94; 95; top; 95 bottom; 96; 98; 99; 101; 104;
107; 110; 112; 118; 119; 122; 124 top; 129; 131 top;
160
Cardus, N (1952) *Cricket All the Year*. Collins, London: 84
Cowley, B (1983) *Cricket's Exiles, The Saga of South
African Cricket*. Don Nelson, Cape Town: 82; 106
Duckworth, LB *Cricket from the Hearth*. Cornish Brothers
Ltd, Birmingham: 70
Frith, D (1978) *A Hundred Years of County Cricket*.
Lutterworth Press, Guilford, Surrey: 34 left; 43 left;
53; 73 top
Grace, WG (1891) *Cricket*. JW Arrowsmith, London:
15 right
Lee, HW *Forty Years of English Cricket*. Clerke and
Cockeran Ltd, London: 59 bottom
Luckin, MW (1915) *A History of South African Cricket*.
WE Hortor and Co: 14; 16; 20; 42; 43 right; 47; 49;
54 left; 55; 58; 61; 62; 71; 72; 73 bottom; 85
Various (1896) *Our Cricketers, Past and Present*. AD Jones
and Co: 21 left; 28; 29; 33; 38; 65
West, SEL and Luker, WJ (1965) *Century at Newlands
1864—1964, A History of the Western Province Cricket
Club*. Western Province Cricket Club, Cape Town:
34 right; 35; 39 right
The Memorial Biography of WG Grace. Constable and Co
Ltd, 1919: 24
Vintage Elevens: 117

Photograph on page 156 courtesy Maureen Payne

INDEX